SHOULD I GO

TO GRAD SCHOOL?

SHOULD I
GO TO
GRAD SCHOOL?

41 *Answers to an Impossible Question*

**Edited by
Jessica Loudis, Boško Blagojević,
John Arthur Peetz, and Allison Rodman**

B L O O M S B U R Y
NEW YORK • LONDON • NEW DELHI • SYDNEY

Published by Bloomsbury USA, New York

Bloomsbury is a trademark of Bloomsbury Plc

All papers used by Bloomsbury USA are natural, recyclable products made
from wood grown in well-managed forests. The manufacturing processes
conform to the environmental regulations of the country of origin.

LIBRARY OF CONGRESS CATALOGING-IN-PUBLICATION DATA HAS BEEN APPLIED FOR.

ISBN: 978-1-62040-598-7

First U.S. Edition 2014

1 3 5 7 9 10 8 6 4 2

Typeset by Hewer Text UK Ltd, Edinburgh
Printed and bound in the U.S.A. by Thomson-Shore Inc., Dexter, Michigan

Bloomsbury books may be purchased for business or promotional use.
For information on bulk purchases please contact Macmillan Corporate
and Premium Sales Department at specialmarkets@macmillan.com.

To our parents

CONTENTS

Introduction

THE FIRST THING TO say about this book is that when we refer to "grad school," we're not talking about programs in the life sciences, law, engineering, or business. What we mean are master's degrees in things like English and history, MFAs in art and poetry, and doctoral degrees in the humanities, cultural studies, and social sciences. Unlike a medical or law degree—or, really, any degree required to advance in a field other than academia itself—humanities and arts degrees run a high likelihood of not paying off on the investment. Master's degrees are routinely derided as cash cows for universities. Doctoral programs, if they do offer stipends, provide less than most entry-level salaries, and only a lucky few can hope to land academic jobs afterward. Finally, there's the problem facing every writer and artist considering an exorbitantly expensive MFA: If you don't need a degree to do what you do, then why get one?

If this book approached grad school from a purely economic perspective, it would be much shorter and far more depressing. The crisis of higher education is a critical issue these days, but this book is not about plundered personal bank accounts, struggling institutions, or the rise of credentialization—at least not directly. It's about what drives people to consider going back to school in the first place, the point at which rational choice intersects with personal predilection, unpredictable circumstances, and anxiety about the future. As Heather Horn noted in a 2013 *Atlantic* piece about why doctoral programs persist against all statistical odds, "Asking why young people keep entering PhD programs is a lot like

1

asking why young people keep moving to New York planning to become actors."

Grad school certainly held an appeal for us. We four editors began working together in 2012 through Platform for Pedagogy, an organization that publicizes and promotes free public lectures, symposia, and cultural events around New York City. Though none of us were enrolled in school at the time—we were all only a few years out of college—we attended university conferences and talks in our spare time, browsed course catalogs, and flirted with the idea of going back. (Since then, one of us has.) We all work in different fields—literary magazines, programming, the art world—and *Should I Go to Grad School?* grew out of conversations about how and why degrees matter in our respective professions, as well as what the future might hold without any extra letters after our names.

The purpose of this book is to provide a broad, unempirical look at how a variety of people in the arts, academia, social sciences, and humanities have personally engaged with the problem of grad school. Rather than solicit a yes-or-no answer to our titular question, we wanted each writer to reflect on his or her own history. Contributors who did go were asked to discuss the issues, exhilarations, and traumas they confronted while enrolled. We were lucky to receive many excellent essays and were struck by the fact that no two stories are the same (though certain themes—the effects academia can have on writing, the decision to spend one's twenties in New York City, the theories of French sociologist Pierre Bourdieu—do appear again and again). There are accounts of coming to terms with one's priorities, struggling through—or abandoning—a dissertation, and returning to school after more than a decade away. People wrote about the joys of learning to speak the language of academic specialization, the bizarre interpersonal dynamics of MFA writing workshops, the subtle psychological conditioning integral to doctoral programs, and the freedom, thanks to school, to finally finish a book or relocate to a new city.

While the majority of the people in this book did go to grad school—sometimes more than once—a number of our contributors didn't, never considered it. Sheila Heti told us that going back to school never occurred to her: Instead, to satisfy the need for creative and social stimulation, she ran a salon of sorts out of her apartment in Toronto. Kenneth Goldsmith and Andrea Fraser noted that when they were starting out in the art world, nobody would have ever thought to get an MFA; people just moved to New York and joined the scene.

In casting a wide net, we aimed to reflect both the realities of various kinds of academic programs and the range of opportunities available to people who choose to forgo them. Our youngest contributor is barely in his twenties (though he's already founded a company); our oldest contributors have upward of five decades of experience in their respective fields. In addition to academics and writers, we asked journalists, sociologists, painters, poets, programmers, historians, activists, novelists, an actor, and a mixologist.

We had no agenda when we set to work on this book. There was no bias for or against grad school, no intention of proselytizing about higher education, or of offering career advice. Our goal was to assemble an array of voices in the hopes that this might broaden the conversation about grad school in the arts and humanities, and to assuage the anxieties of anybody in the process of deciding whether to go. There are, of course, no obvious answers to the question of this book, only examples to be considered and mistakes to be learned from. But if there's one message that we've come away with in the process of working on this book, it's that so long as you surround yourself with the right people and questions, it's possible to lead a meaningful and intellectually engaged life no matter what you decide.

—Jessica Loudis

Stephen Burt

A CHOOSE-YOUR-OWN-NOT-SO-ADVENTUROUS ADVENTURE (WHICH YOU CAN ALSO READ STRAIGHT THROUGH)

1. Are you considering a PhD program in the humanities, such as literature or art history; an MFA in a literary art, such as poetry, fiction, or creative nonfiction; or something else, such as an MFA in a visual, musical, or performing art; a PhD in the quantitative social sciences, lab sciences, or mathematics; law school; medical school; divinity school; etc.?

If you answered yes to a PhD program in the humanities, go to 3. If you answered yes to an MFA in a literary art, go to 4. If you answered yes to something else, go to 2.

2. Skip to the next essay in this collection. I might have advice for you if we meet in person, but my own experience won't help you here. THE END

3. Do you like teaching? For example, have ever been put in charge of a room full of high school or middle school students? Did any aspect of that charge seem fun? If you led groups of your peers in college in any sort of educational activity—including non-classroom activities, such as running a college newspaper or college radio station—did you like doing that? Do you wish you could do it again? Did you watch teachers in college (including teaching fellows) and think about how you could or would do what they did?

If you answered yes, go to 5. If you answered no, or not often, go to 6. If you answered I don't know, because you've never had an experience that resembles teaching in any way, go to 7.

4. Do you expect that your MFA program will lead, as professional degrees (from med school, law school, education school) are designed to lead, to a full-time job (in this case, teaching)?

If you answered yes, go to 8. If you answered no, go to 9.

5. Are you willing to teach college students, correct their writing, and work on how they learn for five or six years, making only whatever the normal graduate stipend in your field is, while also researching and writing a book?

If you answered yes, go to 10. If you answered no, go to 11.

6. Are you willing to write a relatively specialized book with no guarantee that many people will read it? I mean *really* want, in the sense that you're willing to give up nights and weeks and months when you could be dancing or traveling or painting or earning more money or playing with your children, in order to research and write a book that holds your interest and the interest of a few hundred other people but may never hold the interest of thousands (let alone millions)?

If you answered yes, go to 5. If you answered no, go to 16.

7. If you've never had an experience that feels in the slightest like teaching, you may want to find out how it feels before you sign up for four, or forty, years' worth. Consider tutoring underprivileged or overprivileged teens, or try running a book group or a more ambitious DIY arts project, or volunteer to work at a museum. You may also be so introverted, so committed to solitary problem solving, that you won't enjoy teaching. On the other hand, that same introversion may help you when it's time for the dissertation.

Go to 6.

8. Many jobs in creative writing now require that their applicants already have a book published as well as a graduate degree, and many graduates of elite programs never get full-time teaching jobs, especially if they're restricting themselves to one region (e.g., the Northeast).

Go to 4.

9. Go look up the technical term *opportunity cost*, and be sure you know what a low-residency MFA program is (e.g., the one at Warren Wilson College). You can then compare such programs, which allow you to go on with your adult life, against the full-time residential programs and make an informed choice about where to apply. If all you got from your program was time to write plus a couple of thoughtful peers, would that be enough?

If you answered yes, go to 14. If you answered no, go to 15.

10. Do you know what sort of book you might want to write in your chosen field? Can you imagine a title or an argument or a topic (or two or three) for yourself, right now?

If you answered yes, go to 12. If you answered no, go to 13.

11. It sounds like you've got something you'd rather do—a job that's more rewarding, or a chance to make art that's more liberating—than what the academy can give you right now. The opportunity cost of a full-time graduate program might be too high for you. Can you dip your foot in without total immersion?

Go to 16.

12. Do you know who else writes that kind of book, what thinkers, scholars, or writers you'd want to meet, to emulate, to shadow intermittently

until you can learn how to do what they do? Just a few names (of people or books) will suffice.

If you answered yes, go to 17. If you answered no, go to 13.

13. It sounds like you might enjoy graduate school once you get there, but you probably need more focus, or more background, in your chosen field of study in order to thrive intellectually (not to mention getting funded, or getting in). Can you read more on your own? If your friends read or write what you want to read or write, can you organize an informal reading group? If not, can you take one class somewhere, or enroll as a part-time special student at an affordable rate (my former students have had good luck with that tactic at the City University of New York and at the University of Chicago, in particular), and then ask yourself the same questions again next year?

If you are still an undergraduate or just out of undergrad, go to 26. Otherwise, go to 16.

14. It sounds like you're ready. Find out where the writers you like teach, figure out whether you could stand to live in the places where they teach for at least a few years, and figure out whether there's any other program you'd like to consider even if you don't much like the writers who teach there (e.g., it's in your favorite city, your peer group is already there, or the institution may fund you).

Go to 20.

15. What else are you seeking? A teacher who will take a special interest in your work, rather like what you had in college, especially if you attended a small and selective college? Professional connections that will help you publish the book you expect to write? Something else?

If you answered yes to a teacher, go to 18. If you answered yes to professional connections, go to 19. If you answered yes to something else, go to 21.

16. You probably liked school when you were enrolled, and you might miss it now. You may be less than totally fulfilled (who does feel "totally fulfilled"?) in your current job, whether it's a job with a career track or something-I'm-just-doing-for-now. You might very well be right for any number of graduate programs—including an MFA—but not, as yet, for a PhD. Go to the next essay in this collection, which can probably help you more than I can right now, or go back to 13 and consider those suggestions seriously. THE END

17. Where do the writers or scholars you like teach? Do they teach? What do you know about the programs in which they teach? Go research those programs, at least on the web.

Go to 20.

18. Some people in some grad programs in the humanities find a truly supportive, charismatic and yet intimate, ideally attentive mentor. Most don't. The figure who likes your work most may not be the one whose work you like, and the people whose work you like may not be *people* you like once you get the chance to work with them. Can you live with a professional, slightly distant, but admiring relationship with mentors, teachers, and supporters who will treat you like a grown-up—and sometimes like a valuable employee? Or do you need something different?

If you need something different, go to 13. If you can live with that, go to 17.

19. Some MFA programs do very well in providing students with professional connections and clear avenues to publication; some don't. Research the individual program—here gossip is useful, and campus visits (after you get in, if you get in) are invaluable—and research the genre, too: A program that gives literary novelists clear ways to meet agents and avenues into trade presses may do absolutely zilch for poets, and vice versa.

Go to 14.

20. Perhaps you should go to grad school. If you do go, you'll be giving up years in which you could be doing something else, so you should think about what "something else" might mean, and whether the other things you want to do in your twenties or thirties or right now seem compatible with a time-consuming commitment to libraries, classrooms, and writerly discipline.

For me, "something else" turned out to mean going to lots of rock shows, traveling long distances to visit friends, doing a bit of amateurish music writing, wearing girls' clothes to a dance club on alternate Sunday nights, and writing my own poems, all of which I found I was able to do while taking classes and writing a dissertation at Yale. I had the good fortune of meeting the love of my life and moving to New York City with her soon after I finished taking classes and started writing my dissertation. On the other hand, "something else" could have meant, in the mid-1990s, learning to play rock music seriously, finding a band and going on tour, doing a lot more music writing, doing a lot more cross-dressing, and working full-time on political campaigns. Going to grad school meant I probably missed my chance to do those things.

I don't regret it—every decision has some opportunity cost—but I'm conscious of it; that's why I treasure the year I spent on a fellowship (not a famous one, but a well-rewarded one) living in England and studying toward no degree. I found it frustrating, at times, to work alongside people who had literally never been out of school; and I found it helpful to work alongside people who had been in the workplace, the "real" (that is, the nonacademic) world, who could put the demands and the privileges of academia into better perspective.

What else would you like to do with your life besides write a book and teach college students? Can you do that while teaching and writing a book? If not, which one should you do first?

Go to 24.

21. What?

Go to 16.

22. Go ahead and apply. Line up your recommendations, bother your recommenders repeatedly as the deadline approaches, write a personal statement that shows how you see yourself in ten years as a member of this profession, and remember that your writing sample—the work that shows what you can do—matters more than your statement. Don't let any of it keep you up all night.

Go to 23.

23. Applying isn't the same as getting in. You can always say no if they accept you, you can always reapply if they don't, and you can definitely comparison shop. Find out how the advanced graduate students feel at the programs that want you (would they go there again?), and find out how they fare (whether they get jobs). Then find out whether they're funded, and how well they're funded. How's your funding?

If it's enough for you to live on, given your habits and your other resources, go to 29. If it's not enough, go to 28.

24. Are you now a college undergraduate or a recent (within the last year) college graduate on a traditional collegiate timetable (i.e., straight from high school to college as a full-time student all the way to your degree)?

If you've been out of college for more than a year, or if you took any time off during college, or if you started college as an older-than-usual student, go to 22.

If you are now an undergrad, go to 25. If you just graduated from college, having completed a traditional timetable, go to 26. If you do not hold a BA or equivalent first degree, go to 27.

25. Do you have legal or other personal reasons for remaining a full-time student without a break in your education? For example, do you want to remain in the United States but can do so only with a student visa?

If you answered yes, go to 22. If you answered no, go to 26.

26. Many people in PhD programs, and a few in MFA programs, choose to leave before completing their degree or find themselves just unable to complete it. Many of them leave at the master's degree point (typically one or two years in), and many others wish they had. If you make it all the way through a PhD program, or go on the teaching-job market with an MFA, you may then face a choice between taking a job at the University of Undesirable Remote Location, and X, where X equals what you would do if you left academia.

That means that in order to get what you can out of graduate school, and not regret your decision, you'll need to know some possible values of X. You need to know what you would do if you weren't in school in order to know whether to stay in school. You need to know what you would do if you weren't a professor in order to have some clue what you're willing to give up—in location, time, and energy—in order to be a professor.

If you're still an undergraduate, or if you're just out of college and less than twenty-four years old, you probably don't know. Come back in six months to a year, and keep in touch with your favorite professors. You will want them to remember you next year. And, since they know you, you should trust them more than you trust me. THE END

27. You will need a BA or equivalent first degree for selective graduate programs in almost anything, though some MFA programs may not require them. Carole Fungaroli wrote a good book in 2000 about how you can, and why you might, go back to school full-time at a selective college as an adult, and it's still worth a look now. THE END

28. Do not take out large loans in order to begin graduate study in the humanities. Top PhD programs will always fund you if they truly want you, as will most of the best MFA programs (Columbia University is the only exception I know). This is due, in part, to the fact that large schools need people to teach undergraduates, and graduate students are cheaper than faculty. If you can pay your own way, try to find out whether the program really welcomes you and views you as a good risk before you begin. Otherwise, apply again next year. I know of several successful professors who had to apply to top grad programs more than once. THE END

29. Cool. Do you really want to do this? Do you know what—in time, friends, and attention to nonacademic projects—you will be giving up?

If so, go to 30. If not, go to 26.

30. Okay. Stay in touch with your nonacademic friends and with your nonacademic interests; you'll need them. Visit the schools that let you in, if you can. Meet grad students *and* senior faculty. And calm down. This is what you want to do. Most important, you can spend more time reading what you love.

Do you have other people (children or adults) who live in your house or depend on your care? If so, go to 31. If not, go to 32.

31. Being responsible for others while being a grad student is tricky, but it can be done if you're organized and if you ask for help when you need help. People have made it through dissertations and on to fine jobs while their kids make it from infancy to afterschool musicals. Find out what resources your school has for parents or other caregivers before you go.

Go to 32.

32. You have a few years ahead of you in which, first and last, you will be expected to learn and study books (and articles and stand-alone poems and paintings and cars and websites and live recordings and scores, etc.). Start multiple projects; build up as many notes as you can that might become projects or courses or essays or stories or poems or plays five or ten years from now when you will have less time. Remember that you are, or will be, writing a book.

Go to 33.

33. Graduate school in the humanities need not be a reboot of your life, but it is a chance to reorganize. It allows you time and resources, much more than you would get elsewhere, to read and to write, even as you learn

to do other things the institution wants you to do (teach undergraduates, manage money, organize a conference). Remember that it's a gift. An annoying, demanding, mazelike, beautiful gift.

Go to 34.

34. Jonathan Richman wrote a great a cappella song called "Don't Let Our Youth Go to Waste," and Galaxie 500 covered it by surrounding the vocal line with fuzzy, dreamy guitars. The first version's all about frustration and independence, the second about collaboration, about wistful, almost reluctant interdependence. Why bring up these two songs? Because the slogan and the chorus have opposite meanings in them, though the moral import is the same. For some people, going to graduate school would be letting your youth go to waste. For others—and I was one of them—it would be more wasteful not to go. THE END

Stephen Squibb

Like "Should I have sex with my co-worker?" "Should I pursue a career as a politician?" or "Should I try cocaine?" the question "Should I get a PhD in the humanities?" can be safely answered in the negative. No, you probably shouldn't. Some of these things might take place anyway, and they won't always end in disaster, but that still doesn't mean that pursuing them is a wise idea. Furthermore, nobody should be encouraging you. If you are doing cocaine on someone else's advice, both of you need more help than I can provide.

Given the academic job market, that's the responsible thing to say to somebody considering grad school in the humanities. When people say it, they mean to relieve themselves of any responsibility for diverting you from some unspecified, upper-middle-class fate that would presumably be yours if you didn't go. And yes, it's true that if you get a PhD in the humanities, you almost certainly won't make much money. The economics of academia might be why so many grad students return to school thinking that they've already made the only sacrifice that their profession will demand of them. But universities are not free from the *other* pitfalls—the personalities, the politics, the absurdities—that are found in all institutions where people think and write for a living. The mistaken assumption that academics will somehow be liberated from these mundane concerns is likely responsible for the overwhelming negativity that is endemic among humanities grad students.

So be aware that grad school will present various kinds of practical trials in addition to the monetary kind, but know also that getting a PhD in the humanities is by no means a professional death sentence. A recent report by the National Endowment for the Humanities revealed that the unemployment rate for individuals with PhDs in the humanities currently hovers around 2 percent. If this statistic seems shocking, it's because it includes the many PhDs who work outside the academy. The landscape for academic jobs may be grim, but there is no law mandating that getting a PhD means you have to become a professor—though graduate programs may try to convince you otherwise—and it's worth noting that humanities PhDs in nonacademic professions have some of the highest job-satisfaction rates of any demographic.

In my case, I suspect I always knew that I would end up in grad school. In the five years between securing my liberal arts degree and returning to the university, I lived in New York. While there, I edited an "online magazine of cultural praxis," produced performance installations that "rejected the dominant understanding of theater as a static monologue," worked for an artist on projects with names like "Meta-monumental Garage Sale" and "Proposed Helsinki Garden in Singapore," and associated with a literary magazine whose staff split evenly between PhDs and MFAs. For money I did stage carpentry and electrician work and wrung whatever I could from writing and editing. I was fired, justly, first from my position as a facilities manager at a theater company in Manhattan and then from a "fellowship" at an "institute" that was really a "job" at a "gallery." Before that, I lasted a month as a barback at a preshow lounge on Fiftieth Street, a day as a waiter in a fine-dining establishment, and two months in an emotionally fraught if technically lucrative position as a real estate agent in SoHo. I had been on and off unemployment for two years.

When compared to my life in New York, getting a PhD seemed reasonable, even wise. It helped that the stipend and health insurance alone constituted the best salary and benefits I had ever received. Admission felt like winning the lottery, and the prize was a contract: In exchange for reading, writing, teaching, and displaying a working knowledge of two foreign languages of my choosing, I would be paid a certain amount of money in addition to receiving the time and attention of the faculty. This might seem like a vulgarly pragmatic way to think about things, but even by that standard, grad school was not a terrible decision.

I did not go to grad school because it was the responsible thing to do, though the decision did come as a relief to my family. None of my New York endeavors had ever fully escaped the local idiom; I was perpetually explaining to those at home what I was doing, and why my projects were interesting or significant. As in all relationships with demanding partners, the depredations of the city are more apparent from without. After all, how fulfilled could I really be in a place that could not find me health insurance? What work was so important that I could not be paid to do it? When we are young and stupid we often perceive love as something free from banal reciprocity, relying on suffering to confirm our seriousness to ourselves. This was why going to school felt most like a betrayal precisely when it presented itself as the most healthy and reasonable thing to do. Two years later, this choice still makes me anxious. Despite my hapless unemployability in New York (or perhaps because of it) I am still at home in the city. We still see each other on weekends, are still in love.

No, I went to graduate school when my anxiety about leaving was surpassed by a fear about what might happen if I stayed. I had known for a while that I needed time and space to read and to write, that I had ideas I wanted to develop, and that I needed a place to develop them. What would become of me if this space wasn't found? I could see my autodidactic enthusiasm aging poorly, its charming, vagabond eclecticism growing more eccentric and sad. I was already a liability in conversation, quick to drown otherwise innocent exchanges with inscrutable pronouncements and pseudospecialistic qualifications. Crackpottery loomed. And so I went, not to abandon my commitments in New York, but to save them, to release them from the burden of being something they were not. I went to see if I could read deliberately, learn to teach, and to grind into a lens a manic sandbox of ideas.

It was the right decision for three reasons. First, there is no substitute for having even a relative degree of control over one's time and interests. That this freedom often arrives, as it does in academia, with its own set of peculiar and consuming demands doesn't change what it is. Grad school is a place overrun by people who love and care about what they are doing— sometimes to excess—and who maintain deep personal connections with their work. This is incredible, and it's also why the restrictions and pitfalls you encounter there can feel so magnified. But anywhere people have a serious investment in what they do there will be madness and anger besides. This is as true in New York as it is in the academy. I have not always read exactly what I wanted to, nor written exactly as I might have, in either place, but I find the support of the university to be more than worth the price of its constraints.[1] And, second, now that I'm in and out of New York, the city is once again a place of freedom, its projects choices rather than demands. Third, and most important, I'm learning that I love to teach. It keeps me honest and provides a space for ideas and interactions that do not satisfy any other standard and yet feel more important than most of those that do.

There have been adjustments, some more painful than others. As a genre, academic writing is different from journalism or literature; its audience is smaller but typically more dedicated and knowledgeable. It is the difference between writing something that will be read quickly by thousands for a week and something studied closely by thirty people for a decade. Not all scholarship is interesting, but 90 percent of anything you dedicate your life to—art, theater, the Internet, professional wrestling, American history, high fashion, the ballet—will become mundane and familiar, even if it isn't at the start. The trick is finding something, or better, many somethings, worthy enough that sorting through their lesser examples day after day still feels like freedom. If this leaves you at the gates of the academy, the challenge will be the same inside as it is anywhere else: remembering what brought you there in the first place.

In sum: If you have chosen your discipline carefully and you know that you like reading the literature in question; if you have thought in terms of practicalities, with *Who will I study with?* and *Where will I study?* being at least as important as *What will I study?* in deciding your field;[2] and if you can live with less money than most, then you will find happiness. But prioritizing places, people, and projects over money and titles is the recipe for happiness anywhere and at any time. You don't need to go to grad school to know that.

---

1 Speaking of price, do not, under any circumstances, pay for an advanced degree in the humanities. If necessary, continue applying until you secure funding.
2 It might, for example, be better to study art history with a supportive adviser at a well-funded institution than to try to make a last stand on the barricades of comparative literature.

Amy O'Leary

IT HAD COME TO this: I was making snow globes for strangers.

I was twenty-four and this was the most satisfying part of my life in Saint Paul, Minnesota. The raw materials for snow globes—tiny figurines, ersatz snow, glue, glitter, and a hundred little plastic domes—nearly hid the other evidence in my apartment that my life had taken a detour toward a particularly quirky kind of dead end.

GRE study books were there, too, scattered on the coffee table. Mathematical reasoning scores dangled from the fridge. If you'd asked me back then, I couldn't really tell you what the course catalogs, one from Columbia's Teachers College, another from Yale's history department, were doing in my life.

At the time, I was working for a small software company. I made elaborate PowerPoint decks and wore a company polo shirt to conferences in Las Vegas where I spoke with middle managers who always looked sweaty and flushed. At home, in my small studio apartment, I would glue and paint and patch together miniature, fantastical dioramas of moonscapes and street scenes and even one bloody Civil War bayoneting, set in winter. Then I would drown them in liquid and give them away to people I barely knew.

Absent other rituals in our culture, adulthood hits most of us the moment we understand that we are solely responsible for our own lives. It is a thrilling and intimidating moment. But the absolute terror that comes along with this knowledge only really hits after your first try at building a life goes horribly wrong.

I had spent most of my high school and college years wanting to be a newspaper reporter, lusting after a byline in the New York Times. After graduation, I took the first job I could find at a twice-weekly paper in "outstate" Minnesota. I covered city council meetings, planning commissions, feedlot zoning, and the development of a big new Target store in town. I was so proud of my stiff little business cards.

A few months into the job, I learned that my stories were being faxed to a bald man named Clancy. He owned the largest car dealership in the county, right next to the Target. He was the paper's biggest advertiser, and he didn't like my reporting. At night, unbeknownst to me, he would receive drafts of my stories and fax in edits that the paper made without my approval. The printed articles were a jumble of hearsay and misinformation. My sources were furious. When a colleague in the advertising department showed me one of these faxes on the sly, I was crushed. My editor had sold me out.

I had been making $18,500 a year and I had no savings or backup plan. But I still quit in protest without thinking twice.

The next three years were characterized by a series of accidental relationships and career moves that spun me further and further away from whomever I was supposed to be. I dated a charming but highly irresponsible drummer. I found a job at a tech company. I coauthored a programming book.

Naturally, graduate school seemed like just the sort of thick, expensive balm that would calm my anxieties and channel my energies into something that looked like success. I took the GRE and ordered course catalogs from elite universities and wondered whether I should study history or education or something else, and how I would pay back my loans after graduation.

*

It was October and already dark outside the evening I set out for the Ruminator bookstore after work. The Ruminator was one of those doomed little miracles of a shop, and it would disappear two years later. But before it did, I had a habit of going there for readings—with an ulterior motive. The authors who came to town were usually from New York or San Francisco and were stuck in Saint Paul for a night. I was stuck in Saint Paul every night, desperate for conversation. At the end of the reading, I would suggest that we both might use a drink. They almost always said yes.

That time, it was Gabe Hudson. He was a lanky, blond ex–Marine rifleman with wire-rimmed glasses, an MFA from Brown, and a new book of short stories on offer. He walked up to the podium and shuffled through a few jokes and excerpts for an audience of maybe six. Afterward, just as the room became awkwardly empty, I made my pitch. Just a beer or two. Down the block. No big thing?

Sure, he said.

As we finished off a couple of Leinenkugels at a dark-paneled bar nearby, he told me that sometime during his MFA he had set himself a simple goal: He would publish a book by the time he was thirty. And here he was, thirty-one, with a drink in one hand and a book the other.

"Huh," I said, watching his relaxed posture, and something like actual satisfaction on his face. We ordered a second round. I kept staring down at my signed hardback, thumbing the gloss on its cover and feeling the physical weight of an actual accomplishment in my hand.

Over the next two hours, I came to understand that I was in serious trouble. The half-baked ideas, the art projects, the course catalogs, the snow globes—all of it was a slowly accumulating snowdrift of indecision that would eventually bury me in Saint Paul until I woke up one day at forty-five, with two kids, a thousand snow globes to my credit, and nothing but a chirpy profile in the Saint Paul *Pioneer Press* to show for it.

As Gabe slung back the last of his beer, a stunningly obvious notion hit me: By simply choosing *something*, he had ended up with a book in his hand, living a life that he had made for himself.

I realized that I also had to choose something and focus on it intensely. Graduate school was just another stall tactic. I wasn't hungry to publish or teach. It just seemed like a nice-enough way to spend a few years while I stewed in indecision. Something else was responsible for my restlessness: I had no idea what the hell I even wanted.

For a secular person like me, help can be found in humble places: in a conversation, a punch line, and sometimes, if I'm being really honest, in the self-help section at a Barnes & Noble.

When I have felt unanchored, I have occasionally landed there, hoping to absorb the easy confidence of these books. Not long after meeting Gabe, I ended up in the stacks, my fingers skimming spines promising *Whole Life Transformations* and *Authentic Happiness* and *True Callings*. But when my eyes rested on a book that barked, *Follow Your Bliss*, they narrowed in rage.

Fuck bliss, I thought. Because if you're lying in bed in the brittle dark of an October night in Minnesota and you cannot find any bliss, these people make it feel like it is your fault, your failure of imagination, your failure of will. They traffic in a cruel Calvinism.

And then, like a gift, or an antidote, another book with a deceptively simple name came into view. It was called *I Could Do Anything If I Only Knew What It Was*, and upon seeing its title, I nodded naturally in agreement. I finished it right there on the floor of the Barnes & Noble, only to arrive at the second simple realization that would soon change my life: I had never tried to do anything that I might fail at. I had never even stopped to consider what my life might be like if I let myself pursue something risky and ridiculous.

I bought the book and drove home right away. When I got back to my small studio apartment I drew up a list of all the crazy, embarrassing-to-admit jobs that seemed like they would be pure pleasure to do and sheer terror to fail at. The list included entries like this:

Be an Academy Award–winning actor
Own a vineyard
Be a producer for This American Life
Teach kids who really need it

Own a Vespa franchise
Work for social justice in the developing world
Run a restaurant
Make a movie
Write a book

I made an x-y graph on a legal pad and listed at least a dozen of these improbable jobs on one axis. On the other axis, I wrote these questions:

Who would respect me if I did this?
Who would love me if I did this?
Would it flatter my vanity and satisfy my ego?
Would it satisfy my need for meaning?
Will it help introduce me to people I could love?
Will it lead me to other, surprising things?

And probably most important,

What would I be willing to give up for this?

I weighted and ranked the questions, then analyzed my responses. One answer emerged by a mile. It wasn't a revelation. It wasn't my life passion. But, because it was a beautifully functional chart, all the numbers pointed to a single thing: I had to be a producer for the public radio program This American Life.

I laughed. It seemed absurd. I was drawn to the show because it seemed to have the kind of heart and intelligence that was nowhere to be found in small-town Minnesota newspapering. But I had no background in radio. The show was so popular that hundreds of people applied for each single internship. Award-winning journalists wanted to work there, and there were only seven jobs—all presently filled. It was the very definition of a long shot. But that was the point. Now I just had to find a way to do it.

First, I set up some ground rules. I was nearly twenty-five. Thinking back to Gabe Hudson's declaration to publish a book by thirty, I was going to give myself five years to throw everything I had into becoming a producer for This American Life. If I hadn't gotten anywhere by then, I would return to the world of software start-ups and corporate communications.

With that decided, everything that came after felt easy.

I dedicated myself to research. I studied every producer the show had ever hired and discovered that nearly 10 percent of them had been interns there. I researched every intern whose name was mentioned in the program's credits and discovered that nearly 10 percent of them had gone to a four-month-long radio training program in Maine. I applied to the program in Maine. I taught myself audio editing. I bought gear.

I moved to Portland for the training program, and then to New York. I studied every episode of the show, and in my spare time I memorized speeches that staffers had given about how to make radio. I spent a full year working on the perfect internship application, creating elaborate, full-color diagrams that I printed at Kinko's at great expense. When I wasn't accepted the first time I applied, I tried again. (I had five years to keep trying, after all). For my second application, I commissioned a comic book artist to draw strips about what an eager, committed intern I would be. While I was waiting to hear back about that application, I went to the show's Brooklyn office and offered to work for free. I was on the brink of being turned down yet again when the producers offered me a deal: If I transcribed thirty hours of warped cassette tape, they would let me watch them edit that story. During that process, I made friends with a producer named Alex, who recommended me when they were choosing their next intern.

When I got the call to join the show that spring as an intern, it was a total shock. I was walking down Fifth Avenue in Manhattan, coming home from a temporary gig making audio tours for a museum. I could barely believe the news. In a euphoric daze, I called everyone I knew, walking for more than seventy blocks before I could do something as mundane as get on the subway.

That was the beginning. From start to finish, I spent a total of three years researching, interning, freelancing, and waiting. During that time, I sold my car, amassed $15,000 of debt, moved twelve times, made two new best friends, broke up with one boyfriend, and fell in love with another. When it was all over, they made me a producer.

At the end of a long pier in Chicago, sequestered in a small office, I spent my days poring over hours of audio transcripts, editing out breaths and stammers. During my first week at This American Life, I made a sign that I taped over my computer monitor. It showed an aerial shot of Rose Bowl Stadium, replicated eighteen times—the combined seating capacity being an approximation of the show's 1.6 million listeners—with the caption "Don't fuck up."

I was busy and learning, but rarely happy. Much of the work was lonely, and so was I. But I was glad to be there. Every morning I walked briskly to the office, looking forward to the day. Being there was proof that I had taken on something terrifying and risky and figured out how to make it work.

It was a year that changed me, but it was only a year. Just as my contract was about to be made permanent, a beloved producer from the show's early days came back from overseas and asked to return. She had been a mentor of mine. Ira Glass called to kindly explain his decision to give her the permanent slot I'd been hoping to have.

It was tough to see my crusade end like that, but in a way, I'd already gotten what I came for.

The week I learned I would be leaving This American Life, I sent my first letter to the New York Times, explaining why they might be able to use somebody like me. A year later, I was hired as the paper's first-ever audio producer. Now, I'm a staff reporter at the Times—the job I dreamed of when I was seventeen years old.

Today, journalism students often ask me how I became a reporter. I usually smile and tell them it's a long, hard-to-replicate story. But the simpler answer is this: A small-town newspaper broke my heart, and for a while, I was lost. Eventually, I plotted out the pieces of my heart on a grid, and that process gave me the confidence to jump at what came next.

I haven't made a snow globe in a very long time, but I do keep a jar with the tiny painted figurines I made during those days on my desk at home. There are about fifty workers, commuters, soldiers, parents, and children lying in that jar. I never finished their worlds—instead, I made my own.

Eben Klemm

IT IS AROUND FOUR A.M. in the Old Absinthe House, and in a crowded corner, Thomas Waugh is doing his Mick Jagger impersonation for the consideration of Harold McGee. These shenanigans are fairly welterweight for Bourbon Street on a Saturday night, but these are not two boys on leave from the LSU chapter of Delta Chi. Thomas, who has RAF hair from a World War II movie and the slight, permanent smile of someone who appreciates the pranks pulled on him, bartends at the New York City bar Death & Co., which six hours ago won the award for Best Cocktail Menu in the World at the Tales of the Cocktail Conference held annually here in New Orleans. McGee, whose sprightly eyes seem to be broadcasting a wish to do anything other than watch Waugh prance around like a methamphetamined flamingo, is the author of *On Food and Cooking: The Science and Lore of the Kitchen*, a book that leaves everyone who cares about food and beverage in mouth-drooling awe.

These days, the only way I can survive the requisite four days of nonstop cocktail consumption the conference demands is to switch on the last day to a strict regimen of cold beer and warm Campari. I chase a latter with a former and shoulder my way back toward the two to regulate the proceedings. The reason Thomas and I have McGee's company is that about twelve hours ago, along with the food technologist Dave Arnold, we presented a talk titled "The Science of Stirring" to a roomful of the world's top craft bartenders. The talk was larded with graphs detailing hundreds of hours of experiments concerning technique, temperature, and dilution. This, along with a sister lecture on shaking we'd given the previous year, have upended much of the current thinking about good bartending techniques. We've burst some bubbles. We've pissed some people off. We're pretty fucking pleased with ourselves.

At the age of sixteen, my path toward curing AIDS and winning a Nobel Prize seemed pretty clear and unobstructed. But as further maturation exposed me to other realms of inquiry and diversions, these convictions declined at a rather geometric rate until the primary feeling I had upon receiving my bachelor's in biology was relief. With degree in hand, I bummed around the labs of Boston's lesser biotech companies for a few years, mostly interested, in no particular order, in home renovation, drinking, and writing the most important poem in the English language since *The Wasteland*. Two out of those three have worked out for me. But at the age of twenty-five, I was working on the outskirts of Waltham, Massachusetts, for the worst genomics company in the world, and I had no idea what I was supposed to do with my life. Biology, a field of inquiry I had once loved, something I had decided I would spend my entire life pursuing, seemed like a dead end. I really didn't know what to do next until, talking to a trusted elder in the business, I received the advice to not give it up until I'd worked in an academic lab. My friend Bob told me, "You're probably going to do something else anyway, but this will change the way you feel about what you have been doing."

So I took a pay cut and became the first employee of David Schneider, a new fellow at the Whitehead Institute at MIT, and the next three years of work redeemed the previous four. For the first time in my professional life, work was about curiosity and problem solving, carried out in a building full of people who were doing the same thing. My boss had (and still does, fifteen years later and a continent away) a unique field of study, a novel approach to using insects to study human infection, and was someone who understood that our research agenda included taking a couple of hours out in the afternoon to watch movies like *Starship Troopers*. What I had before were co-workers, now I had colleagues: buoyant Germans, reedy Indians, sarcastic Aussies who came to work with purpose. In the elevator, Nobel

Prize winners complimented my dorky essays in the institute's newsletter about Whitehead's art collection. The lens of time, usually soft-focus, won't let me pretend that the building perpetually hummed with esprit de corps, but most of the people I worked with then had a sense of belonging and a sense that they had something important to complete. After a couple years, I had proved my enthusiasm and work ethic enough to David that he was willing to help me get into grad school, into MIT.

Which is when I sold my house and moved to New York to seek my fortune as a bartender.

Since then, various PR teams tasked with getting me press have made a little too much hay of my previous profession—*The mad scientist of the bar! He applies the science of MIT to the art of mixing drinks!*—and I've uneasily allowed this, needing a public underwriting of my career change to abate my private anxieties about it. Look, I'll never be able to precisely determine whether those years in the lab had any effect on the success of my later career; and if so, how, still, this narrative omits too much. It doesn't account for the cultural shift in urban drinking that started right when I needed some spending money, nor does it consider that I and a few others—and then the ones we trained— were lucky enough to be around at just the right time to invent something altogether new. But it is true that during this time, we created a decade's worth of the most creative and inventive cocktails ever seen in the history of the profession. Now, inventing cocktails isn't exactly brain surgery—or what I had been doing: performing bacterial enemas on *Drosophila mela-nogaster*, which also wasn't exactly brain surgery—but this is what our generation of craft bartenders did do: We created new cocktail aesthetics, techniques, and schools of thoughts; we invented new spirits and revived old ones; we discovered new things to mix, did historical research where there hadn't been any before, shaped an international palette, became famous, became pariahs, formed alliances, and suffered schisms. Now looking back at all this, doesn't it sound a little, well, *academic?*

What I learned from observing Schneider and all the other researchers and postdocs and grad students down the line was that all of them owned one specific question, one problem that they were willing to spend their life pursuing. I liked the work, loved it even, but work was never the question. At that time, I didn't have one thing I wanted to spend my life thinking through. That was why I didn't go back to school in the end, because I did not have a precise enough idea for myself. I am exceedingly fortunate to have found and helped form a community, which, as silly as its aspirations may be, has gradually assembled a set of questions and goals and a means to reach them while taking the work very very seriously. No matter whether it's the London bar owners who use equipment so expensive few others can duplicate their work, the San Francisco bartenders who grow absinthe herbs in their backyard, or, say, the zealots of the Japanese school of bartending whose tenets I've rather mercilessly skewered, there's no one involved who hasn't tried to make a better product, and many who have made a lot of people happy during that process.

Granted, given the particular aesthetics of our age, we could easily comb back through the last two paragraphs and trade out the references to mixology with *artisanal cheesemongery* or *bookbinding* or any number of the hip trades that the supremely overeducated seem to get attention for doing these days. But I don't think that undermines my story at all. These days, I have a fairly awesome job. I sit at home and wait for clients to e-mail me requests for new cocktail menus and I make site visits to help them open up new restaurants. I'm published. I'm big in Bogotá. Would my life be more or less complete, would I be better or worse, richer or poorer, doing more or less good if I had gone to grad school? Yes to all of the above. Anything can become a serious, almost academic pursuit if you care to work at it deeply and honestly (or dishonestly) within a community of similar individuals who choose to care about it as much as you do. You just have to find them. The important thing is to be sure of the questions that you are willing to pursue forever, and to determine the best ways and institutions that will allow you to do so. Other people are waiting for you.

I manage to peel Thomas away from McGee, reminding him of our seven thirty A.M. out of Louis Armstrong International, and of the absolute joy a shower before the flight might bring. McGee and I step out onto the sidewalk into the loud and fragrant air. There's so much I want to ask him. Over the past couple hours, I've thrown him as many questions as Thomas did dance moves. I'm getting him a cab. "By the way," I say, "In whose lab were you in at Yale?"

He shrugs, "I studied poetics. With Harold Bloom."

Naturally.

David Orr

IF YOU'RE INTERESTED IN poetry, the question isn't "Should I go to grad school?" It's more along the lines of "Would it be crazy not to go to grad school?" After all, American poetry "has been all but entirely absorbed by institutions of higher education," as scholar Mark McGurl puts it in The Program Era. Which seems fair enough. In the 2012 edition of The Best American Poetry, almost all of the seventy-five contributors have taught poetry in universities, have earned an advanced degree in poetry, or (more frequently) have done both. The fifteen chancellors of the Academy of American Poets have all taught creative writing at one time or another. And the Association of Writers & Writing Programs (AWP) claims to have more than five hundred member institutions, up from only thirteen in 1967.

There are reasons to be pleased about all this. Poets have been the hoboes of literature for ages, shuffling with our little bindles from rich patrons (Rilke) to odd jobs (Whitman) to positions as stamp distributors (Wordsworth). So it's nice to finally have a place to call home, particularly a place that offers health insurance and, for a few lucky souls, tenure. And of course, should Earth be invaded by aliens who can only be defeated by group critiques of their haikus, we now have a small army of creative writing professors to throw at them.

But the explosion of university-based poetry—and the parallel diminishment of poetry pretty much everywhere else—leaves people like me in an odd position. I'm a poetry critic. I'm also a poet. In combination, those two facts mean that I should have either an MFA in poetry (the standard degree for poets) or a PhD in English or comp lit (the standard degree for people who want to talk about poets). I might even have a PhD in creative writing (which I guess is the standard degree for poets who want to talk about themselves).

But what I have instead is a law degree. I've never taught creative writing at a university. I took two creative writing classes in college, which served mostly to prove to me that I don't function well in groups, at least where poetry is concerned. I remember asking one of my professors whether I should consider grad school, and he said, "I don't think you would . . . like it." He was probably right.

So I went to law school in order to give myself a way of making a living that was completely independent of poetry. The idea was that this would allow poetry to remain, well, *poetry*. It's a romantic and possibly naïve way to think about art, but I'm still not sure it's entirely wrong. And of course, I was young and arrogant, and I'd read just enough to think that I could teach myself better than anyone else could.

I couldn't, naturally, and I'm sure I'd have benefited from some time in an English department. Still, there are some advantages to being young and outside the reach of a system that tends to discourage the publication of pointed criticism. You often say what you actually think, for one thing. Many of the things you think will be ridiculous. But some of them will be true, and that's something poetry always needs.

I wrote my first review for *Poetry* magazine as a second-year law student. Three years later I did my first piece for the *New York Times*, and a couple of years after that, I became the paper's primary poetry critic (not that my services are needed on a daily basis). Along the way, I managed to get poems published in *Poetry* and the *New Yorker*, among other places.

Would this have happened, or happened any faster, if I'd gone to grad school? I think not, actually. I'm an impressionable person, and if I'd become enmeshed in the university when young, I believe it would have been harder for me to understand some of the limitations that it can impose on your thinking. Don't get me wrong: English departments and creative writing departments are the lifeblood of poetry today. We can't live without them. But we also can't live with nothing but them. Like all systems, the university wants to perpetuate itself, and the interests of the massive, wealthy American educational complex aren't necessarily the interests of poetry, that fragile creature. But when you work for the former, it's easy to fool yourself into thinking that you're defending poetry when what you're really defending is the authority of your discipline.

Take the perennial debates about the so-called popularization of poetry. I can't even count the number of times I've heard someone—always a professor or grad student—complain about poetry being "dumbed down" in some general-interest publication in order to make it, horrors, "accessible." These same people will then get up the next day and, with no sense of hypocrisy whatsoever, do their absolute best to make Wallace Stevens interesting to a bunch of bored eighteen-year-olds who spent the previous evening throwing up on each other. And they will collect a paycheck for doing so. But this, of course, is not popularizing poetry by trying to make it accessible to people who don't know anything about it. This is teaching, don't you know.

A few years ago, an MFA student asked me if I ever got any grief because I don't have a "poetry background." I knew what this person was trying to say, so I let it pass. But part of me was cringing. Part of me wanted to reply that the only background a poet or critic needs is whatever happens to work, whether that involves learning from a professor or learning from a library or making a lot of very bad decisions, and then learning from those. Our job is to say something interesting, however we can manage it, not to flourish our credentials. We're nothing but what we leave on the page.

To which the MFA student might have replied, "That's all well and good, but don't you think you're acting as if you care about practicality, when what you obviously really care about is a slightly crazy notion of purity or solitude or something?" That would be a fair response, and I would have said so.

But I wouldn't have really believed it. And that's why I never went to grad school.

Maggie Nelson

I GRADUATED FROM COLLEGE in 1994, and at times I wonder if my generation of American writers was among the last to whom the notion of enrolling in an MFA program simply never occurred. The presumption, at least with the people I knew, was that if you wanted to become a writer, or at least a certain kind of writer, you had to move to New York City and "make the scene." During my freshman year, I had hooked up with a senior, a poet named Cynthia Nelson, who became both my first girlfriend and my guide to the downtown NYC poetry scene and all its lore. During my summers, I trailed her, living in her apartment at 49 St. Mark's Place, where I sweated, read all the books I bought at St. Mark's Bookshop, and wrote poems on an old typewriter propped up on a milk crate. I went to see the poets at the Poetry Project at St. Mark's Church and at CBGB and ABC No Rio and the Knitting Factory and other venues. I had dreamed of being among them, and I was.

After I graduated, I went straight back to the Lower East Side, this time to the corner of Orchard and Broome (a neighborhood and corner that was completely not what it is now, of course), and my poetic education began in earnest. Apart from my own reading and writing, my education consisted of a kerjillion workshops with the poet Eileen Myles downtown, and a day job as an assistant to the poet David Lehman uptown. (There were many other jobs, all in food and beverage service.) My colleagues in Eileen's workshops were amazing artists and dancers and fellow writers, each of whom represented a different way of being an artist in the city. I was a dancer then, too, and I went to class at Movement Research in the morning, Judson Memorial Church on Monday nights, and weekly contact improv jams at PS122 that a boyfriend at the time disparagingly called "touch club." It was pretty fantastic. Drug addled, romantically disastrous, rodent ridden, and clichéd in ways that were happily lost on me, but fantastic.

Eventually, after about five years, I noticed my mind feeling soft. Exuberant alcohol and drug use by friends and lovers had soured into naïveté-busting rehab. Dancers who had seemed like geniuses suddenly didn't seem quite as smart, even if they did use text in their work. Our rent was on the rise on Orchard Street, and my longtime roommate suddenly announced he was applying to a master's program in public policy at Columbia. Having studied for years with Eileen and an offshoot group, I was sick to death of writing workshops. And I was realizing that I had more things to say than poetry could express. I am one of the handful of humans on earth who enjoys writing critically, and I missed having a reason to do so. Like many English majors in the early nineties, I had had a lot of "dessert" in the form of entrancing critical theory but very little basic education about the history of literature. I had to force myself to remember that "eighteenth century" didn't mean the 1800s. I was embarrassed to admit that I had never read much of the work the critical theorists I loved were writing about, be it that of Freud or Henry James. Spotting Patti Smith buying a paper at Gem Spa and tearing up at the commemorative literary plaques at the Chelsea Hotel were no longer enough. Also, I knew that if I wanted to teach literature at the college level—which, in the back of my mind, I guess I always figured I would do (What else would I do: Wait tables forever? Teach yoga?)—an MFA wouldn't be very useful. I had heard through the grapevine that you could actually get *paid* to study if you went for a PhD, whereas MFA programs cost money that I didn't have. I had been a successful student in college; maybe I could get into a PhD program and find someone to pay my way?

Before long, my roommate and I were studying for the GRE together on our grimy kitchen table. To prepare for the subject test, I used the stacks at the New York Public Library to make flash cards about Chaucer, the Reformation, and diasporic English that I would then study on the subway.

I was in heaven. I love nothing more than placing the life of my mind against a teeming metropolis indifferent to my contemplations.

Thankfully, I have forgotten many of the details of the personal statement I sent with my applications, but I do remember that I centered it on Susan Sontag's famous proclamation in *Against Interpretation* that "in place of a hermeneutics we need an erotics of art." I said that I wanted to go back to school to address Sontag's question "What would criticism look like that would serve the work of art, not usurp its place?" I made it clear that unlike many people who want to call us back to "criticism that matters," or who lament the loss of the "public intellectual," my idea of criticism was not to react against the ascendancy of things like critical race theory, feminist theory, queer theory, and so on. I wanted to be a formalist, but a progressive one. A public intellectual, sure, but not at the price of dumbing things down. I was younger then, but in many ways, my priorities haven't changed.

I can't remember how it all shook out (I've repressed the rejections, of course), but I was lucky enough to get good offers from UC Berkeley and the City University of New York. When I asked my college professors for advice, they all pushed for Berkeley. Their reasoning—which was sound, albeit besotted with the norms of academia—was that the job market for new PhDs was so competitive that you simply *had* to go to one of the top-ranked schools or you were never going to get one of the highly coveted jobs in the field. I didn't really know then what the "job market" or the "field" meant, which was just as well. I didn't have my eyes on any prize. I wasn't even totally sure I wanted to be a professor. I wanted to be smarter and a better writer and to talk to people whose intelligence blew my head off. I wanted financial support to do what I loved, even if for a handful of years.

When I went to visit Berkeley, I suddenly doubted my plan. Nobody with whom I spoke was encouraging about my being a creative as well as a critical writer. In the class I sat in on, the students seemed obnoxious and competitive. (I later learned this was not at all specific to Berkeley.) Someone in the class I visited said, "Here's where the rhetoric simply balloons," and I scribbled down the phrase, thinking it the epitome of pretentiousness. (I've since used it several times, without irony.)

I sought out the poet Thom Gunn to ask advice. He reclined in his sunlit office, in his trademark snug T-shirt, and said, "Well, you should come here, if only for the weather!" I told him I had grown up in the Bay Area and was actually smitten with the seasons in New York. He smiled and said, "Well, then you should stay in New York, for the culture!" And then there were the hacky sackers, hacking away all over Sproul Plaza. I went to high school in Haight-Ashbury, and ever since, I have been on the run from the hacky sackers.

Before I'd visited Berkeley, I'd spent a day visiting the English program at CUNY, which was then housed on the fortieth floor of the Grace Building, right across the street from Bryant Park and the New York Public Library. First I sought out Wayne Koestenbaum, whose 1993 book on opera and homosexuality, The Queen's Throat, I had loved. Wayne said, "Go visit Berkeley, and look at what the people there are wearing. Then come back here and look around." This comment came back to haunt me as I watched the hacky sackers. Could I really decide on graduate school based on student fashion? Yes, I could, if style is indeed a form of substance. I also visited feminist critic Nancy K. Miller, whose work on autobiography had been important to me in college. When I told her that I really liked CUNY but worried that Berkeley was the more highly ranked program (imagine my audacity!), she rolled her eyes and said, "Have we come so far from the phallus only to cling to it in the final hour?"—a line that still makes me smile and has reverberated at several critical life junctures since. From there I wandered into Bryant Park and asked the seated Gertrude Stein, cast in bronze, what to do. Stay here by me, she said, as if I were one of her dogs. I obeyed.

It was a terrific decision, one of the best in my life. I loved CUNY, loved PhD school. In penance for my undergraduate woes, at first I prohibited myself from taking classes that seemed like "dessert," and instead I studied early American literature (colonial, federalist, nineteenth-century, Native American, the whole bag). I audited courses on literature from the seventeenth and eighteenth centuries so that I had at least cocktail party knowledge of the eras, even if they didn't do much for me. I vowed never to take an incomplete, and I didn't, which meant I was reading and writing papers nearly all the time. At some point I even figured out a way to read in the shower.

I wanted teaching experience, but I couldn't bring myself to work for the pittance paid to CUNY instructors to teach composition three days a week at faraway satellite campuses, so I kept waitressing and bartending at a restaurant on the Bowery. After my poetry book *Shiner* came out in 2001, I got a job teaching literature in the New School's MFA program. It was a tad humiliating to have to wait on my New School students from time to time, but I made as much bartending in one week as I could have made teaching at CUNY for an entire semester (plus I ate and drank for free), so I just suffered through.

Part of my attraction to CUNY had been the fact that unlike most doctoral programs, it didn't offer a master's degree along the way. It was all or nothing. This perversity kept me going, as I knew that each year that went by would be a degree-less waste should I quit. Eventually I got it into my mind that I had to get my doctorate before my thirtieth birthday, and I worked like a dog to do so. It was a time of striving. I took my composition exams in the midst of a menacing late-summer storm, my orals just weeks after the September 11 attacks. Afterward, my committee agreed that the kind of intellectual conversation we had just had was worth living and dying for. During the months that followed, our building was repeatedly evacuated due to bomb threats at the Empire State Building. Over the next two years, I wrote a dissertation I loved on women and the New York School that combined everything I'd learned from Eileen Myles and David Lehman prior to graduate school with everything I had learned there. A few years later, I edited it and published it under the title *Women, the New York School, and Other True Abstractions*. I likely won't write anything as academic again, but I stand by it.

In retrospect, it was all pretty euphoric, though I'm sure I bitched my way through, like most grad students do. I'm pretty embarrassed now to think of what a jerk I was in some of my classes—something about being a grad student really brings out the bitchiness in people. It's probably the fact of being an adult placed in the somewhat infantile position of student, I'm not sure. This is why now I don't worry too much when my graduate students express dissatisfaction with the program, their teachers, or their peers—I know from experience that the positive effects of one's education are not always legible in the moment, and they often take months or years to unfold. The lessons one learns are not always those that one imagined learning, or that one thought one needed to learn, and that is part of their virtue.

Nowadays many more poets and writers are getting PhDs rather than, or in addition to, MFAs. There has also been a rise in something called the PhD in creative writing, which didn't substantively exist when I was contemplating grad school. These trends make sense insofar as the job market for creative writers has become steadily more competitive, and people think that a PhD might give them an edge. And why would anyone want to be out looking for work or incurring gobs of student debt during the Great Recession? Against the dog-eat-dog backdrop of contemporary capitalism, the sheltering wing of a well-funded PhD program can seem like a last bastion of civilized society. If it suits you—and really, it doesn't suit everyone—time spent in a doctoral program isn't just preparation, it's a perfectly wonderful way to spend the days of one's short life. It also resembles the life of a professor quite closely, save that as a professor you're (hopefully) no longer striving for anyone's approval, you make up your own syllabi, and you must pick up the check if you meet one of your students for coffee.

So I guess this is a ringing endorsement, with the caveat that it's just my experience and that I was very lucky in grad school, having had good financial support, a natural/nerdy affinity for the classroom, and no felt conflict between my "creative" and "critical" pursuits. In fact, knowing myself to be a writer first (rather than an academic) has always served as a form of emotional insurance, keeping me hovering apart from the bizarre exigencies of academia proper. Now that I teach in an MFA writing program, and one with high tuition at that, I could write a hundred more pages on the ethics, utility, excitements, and injustices of getting an MFA in art or creative writing. But I'll leave that alone for the time being and just say that I continue to believe that each day on the planet spent studying or making art is a good day, and perhaps an ethically defensible one, if, as Sontag says, you can't think and hit someone at the same time. Of course, you can, sadly, think and become a victim of a deleterious student loan system at the same time. The answer to such conundrums, to my mind, lies in empowering the students of the present and the future to demand a more just, wild, and free world, not in denigrating the notion of higher education, nor in calculating the cash value of a life spent devoted to scholarship or art making.

In closing, I'd like to thank all my teachers, who have meant everything to me, and to encourage anyone who's contemplating similar choices to drop me an e-mail. For if there's one thing that has become clear to me in writing this piece, it's the value of advice. Not because that advice needs to be followed—to the contrary! Rather, because figuring out when and how to follow, ignore, collage, or reject the life shapes offered to you by others helps in honing that indispensable skill—critical in grad school and beyond—of taking what you need and leaving the rest behind.

Meehan Crist

I REMEMBER THE MOMENT I knew my life had changed. I was lying on my back swaddled in white hospital blankets, ears muffled by plugs and some sort of soft padding, my body buried inside one of the world's most powerful experimental magnets. I was twenty-eight years old, in my third year of graduate school, and this was my second MRI. The familiar smell of plastic and the dull glare of fluorescent lights erased any sense of the spring day outside, but I was happy to be in the lab. I wasn't getting a brain scan because I was sick; I was getting a brain scan because I was curious.

Getting extracurricular MRIs was not what I had in mind when I applied to MFA programs in writing. Back then I was still living in Quito, Ecuador, a city so close to the sun that it's bleached like an overexposed photograph. None of my friends spoke English, much less read or wrote in English, and though my Spanish was eventually passable, I spoke not a word of it when I first arrived. Actually, that's what I always tell people, but it occurs to me now that it's not true. For years before going to South America, I had worked summers as a waitress in California, which meant I had to learn some Spanish. The first words I learned were probably "*Mas sopa roja, por favor*," which I was supposed to yell across the kitchen to the line cooks, who would send one of the Mexican or Guatemalan or Ecuadorian guys out with another huge silver pot of that day's "red soup."

So maybe, a few years after college, when I decided to escape the United States for a while, the scales were already tipped in favor of the decision to move to Ecuador, where I tried to write fiction but kept getting distracted by writing about the world around me. I was working on short stories (puppets with strings visible all the way up to the puppeteer's hands) and, on the side, writing about getting teargassed at a soccer match or finding fresh cougar shit in a farmhouse where I slept for a few nights or watching a herd of horses explode out of the park and gallop down the main boulevard at dusk. Living sometimes felt like dreaming, and, over time, I began to see the stuff of the imagination and the stuff of real life as just different materials for the same art.

Maybe all this is why, when I decided to go back to the States to get an MFA in nonfiction, the fact that I spoke Spanish helped me get a fellowship to research the Puerto Rican poet and statesman Luis Muñoz Marín for a journalism professor, a fedora-and-trench-coat type who had never gone to grad school for writing or anything else, but who had edited one of the nation's most powerful political magazines and written some seriously impressive books. By then, I'd been in grad school for a year, and he took one look at a draft I'd turned in to my workshop (and for which I had been showered with praise) and urged me to look outward before turning inward.

Up until then, I had been writing about my mother and a brain injury she suffered when she slipped and fell while ice-skating. I can't remember now if this professor specifically told me to look into the science of brain injury before writing more about my mother, but after that conversation I began to imagine a continuum with science on one end and personal experience on the other, certain that I had gone too far toward the personal end of the spectrum and that I needed to turn my attention completely toward the other in the hope that my writing would end up balanced somewhere in-between. Because I was on a college campus, I started taking neuroscience courses. I started hanging around labs, going to conferences, and interviewing experts. This is how I eventually found myself in an MRI machine, hoping for images of my brain that would look like exploded balls of colored yarn.

"It is easy to see the beginnings of things, and harder to see the ends," Joan Didion writes at the start of "Goodbye to All That." But the opposite is often true: It is easy to see the ends of things, and harder to see the beginnings. One day, you wake up smack-dab in the middle of your life and think, "How did I get here?" Then, you try to sit still inside an MRI machine while radio waves bounce around your skull and you wonder how you became the person you are.

Would I be who I am today if I didn't get a graduate degree? Probably not. I can imagine versions of my life that would have been better. I can imagine some that would have been worse. (I certainly can imagine a life without the debt I now carry.) But it's hard to draw a straight line that begins at my decision to go to grad school and continues to the present. I did not intend to write about science, or to become a "science writer." But that is what seems to be happening—what has somehow already happened.

If you are thinking of applying to grad school, you may hope that it will change your life. And it probably will, though maybe not in the ways you expect. While it's easy to say that grad school changed the course of my life—my decision to get an MFA had nothing to do with science, but I might not have found my way to science without it—it's also true that being a waitress and learning Spanish and going to Ecuador and working with a skeptical journalist changed the course of my life. Who we are and who we will become is dependent on more than just one big decision, it is dependent on a serendipitous chain of events, a jiggering trail of minute choices that may not seem to be pointing you anywhere, but which, taken together, are already pointing you toward what comes next and next and next.

Duncan Watts

Just over twenty years ago, I left my job as an officer in the Royal Australian Navy, said good-bye to my family and friends, and hopped on a plane in Sydney toward the United States to start at a PhD program at Cornell University.

At the time, I didn't know a single person in the country that was to become my home, or for that matter, anyone who had ever studied in the U.S. I barely even knew anything about Cornell. This was 1993—still the pre-Internet era—so the extent of my knowledge was a one-page write-up in one of those college guides they used to have in libraries and whatever the admissions office had sent with my acceptance letter. I remember someone telling me that the campus was beautiful and that the winters were long (both true, as it turns out), but that was about it. I didn't even know what classes I would be taking.

I was only twenty-two at the time, still young enough to make major life decisions without thinking too much about them. But as I hugged my sister and my best friend good-bye that day at the airport, the enormity of what I was doing finally hit me. I'm a big guy—6' 2" and over two hundred pounds—and I thought I'd been through some tough moments during my years in the navy, but this was more than I had bargained for. I broke down and cried like a baby, right there in front of hundreds of people in the passport line. I remember feeling horribly embarrassed, but I couldn't help it. I was leaving my whole life behind and I had no idea where I was going, how long I was going for, or what I would do when I got there.

What on earth had I been thinking?

To be honest, I'm not actually sure. It certainly wasn't that I had my heart set on an academic career. During my undergraduate training at the Australian Defence Force Academy, I'd found myself more inspired by the military officers than by my academic instructors, so the idea of becoming a professor wasn't terribly appealing. At the same time, a navy career didn't seem in the cards for me, either. In the final year of my degree in physics, I had stumbled on chaos theory, which at the time had felt like the next big thing in science, and I ended up writing my honors thesis about it. The navy, however, had no interest in chaos theory or in letting me do research of any kind. They also wouldn't let me go to sea on account of my bad eyesight, so I was stuck doing mostly administrative jobs.

Grad school seemed like the obvious way out of this rut. But there were two problems. First, the navy didn't send officers to PhD programs, especially not officers who had only just completed their first degree, so there was a good chance they wouldn't let me go no matter where I got in. And second, I had to get in somewhere.

Oxford had always been a vague dream of mine, but in order to afford it I had to win a scholarship, which effectively meant winning a Rhodes. I applied two years in a row, both times reaching the final round only to fall short. The second year, however, I also applied to some schools in the U.S., which I'd chosen by looking at the addresses of the authors that I'd run across in my thesis research. Cornell was one of them. Given how little I knew about the place, I had always assumed I had less chance of getting into Cornell than Oxford. But a few weeks after missing out on the Rhodes for the second time, I got a surprise letter in the mail telling me that I had been accepted to Cornell's Department of Theoretical and Applied Mechanics. It wasn't my first choice by any stretch, but I figured it would have to do, so I went to my boss with the news that I wanted to go to the U.S. for grad school. Even then it was a long process—I remember the commodore in charge of navy personnel asking me why I would possibly want to go and get a PhD when I already had the best job in the world. In the end, however, they were surprisingly understanding, and they let me go.

It didn't exactly get off to a great start.

Cornell, if you're not familiar, is a big university in a small town called Ithaca, New York, about four and a half hours north of New York City. The campus is as beautiful as I had been told, but it's also pretty intimidating for a newcomer, and very isolated. I didn't know a soul when I arrived, and phone calls back to Australia cost more than a dollar per minute, which on my stipend meant that I couldn't afford to call home more than once a month or so. I remember feeling incredibly lonely.

My program also had some surprises in store for me. For one, I had to teach introductory mechanics, a class I'd never taken myself. Being engineers, all my classmates *had* taken it, so I was already behind the curve. I also didn't realize how many mandatory courses I would have to take on topics that had nothing to do with my actual interests. And worst of all, the chaos theory people whom I'd been looking forward to studying with had all left the department.

So here I was in a strange place with no friends, taking courses I didn't like and teaching courses I didn't understand, feeling totally overwhelmed and wondering how I had managed to misjudge things so badly. The only reason I didn't head straight back home was sheer stubbornness and pride. But I did seriously consider leaving Cornell, even going as far as to apply to a program at MIT that I thought would be a better fit.

Right around this time, a young MIT professor named Steven Strogatz visited Cornell to give a seminar. As a lowly grad student, I wasn't aware that his visit was actually a job interview, or that he would soon be offered a faculty position in my department. I just remember thinking how interesting his work seemed and what a clear and entertaining speaker he was. So as my first year of grad school came to an end, I called him to ask whether he'd take me on as a student if I were to transfer to MIT. That's when he told me that he was actually coming to Cornell—in just a couple of months. I decided to wait.

Up until then I'd been working with a professor in mechanical engineering and had been feeling pretty stuck in my research. He was a very distinguished researcher and was in many ways a kind and caring adviser who was doing his best to help me. But we were on different wavelengths.

On the rare occasions when he actually had time to meet with me, he would interrupt whatever question I was trying to ask by thrusting a pile of books into my arms and telling me the answer was in one of them. Typically, it wasn't, but by the time I'd determined as much the meeting was long over and I'd have to wait another couple of weeks to try again. Presumably I was supposed to figure things out on my own, and I did manage to make some progress that way, but it also made me wonder about the point of having an adviser.

When I met Strogatz, the difference was palpable. Steve's research was on the synchronization of coupled oscillator systems, and he had just published a popular textbook on nonlinear dynamics and chaos, so he was very much doing the work that I cared about. But it was more than that. It might seem strange to talk about chemistry between an adviser and a student, but we just clicked. It didn't hurt that, being relatively young himself and also new to Cornell, he had much more time to spend sitting around talking about research, or to just talk. So with the consent of my original adviser, who turned out to be such a good sport that he even let me keep a desk in his lab, I became Steve's advisee. Neither of us had much idea what we were going to do, but both of us had a feeling that it would be fun and interesting.

And indeed it was. I won't go into the details, but the short story is that we wound up doing something quite remarkable, inventing, in effect, a whole new field of science. We didn't realize that at the time, of course, but our first paper, "Collective Dynamics of 'Small-World' Networks," which was published in the journal *Nature* in 1998, the year after I graduated, quickly became a blueprint for what is now called network science. Fifteen years later—and with more than twenty thousand citations and counting on Google Scholar—it is one of the most cited papers in any field in the past two decades.

At this point, you probably think that I'm going to recommend going to grad school: *Look at me! I went to grad school, followed my dreams, and had a wildly successful academic career. You can, too!* But that would be misleading, for three reasons.

First, the odds of having a wildly successful academic career after going to grad school are about the same as the odds of becoming a movie star after studying acting. This reality is one of those obvious numerical facts that somehow many ambitious students miss until it's too late. Because you spend most of your academic career studying the ideas of famous people and reading highly cited papers, it's easy to fall into the trap of thinking that those are the norm, when in fact the overwhelming majority of papers receive very few citations and don't end up in anyone's curriculum.

Second, the gap between superstar and anonymity is far fuzzier than most of us feel comfortable admitting. As successful and influential as that 1998 Nature paper now seems, the reality is that it came within a hairbreadth of being rejected. How it eventually did get published and what happened after that is another long story, but the short version is that if it had been rejected by Nature, it would likely never have garnered the attention it did. And without that early attention, most of what followed in my career—a book, a job at Columbia, a second book, tenure, etc.—wouldn't have happened, either.

And finally, just getting to that point meant taking some risks that any sensible grad student would regard as crazy. When I told Steve that I wanted to prove the theory that everyone in the world is connected by just six degrees of separation—which in the mid-1990s still seemed like an urban myth—and that I also wanted to connect that idea to problems as diverse as the synchronization of coupled oscillators, the spread of epidemics, and the outbreak of revolutions, he was sufficiently intrigued to let me try, but only after I promised him that I wasn't interested in an academic career. As he reasonably pointed out, everything in academia is organized in terms of disciplines, and what I wanted to do didn't fit into any existing discipline. So even if I succeeded in figuring out something interesting, chances were it wouldn't be the kind of interesting that would get me a job.

As it happened, I didn't care about having an academic career. So I went ahead and did what I thought was interesting rather than what I thought was expedient, and I had a career anyway. But that doesn't mean Steve was wrong. I think that if you do want to have an academic career, it really is a good idea to pick one particular field of interest and be very attentive to that field's priorities, methods, and norms. I just don't think that that's the only reason to go to grad school, or even necessarily the best reason.

Going to grad school as a stepping-stone to an academic career—or to any other career, for that matter—is to treat it as a means to an end; and it can be that. But it can also be an end in itself. And as muddled as my thinking was leading up to grad school, and even through most it, I always thought of it as an end in itself, an adventure that I was going to have solely for the sake of having an adventure.

I don't know exactly why I thought this, but it was an idea I'd had since I was a boy, hanging out with my dad in his lab, looking at all the workbenches and machines and blackboards covered in diagrams, feeling a sense of wonder that this was a place where people figured out how the world worked. I didn't know exactly what that entailed, or even what I would have to do to experience that sensation for myself, but I had convinced myself that if I went to grad school I would find out. It wasn't exactly a plan, but it *was* something like a scent that either got weaker or stronger as a result of any particular activity that I tried. So I just kept trying things and following my nose until I found it. That I turned it into a career after I found it is all very well, but it's also beside the point, because that wasn't what I was after.

So do I think going to grad school is a good idea?

I'm not sure. Certainly it was a great experience for me, but it's not for everyone. Grad students are by nature competitive, analytical types who are already predisposed to overthinking everything, so the intensity and uncertainty of grad school make it a breeding ground for insecurity and anxiety. It's definitely not something you should subject yourself to because you can't think of anything else to do, nor should you suffer through it on the grounds that you'll be happier with the academic career that it leads to. There are plenty of miserable academics out there as well, and lots of great and interesting things to do with your life that don't require a PhD, not to mention the five to seven years that most people spend getting one. Don't sign up for it lightly.

But if you do decide to go, remember that those years are not just a prelude to your life, they are part of your life as well, and in some cases, a pretty good chunk of it. So you might as well make them count. Beyond that, I don't want to get too prescriptive, but here are three suggestions.

First, try to be positive. Grad school may be a time of great uncertainty about the future, but it is also a time when in the present you don't have a whole lot of responsibility, you do have a lot of time to think and learn, and you are surrounded by an incredible depth and diversity of knowledge. There were academic programs at Cornell that I'd never even heard of until I got there, and once I got my feet on the ground, I started auditing classes in completely unrelated programs, such as philosophy and political science, just because I could. My classmates thought I was crazy because I wasn't getting credit for these courses, which also took time away from my mandatory coursework. But I thought they were crazy, because when in the rest of their lives would they ever have the luxury of sitting in on some world-renowned expert's course on a topic that they just happened to find interesting? Grad school is full of these wonderful opportunities to learn about almost anything under the sun. Take advantage of them while you can.

Second, find the right adviser. Unless you meet your future spouse in grad school (which actually is not all that unlikely), the single most important relationship you are likely to have is with your adviser. So it's important, both to your success and even more so to your happiness, to find an adviser who is a good fit for your needs. In part that means that he or she knows enough about your intended field to guide your research. But learning how to do good research is about more than just mastering certain skills or domains of knowledge. It's also about learning how to ask an interesting question, which after a lifetime of answering questions that have been handed to you suddenly requires you to think in a whole new way. You're going to need some help with that.

And finally, find your question. The best piece of advice that Steve ever gave me was that I would know I had found my question when I found myself unable to articulate why it was so interesting to me. That I could go over all the usual reasons (interesting math, practical applications, etc.), but in the end it would be something else, something that—as Steve's mentor, the great mathematical biologist Art Winfree, told Steve— "irrationally grips you by the imagination." I used to do a lot of rock climbing back then, and I was surprised to learn that the thrill I got from the occasional breakthrough in my research was not unlike that of leading a challenging route, or reaching a mountaintop. There's no physical danger, of course, but it's the same sense of pitting yourself—in this case, your mind—against the world, of pushing yourself to your limits and then realizing your goal, of experiencing the beauty of the world anew. You don't have to go to grad school to experience this feeling, but if intellectual adventure is your thing, there's a chance you can find it there. I hope you do.

Elizabeth Schambelan

Should I Get an MFA in Writing?

No, you shouldn't, because getting an MFA in writing is a crazy thing to do. You will devote two years of your life, and perhaps tens of thousands of dollars, to obtaining your degree, and once you've got it you won't have any qualifications you didn't possess in the first place. You don't need an MFA to be a published writer. You don't even need an MFA to teach in an MFA program.

Should I Get an MFA in Writing Anyway?

That's a very complex question. Here are some dos and don'ts that may help you make the call.

DON'T go to grad school to learn. In grad school, you will participate in many workshops. A workshop is a pedagogical situation in which people respond to one another's writing. The term *workshop* is used because *cluster-fuck* lacks euphony. When it's time for one of your pieces to be workshopped, you will be required to sit silently while everybody responds to your writing and to one another's responses. You will feel as if you are trapped in a Saul Bass title sequence, adrift in a psychedelic whirl of aperçus. Sometimes a response will take the form of a long anecdote that moves further and further from any semblance of pertinence. The phrase *my journey* may be used. Dejection will settle on everyone's face as it becomes clear that the speaker is no longer responding—the speaker is sharing. At the end of the workshop, each participant will hand you his or her copy of your piece, with more responses written in the margins. I dug through my old files to offer you this sampling of responses I received:

- *This needs to be smart or stupid, not both.*
- *She has an intense neurotic quality to her voice that is similar to yours.*
- *I'm still not clear on what "nothing" entails.*
- *At first I thought, another story about snorting coke with assholes, but then there's this axial rotation—good job!*
- *I admire your intelligence greatly, although it scares the shit out of me.*
- *Reductive, no?*

Your impulse will be to synthesize all the responses into a coherent whole from which you can extract some knowledge, insight, or heuristic value. Be advised that this is impossible. But it doesn't matter, because MFA programs are not about knowledge, insight, or heuristic value. They're about conflict resolution. After all, if you weren't conflicted—about what to write, how to write, when to write—you wouldn't be in grad school. The MFA program is a system designed to force you to come to grips with your quandaries. It is a clumsy system, to be sure, but, like democracy, it has yet to be trumped by a competing one. So how do all those responders in your workshops help you to resolve your writerly conflicts? The same way that Greek choruses help to resolve dramatic conflicts: by yammering incessantly, sometimes hectoring, sometimes wringing their hands, sometimes airing insights that no one wants to hear, sometimes shaking their heads in sanctimonious disappointment (often scoffed at and ignored by the chief dramatis personae, but generally goading the action toward its climax), and always offering themselves as something to react against.

DO go to grad school to socialize. Meetings, meetings, meetings. MFA programs thrive on meetings. Meetings for drinks, meetings for coffee, meetings during office hours; conferences, study groups, assignations. In these meetings you'll have conversations that, in a variety of direct and indirect ways, will aid you in the conflict-resolving process described above. Indeed, figuring out with whom you want to meet is one of the most important things you will do in your workshops. Who's smart? Who's hot? Who's on crack? Nota bene: Do not have drinks with anyone who meets all three of these criteria.

DON'T go to grad school because you have a story to tell. MFA programs are intended for people who want to write, which is to say, for people who have x number of stories to tell. It's conceivable that $x = 0$, but the point is to solve for the variable. If you already know $x = 1$, you don't need an MFA. I'm looking at you, memoirists. And at you, novelists who are memoirists except for the proper nouns.

DO go to grad school for sex. A friend of mine says that she chose a particular MFA program because she was aroused by one of the faculty bios while she was perusing its website. What did it for her was the fact that the professor in question had edited the selected poems of W. S. Merwin. If you find yourself having a similar reaction to a CV, or to a spirited argument about *Wittgenstein's Nephew*, then grad school may be the place for you. And yes, people have sex in grad school, because while grad school is full of people whose idea of a proposition is *I admire your intelligence greatly, although it scares the shit out of me*, it is also full of people on whom such propositions work. This is really beside the point, though. The point is that where reason is no guide—and in deciding whether or not to get an MFA, it isn't—libido may light the way.

DON'T go to grad school to find your voice. This common formulation—*I want to find my voice*—is problematic, for it suggests that your voice is like a geyser of oil. You just sort of wander around until you finally locate it and then, having located it, you let it rush out in a torrent, cherishing every precious drop. This is not a good thing. After all, when Jack Kerouac found his voice, the result was *On the Road*. If you don't understand why that's a cautionary tale, you need to go to grad school.

DO go to grad school to gratify careerist impulses. You may not think of yourself as careerist, but you want other people to read and like and respect your work. You want an audience, and to find an audience, you need some kind of career. And to have a career, you need what Pierre Bourdieu called a "circle of belief"—a group of "consecrating agents" who like your writing and bestow value upon it through their good opinion. I cite Bourdieu to lend Gallic credence to something you already, on some level, comprehend: You *do* need to know somebody. That said, it might be fine if all the somebodies you know are nobodies—that is, if your circle is just you and your friends—as long as the belief in one another's work is sincere. Such circles have even been known to transform themselves into schools, movements, -isms, and so on. In any case, you need a circle, and an MFA program will facilitate its creation.

DON'T go to grad school to become a better writer. You may find, at the end of grad school, that you are a different writer than you were when you began. You may have different intentions, different tactics, and different tastes. However, the likelihood that you will be a *better* writer is slim. You will be prone to the same foibles, tics, and blockages as always. The best you can reasonably hope for is that you will have learned how to recognize these lapses and either fix them or turn them to your advantage. You will have accepted that doing so takes a great deal of time and effort and, sometimes, ruthless dispassion as well. You will, in short, have become a better reviser.

DO go to grad school to escape. Everyone says you can't run away from your problems, but you can—it's called going to grad school. And here, perhaps, I should offer my testimonial.

My problem was romance. I refer not to an intimate relationship but to a literary genre. It was the year 2000, and I was employed as a fiction editor at a content provider that packaged value-added metadata. To put it in less Y2K-ish terms, I worked for a company that paid twentysome-things to sit around in a big loft on Hudson Street and write blurbs about books, CDs, videos, and DVDs. These squibs were then packaged with information about pricing, release dates, etc., and sold to other compa-nies for use on their websites. It was shockingly remunerative for such an easy gig, but then, this was the height of the tech bubble. Money was everywhere, its heady scent wafting through the air, mixing with the odors of Pirate's Booty and freshly laid industrial carpet to form the distinctive bouquet of an era.

Because I had the least seniority of the several fiction editors (*editor* here being purely an honorific), I had been assigned to cover romances. I was okay with that at first—I assumed that I would find some redeem-ing qualities in these books: a trashy verve, a sex-positive crypto-feminism. I did not. Romance novels, I discovered, though very diverse—there are mystery romances, sci-fi romances, NASCAR romances—are united by an unvarying awfulness that truly beggars belief. As I skimmed and perused and churned out précis after précis, I became inured to the deranged vulgarities endemic to the genre. I was unfazed when I had to summarize a plot centering on a Highland lass's obdurate hymen, and I stoically refrained from editorializing when I encountered a Western romance in which the love interest was a Texas Ranger named Ranger. (Yes: Ranger Ranger.)

When I say I was supposed to cover romance novels, I mean I was supposed to cover *all* romance novels. I was not only charged with writing blurbs about every newly published romance but also supposed to keep chipping away at the backlist until I had generated content about every romance in print. It was a Sisyphean job description, but the company's owner was sure my colleagues and I were equal to such tasks. Rollerblading from one cluster of cubicles to another, hopped up on Red Bull, he would excitedly remind us that within each of us there was a vast untapped reser-voir of content-generating potential. When he said things like this, I would yearn to grab his can of Red Bull and shove it down his throat. But now he seems to me a kind of bumbling innocent, and the whole project—this notion that human industry was somehow equal to the galactic scale of content—strikes me as both touching and haunting, like an ancient civilization's attempt to build a temple as high as the moon. In those antediluvian tech-bubble days, nothing except money generated more febrile delusions than content, and a cosmology had arisen that, from the vantage of our more enlightened present, appears precisely backward: Money, as expressed in the Dow Jones average, was thought to be infinite, and content was thought to be finite. Today, of course, we know that it's the opposite—that money will, from time to time, flamboyantly announce its own limits, while content is a boundless, bottomless sea.

I kept myself afloat well enough until all that typing brought on a whopping case of chronic tendonitis. My readings in voguish political theory had taught me that I was a mere peon of the culture industry, a cognitive laborer with no choice but to sell my brainpower to the overlords of Empire. But why hadn't anyone warned me that being a cognitive laborer would involve so much physical pain? As it became more and more difficult to type, I found that I could no longer do my own writing on my own time. I also began to fear for my ability to do my job, or any job. I knew what an acute shortage of money felt like (having worked as an editorial assistant at a small literary publishing company, where I made $18,000 a year), but I had always felt secure in the knowledge that I would never be entirely without an income—I had skills and qualifications and I would always be able to find employment. Now, though, I realized that all of my skills and qualifications required typing to manifest themselves. There was something profoundly sickening in the realization that, in the end, this was what it came down to. Ultimately, my value resided not in my skills or qualifications or ambitions or desires but in my body and its brute ability to perform its work. I was no different from, say, a worker in a nineteenth-century textile mill who is injured on the job, dies in a garret, and is buried in a pauper's grave.

I started physical therapy, and was informed that my wrists were "strained and inflamed." "Your wrists are a Pavement album!" said a friend to whom I reported this diagnosis. I also found out that I had bursitis in my neck, which was shocking, since I had always thought that bursitis, like impetigo and irascibility, only afflicted old men. The exercises and stretches helped a bit, but the only thing that would cure me, I was told, was rest. Yet this was not an option. I had no choice but to keep plugging slowly away at my blurbs, popping anti-inflammatories in a pair of Velcro wrist splints. My productivity declined sharply, and I waited for someone to notice, but no one did.

Then one day in early 2001 my boss appeared at my desk, exasperatedly brandishing a printout of one of my blurbs. I scanned it in utter mystification, like an Ambien addict surveying her kitchen after a night of frenzied sleep-eating. I will paraphrase it from memory, but first I should explain that the "Regency" is a type of romance novel in which breeches are tight and references to entailment are strewn across each page, as if to neutralize the anachronisms that flourish therein.

Regency fans will love this spicy read, provided they can't read and content themselves with simply staring at its cover. The guy in the tailcoat who looks like George Clooney is Chad Sutherland, a dashing gentleman who, after falling from his horse, develops a mysterious affliction that causes him to vomit whenever he moves rhythmically. His bride, Amber (the Julia Roberts type in the poke bonnet), is upset for all the obvious reasons. But adding to her distress is a wholly preposterous glitch in probate law—it seems that if she doesn't produce a male heir quickly, her husband's estate will devolve to his younger brother. He spies for the French and is effete to boot, or maybe it's the other way around. What to do? I pose the question merely for rhetorical effect, since Regency fans already know what Amber should do: consult a gypsy. But will a gypsy spell be enough to save her relationship? Will Chad's brother get his comeuppance? Will the ghost of Jane Austen vomit even more copiously than Chad, and will it be prevented from killing itself only by the recollection that it's already dead? Pick up this sexy Regency, stare at its cover, and imagine the answers.

I saw a movie as a kid in which a homicidal maniac puts explosives on some roller coaster tracks. The ensuing explosion is small and leaves the tracks curled up just slightly—just enough to derail the roller coaster and send it careening in slow motion through the air. Scanning this blurb, I realized that, in writing it, I'd been attempting to do the same thing to my life. I needed to get off the track I was on *stat*. I had always vaguely assumed I might get an MFA sooner or later. Now it was abruptly obvious that later had become sooner.

This is what might be called the epiphanic model of going to grad school. It involved no cogitation, no weighing of pros and cons—it was a course of action that simply revealed itself to me, and a highly irrational course at that, given that I would obviously need to type a great deal in an MFA program. So I cannot usefully gloss my own thought process in this regard. I can only offer the tips, such as they are, presented above. I can also tell you that grad school did for me what I needed it to do most. It offered me at least a partial escape from the machine—call it capital, Empire, whatever you want—that had entrapped me. I was given a research assistantship, which enabled me to earn my stipend by going to the library instead of by typing, and this, combined with the glacial efficacy of my physical therapy, enabled me to get back to writing.

I returned to the workaday world in 2003, but I did so with a new perspective. My approach to writing had been leached of any romanticism that may have lingered from my adolescence—which is to say, I now understood that writing is a discipline, with all the connotations of rigor and routine the word conjures. Other forms of romanticism I'd harbored without quite realizing it seemed to have vanished as well, though whether this was a kind of imitative magic or simply the effect of the zeitgeist I don't know. Certainly in spring 2003, the neocons of the White House and Pentagon were feeling very bold indeed, and despite the madcap insouciance with which they prosecuted the war on terror ("Stuff happens!"), there was an uneasy and palpable sense of *This is no joke. These people are not fucking around.* It seemed necessary to respond in kind. I would not say, *I will never again write a blurb or its equivalent*, for such dicta are a form of romanticism, a denial of the compromises and deferrals that circumstances may demand.

Astra Taylor

First things first: No one should follow my example. I got a master's in liberal studies from the New School for Social Research, one of the more useless and overpriced degrees that exists. I cannot, in good conscience, recommend that anyone do this. If you want to go into the humanities or the arts, the first rule of graduate school should be: Only go if it is free, or better yet, if they are paying you. And if it is free or they are paying you, you should still think twice.

I didn't heed this advice, obviously, partly because no one gave it to me. I was young and desperate to get out of the South, so enrolling in school gave me a faraway destination and, critically, access to the capital I desperately needed to make the transition, even if it meant taking on a lot of loans (one advantage of being so young was that I didn't bother to think about how I'd ever pay the debt back—I assumed it would all evaporate or that I'd die before I got old). I remember thinking, "Wow, graduate students get way more money than undergraduates!" Clearly, what I needed to be taking was a course in compound interest, not critical theory.

In a way it was worth it, if only because it got me to New York City, which ultimately provided a much richer education than the New School was able to offer. New York City revealed the possibility of an intellectual life outside the classroom. There were bookstores and lectures and people who talked about ideas. For someone from a town where everyone was interested in one of two things—watching football or being in a band—this was a revelation. Before arriving in the city, I had assumed graduate school and, eventually, professorship to be the only viable options for a person with my interests. After moving to the city, I began to realize there might be another way.

But what was that way, exactly? Graduate school didn't say. In the end, the fact I landed an internship and then a job at Verso Books proved to be a more crucial stop along the strange path I eventually took than my pit stop at the New School. At Verso I realized there were writers who didn't have PhDs who still dealt in ideas. I was introduced to unfolding political debates that seemed relevant to my daily experience. It was also where I met many of the philosophers who would later be in my films. I quit Verso well before I got my MA, but not before soaking up a good many of the books that lined the office walls.

Maybe I'm being ungenerous. No doubt, there's a lot I learned in graduate school, much of which I take for granted. I was precocious when I arrived, but also incredibly naïve, a teenage homeschooler from Georgia. I enrolled at the New School at nineteen after a very condensed undergraduate career that was almost ridiculously spotty and postmodern—I could quote Deleuze and Guattari and Baudrillard and Lacan, but I hardly knew anything else. There was so much I had missed. At the New School, I began to fill in the gaps, to move backward. I took a class with Alan Bass where we read nothing but Freud. I studied Socrates and Marx, and Faulkner and Joyce with James Miller. Adolph Reed taught me about race and class and social movements. My education was rounded out, compared to what it had been at least.

Yet even the numerous positive aspects of the program I was enrolled in simply weren't worth the cost, however much it saddens me to say that. Years later I mentioned this to a New School administrator at a social function and he was aghast. "You can't judge an education by that measure," he said, making it clear that he found my buyer's remorse crass. Education, he argued, in the style of a MasterCard commercial, is "priceless." But it was the administration that employed him who put a price tag on my degree, not me. And by doing so, they forced me to apply the logic of the market to my learning. Was my master's degree worth the investment? Was that seminar I took with Derrida worth the hundreds of dollars in interest I paid every month? Not long after I graduated I was adjuncting at an upstate school for $2,000 a class, and I can tell you the answer: No.

But even if I had played my cards better and attended a graduate school that supported me with a nice fellowship, I'm doubtful I would have stuck around academia for long. On some fundamental level, I just don't belong on campus. This can probably be blamed on my upbringing and the fact that I didn't have to go to school as a kid. Maybe I just never got acclimated. A lot of people love school, and many smart people happily spend their entire lives there, from kindergarten all the way up to the tenure track.

In contrast to these folks, the classroom has always seemed odd and uncomfortable to me, arbitrary and slightly alienating. Why meet for ninety minutes twice a week? What was the point? What were we doing there? While I valued my relationships with faculty and was often awed by their erudition, the rigmarole of institutional learning just didn't make much sense to me on an instinctual level. Sure, sometimes there were unexpected epiphanies and moments of insight thanks to comments from the teacher or students. But just as often lectures and group discussions left me ener-vated and uninspired, even when I cared deeply about the material.

While I am grateful that (a dwindling number of) people are employed full-time to pursue eccentric areas of expertise and share their accumulated knowledge, I wouldn't be happy as an academic, despite the fact that there are so many parts of school that I like: I like professors, I like libraries, I like research, I like reading, I like talking about what I've read, and I even like syllabi, which are really useful personal study guides. Yet somehow, I find the sum of school to be less than its parts. Given this, I've done my best to incorporate the most appealing elements of higher education into my everyday life. In a sense, the work I choose is a permanent version of my ideal graduate school. That's part of why I gravitated toward filmmaking and writing (neither of which I ever formally studied), which are empty vessels to be filled with whatever my latest interest or obsession is.

So far, this approach has provided me with the mix of structure and freedom I need. Working on my documentaries *Žižek!* and *Examined Life* enabled me to study philosophy, ideology, and ethics and to collaborate with thinkers I'd long admired. Those films also allowed me to connect with a broader public, an audience scattered around the globe, in a way that an academic project probably would not have. In my writing, I've focused on social movements, economics, and technology, delving into the scholarly literature on these topics while also finding unconventional ways to approach them. In 2012 I decided to apply some of the lessons I learned while writing about protesters and actually become one, helping to spearhead Rolling Jubilee, a campaign that emerged out of Occupy Wall Street. Through buying and abolishing personal debt that is for sale on the secondary market, Rolling Jubilee calls attention to the fact we are forced to go into debt for things like health care and education, which should be public goods. As I write this, I am also finishing a book about the political economy of new media. The process of working on it has been my version of doing a PhD.

If you want to be a scientist or a lawyer or work in public health or if you love teaching more than anything else, then by all means, go to graduate school. But those who are tempted to enroll because they have some vague desire to live a life of the mind should proceed with caution. There are those who attend graduate school for a respite from a depressed job market or existential uncertainty, since a degree program can provide a sense of purpose and steady progress. But given the casualization of academic labor and other factors, these problems come roaring back after graduation for many. Instead of temporarily evading these issues, they should be faced head-on. What if people put the resources they currently invest in graduate school—their time and energy and, yes, money—into building new institutions that could support independent scholarship and creative work for decades to come? What if we worked to build a daring, durable intellectual culture outside academia instead of lazily bemoaning its absence? No doubt, embracing such ambitions is far more challenging than any graduate program that currently exists, but the rewards would certainly be much greater. Maybe, even, priceless.

Samuel Zipp

The temptation here, of course, is to just say no, don't do it. Don't get a PhD. Anyone reading this will have heard all the usual tales of woe. There are no jobs. What's long been true in the humanities now often applies even in the social and hard sciences. You'll spend six or seven years making yourself more or less unemployable in any field but the one in which your carefully composed, meticulously specialized dissertation "intervenes." But there are no jobs. So then what? You'll have sold yourself, for the pittance of a stipend, to a foolish grind: all those years of hermetic training in an obscure craft followed by a lifetime of stringing together adjunct commuter positions that pay by the class. So turn back now. Before it's too late.

That's a crude take on a complex reality, but it's more or less what I tell students. When they show up in my office, enthusiastic young folks hopped up on ideas and expectation, eager to live the "life of the mind" or do "politically engaged scholarship," I tell them to go to work first. Spend two or three years in the world beyond school, figuring out if there's anything else you would be happy doing with your life. If after a while you can't see your way clear to anything else but academic research and teaching, then okay, give it a shot.

But, first, think about where you'd like to be in ten years. Are you so driven to teach and do academic research that you are willing to accept whatever the academic job market gives you? You'll have little control over where you live and little choice of the kind of job you have to take. You might have to fight through several part-time or temporary positions, maybe even accept precarious employment as a permanent condition. Or you might end up working at a state school or small college, teaching indifferent students in a part of the country that might feel like exile from the metropolitan life you expect.

Maybe the most important question I often have for students is this: Are you willing to take a hit in status? Many of these kids—not all, of course—are the classic overachievers we hear so much about; they're well-schooled in the rituals of our rigged meritocracy. Driven to succeed in school all their lives, they know how to "do well" and they expect to be rewarded for playing the game. They were the head of their class in high school; they got into Brown; they assume that the kind of class sorting they've benefited from all along will just continue. They'll go to one of the top schools and then go on to work at another. It hasn't occurred to them that the academic job market doesn't work like this. (I'll never forget a friend, having gone to Columbia for college and Stanford for graduate school, telling some of her nonacademic friends the news that she'd landed what was, by any academic standard, a great first job at UC Santa Barbara. Um, they hemmed and hawed, trying to be supportive, uh, great. So is this good news?)

If you can live with this uncertainty, or don't feel that these risks apply to you, by all means go ahead and apply. But go to the best school you can get into in your field—those otherwise meaningless rankings matter, unfortunately—and think twice if you can't get into one of the top five. And finally, don't go if it's not all paid for; don't let yourself get into debt to do it.

Of course, I deliver this brutally honest and admittedly narrow take to students I already know, whose aptitude for graduate work I've had an opportunity to judge, and who begin with the privilege and good fortune of an impending degree from the Ivy League school where I am equally lucky to have landed a job. (And all manner of exceptions apply, given the student or the field or other particularities.) For those reading this whose situation might not mirror the blessed combination of privilege and expectation that these comments are designed to handle, this stark scenario is perhaps less than helpful.

But beyond all the academic job market worries, there are more fundamental questions that sometimes get lost, questions about what grad school is actually for, and about what you can make it do. I still think it helps to ask yourself who you would like to be in ten years. Will graduate school help you be that person?

Fifteen or so years ago, back before grad school, I wanted to be a "writer." It was pretty ambiguous. I'd come up on James Agee, Joan Didion, and James Baldwin, but there was no clearly marked path to the Elysian Fields where the personal essayists gathered. You simply had to write, to convert the splay and drift of experience into crystalline form, to shape the burst of the world with sentences rendered just so. Simple, right? Of course, I somehow missed the fact that even if you were favored with the innate gift of an ear for prose—a high enough bar I could rarely clear—you still needed something to write about. You had to have something burning in you, some fire in your head that could only be contained by the act of putting words and sentences down over and over again. Much was burning in me, but it was usually just nervous indigestion. There was more smoke than fire; it smoldered and fluttered but never roared.

Just before I went to grad school I worked three days a week as an editorial intern at an Internet news magazine. I fact-checked stories and columns, wrote a bit, and dodged the nerf rockets of the weberati. I could see a way forward in journalism: Working my way up the editorial ladder in magazines or on the Internet, writing or editing; it wasn't a way to fan the burning, but it was a life. (This was just on the cusp of the first dot-com boom. We'd yet to quite grasp how the Internet would disembowel old media journalism and make all this much harder.) But every day when I went to work my gut was in a clench, and I kept missing deadlines. But then there was the prospect of grad school. Get paid to read and write, to think, to consider history and politics and culture in a way that journalism couldn't match. It wouldn't stoke the burning, but it might surround it with tinder, provide something to help a banked fire catch. I called a writer I fact-checked to ask his advice—he'd been a newspaper reporter and now wrote a media column and books about pop culture, technology, and dogs. For him it was simple. You want to be a writer? Write. A PhD wasn't going to teach you to write. Writing was. So just write. Besides, it'll be hard, if not impossible, to resuscitate a career in journalism after six or seven years in grad school.

I listened and nodded to myself and yes-I-see'd into the phone, and then I ignored his advice. I did so not because I knew better—in a lot of ways he was right—but because I was afraid. I had no great desire to go back to school, didn't really want to be a professor, and had little sense of what it meant to train to be one, but I couldn't see any way to go it alone. I felt stuck at an intellectual dead end. I didn't know how to make the world of journalism I saw answerable to the fire I felt but couldn't coax into a blaze. I needed help.

Looking back a decade and a half on, I think this was a safe and stupid decision I'm enormously glad I made. Not only because it's worked out well for me, or because the world of journalism was blithely tooling toward a precipice, but because it turned out to be the right way for me to work toward becoming the writer and thinker I thought I might eventually be but couldn't envision or even imagine how to become.

It turns out that I am not good at selling myself, or multitasking, or writing short sentences. I take a while to come to my ideas, and I'm not overflowing with them—no bloggy, Twitter-fed, Facebook-fired writing life for me—but I no longer get that grip in my stomach when I go into the office. I'm better with deadlines, too, maybe because they come around less often.

This is not to say that grad school did this for me. I had to make it so in the teeth of an institution that isn't much concerned with my little writerly dreams.

For all the other writers out there, here's the obvious: Grad school will not help you hone your prose or cultivate an audience or even, unless you are lucky, provide you with a community of folks who want to read and write prose. Quite the opposite, in fact: At its best, grad school is supposed to instill in you a language for participating in a profession. Depending on the discipline, this language can be straightforward and unadorned to explain results, baroque and convoluted to handle close readings, hermetic and jargony to make meaning strange, earnest and hectoring to rally for a cause, precise and relentless to reveal the logic of argument, or pedantic and plodding to lead the reader through evidence. Sometimes it's more than one of these things at once, but rarely is the end result lovely or a joy to read. Still, this profusion of intellectual modes carries within it an implicit challenge, a chance.

For those who want to be writers as much as scholars, grad school offers the opportunity to make, not find, a voice—a chance to bend and reshape the resistant languages of the academy in that inner fire, to make them do work they're not quite supposed to do, and thereby produce new kinds of hybrid writing, writing more strange and more galvanizing and more kinetic and complex than either conventional academic or journalistic prose; writing built to handle both analysis and narrative, close reading and character studies, evidence and description, theory and practice.

Those are the big stakes, but in many ways it's the small stuff, the every-day demands that will loom largest down the road.

There are a couple things that I never quite grasped until I got a job in academia. They're obvious, when you think about them, but they're things they soft-pedal in grad school in the humanities, and they remained fuzzy to me throughout school. The first is pretty simple: Grad school is designed to nurture your "project." The whole enterprise hinges on the idea that you've got some special talent that needs care and feeding. When you get a job, however, a host of new day-to-day duties rush in, ones you will be only partially or not at all trained to do: teaching, of course, but also curriculum development, program design, academic advising, and various forms of university and college administration. Think about whether you want to do these things.

The second is even more basic: In many cases, grad school in the human-ities, in some fundamental way, often doesn't prepare you at all for what universities actually do. The university is designed to produce research. It's designed to train you to specialize in some arcane corner of the vast world of knowledge and to be content to stack your discrete, well-considered morsel on top of the pile of accumulated knowledge in that field. The truly ambitious and nervy hack a part of the pile away before putting their morsel down, but they're still contributing to the pile. Someday, the story goes, the pile will be finished, and we'll know all there is to know.

Okay, so you might respond that this is a caricature of a more complex reality, and besides, it's outmoded; nobody believes in it anymore except for scientists and the odd historian. My degree is in American studies, and like all the other studies programs, we are interdisciplinary or even postdisciplinary. We long ago demystified the ideology of objective knowledge, interrogated the myth of progress, and identified the way that the production of knowledge always constructs power and disciplines the unruly world by specifying the known from the unknown, the valid from the invalid. Sure. That's what we tell ourselves, but the truth is that it doesn't matter. The university doesn't care. It's designed to produce knowledge. That's its very form. Knowledge production is how it assigns and withholds value, how it disciplines the workers it cradles in its velvet-lined grip. Critique is nothing if it can't pass as knowledge. There's a vast apparatus of deans, administrators, trustees, grantmakers, foundations, accreditation boards, and government agencies that makes sure it's so.

Some in the humanities delight in this disjuncture; they take pleasure in the thought of being a ghost in the machine, pulling one over on the administrators. But when one doesn't fully believe in the institution one is working hard to make a career in, defiance can start to feel hollow. Again, a stark scenario—there are plenty of ways to find a less constrained path—but consider yourself warned.

In the end, lots of folks, like me, go to grad school for the wrong reasons. Some have grandiose writing dreams; some just want to write a book. Some want to find the life of the mind; some really want to be activists. Many stumble into it one way or another as a way to do something else. This can work out, but just remember that you might find yourself fighting with the decision the whole way, so take the time now to consider which fights you want to be having ten or fifteen years down the road.

Andrea Fraser

I DROPPED OUT OF Berkeley High School shortly before my sixteenth birthday, about two weeks into my junior year. I spent a month and a half cramming for the SATs and the California state proficiency exam while I got a portfolio together. I took the tests and moved to New York in November, where I joined my older brother and sister in the East Village. Once in New York, I applied to the School of Visual Arts, where I started in January 1982. After two years of course work at SVA I look a leave to attend the Whitney Museum of American Art's Independent Study Program. The Whitney is not a degree-granting institution, and SVA would not give me any credit for my year and a half there, so I did not return to SVA. Instead, I began participating in reading and study groups, such as the New York Lacan Study Group (which included people with MDs and PhDs in psychiatry, psychology, philosophy, literature, and cinema studies), and a group that read psychoanalytic and feminist texts (which later became the performance group V-Girls). There was also a group that read Marx's *Capital*, a group that read about groups, and I vaguely recall participating in something called the Second Sunday Salon. My immediate peer group was already developing a network and beginning to publish and show. I published my first essay in *Art in America* while I was still in the ISP; the year after I finished, I did my first gallery talk/performance at the New Museum. Getting an MFA was not something I ever even considered.

In many ways, this kind of narrative is inconceivable today. The New York art world was tiny then compared to now. There were far fewer competitors for the attention of critics, curators, and older artists looking for assistants. The absence of MFA programs meant that such attention could only turn to younger artists in or just out of undergraduate programs. What we have seen since the 1980s with the growth of MFA programs, and more recently with the rise of art practice PhDs, is not only an expansion of educational opportunities but also the inflation of educational qualifications. The prevalence of MFA programs has led to the devaluation of undergraduate degrees, just as the rise of PhD programs in Europe and elsewhere is leading to a devaluation of the MFA. In the U.S. context of mostly private nonprofit and even for-profit higher education, the expansion of MFA and art-related MA programs has been driven largely by financial calculations: These programs are cash cows for universities and art schools. They are among the most expensive degrees offered and they often provide little financial aid. Compared to traditional professional degrees in law, business, or medicine, which must compensate faculty highly to compete with the private sector, art programs are cheap to run on the low-wage labor of adjunct instructors drawn from an enormous pool of underemployed artists. Nevertheless, despite their high costs and the slim chance that degrees will be converted into income to pay back loans, the market for MFAs has become huge.

While much reflection on the explosive growth of the art world over the past decades has been focused on the expansion of the art market and of art institutions, the art world explosion would not have been possible without a parallel growth in the ranks of those who aspire to become artists, critics, curators, dealers, or to find other roles in the art field. It may be that, through MFA and MA programs, universities and art schools have learned to exploit what Pierre Bourdieu described in the late 1970s as a "new system of structural instability in the representation of social identity and its legitimate aspirations" that "favours the development of a less realistic, less resigned relationship to the future." On the level of education, Bourdieu characterized this system as marked by students "overestimating the studies on which they embark, overvaluing their qualifications, and banking on possible futures which do not really exist for them," often under the guise of rejecting the hierarchies, limits, and forms of social determinism—impulses that have been central to the artistic ethos for more than a century.

Of course, the art world, including its MFA programs, can provide for possibilities that do not exist in other fields. In what other discipline could a high school dropout with no degrees like myself become a tenured professor at a top research university like UCLA? (One of the reasons I turned to art at age fifteen was that I figured no college but an art school would have me.) On the other hand, the economics of art education are clearly imposing new determinisms on artistic trajectories, often by burdening MFA graduates with debilitating debt. These economics have also transformed the futures on which MFA grads increasingly bank, with the highest-priced programs implicitly promising get-rich-quick art stardom and even graduate-studio sales to recoup tuition costs. Indeed, expensive MFA programs have become an important factor in the marketization of the art field.

However, the expansion of the art world also means that, increasingly, we must not speak of just one art world but of many. In addition to the market-based world of commercial galleries, fairs, and auctions, there is also the exhibition-based and discourse-driven art world of nonprofit and public institutions, and the extra-institutional and often politics-driven world of cultural activism and DIY art initiatives. There is also an expanding academically based art world, represented not by the growth of MFA programs so much as by the emergence of art practice PhD programs and the development of the field of art research. Along with the fragmentation of the art world into these increasingly distinct and autonomous subfields, we are seeing the differentiation of art education in ways that correspond to these different worlds and their radically different economies, discourses, values, practices, and aspirations. While expensive New York–area schools continue to feed painters and other object makers into Chelsea galleries, the larger field of studio-art education has diversified: Programs at public universities and art academies in Europe and the United States are increasingly focused on the development of discursive, political, public, and social practices; European MA programs in art research orient students toward PhD programs; and a growing number of free or inexpensive artist-run academies serve the

DIY field, perhaps in the same way that reading and discussion groups served my generation in the mid-1980s.

As a professor of art at UCLA, where I guide students to degrees that I myself do not have in a historical context that is radically different from the one in which I developed, it would be presumptuous to prejudge my students' trajectories. Instead, I see my role with undergraduates as being primarily one of helping them clarify and articulate their own values and goals. This includes providing them with a broad perspective on the art field that will enable them to make informed choices about the trajectories they pursue and to reflect critically on the aspirations they have already developed—which are often based on highly idealized representations of artists, whether as geniuses, celebrities, or revolutionaries.

What is it that you really want from art, I ask? Do you really love to make things? Do you want to change the world? Do you have a need to communicate? Are you driven by a desire for recognition? For legitimacy? For fame and fortune? By a love of beauty—or fashion, or design? By the pleasure of performing? Is art an escape from intolerable conformity? From the symbolic and material violence of cultural and economic domination? Of racial prejudice? Of gender and sexual normativity? Is art a platform for politics? For social struggle? Is art a way of building community? A place of belonging? Is art a means to achieve or perpetuate a lifestyle? To gain access to a desirable social world? Is art a means of knowledge production? Of self-realization? Is art an outlet for aggression? An opportunity for redemption?

There are many other questions I might ask, each of which might generate responses that would indicate radically different aims and radically different artistic trajectories—including educational trajectories. While I personally favor some of these aims over others, my primary concern is that art students recognize and reflect honestly and openly on the full range of their motivations and investments. Art education too often expands on what is already an enormous gap between what we do in the art field and what we say about what we do, reproducing legitimizing discourses that have little to do with what art is and what motivates art practices. This can only lead to the development of positions that are politically and artistically incoherent and often deeply contradictory. On an individual level, it may also produce or exacerbate conflicted investments that can lead to a life of cynical denial or self-defeating struggle. This is probably what I would hope to spare my students from above all—but I would also hope that they spare themselves from going deep into debt for an MFA degree.

David Levine

My father was dead, and by the end my mother couldn't stand him, so technically there was no reason for her to compel me into his line of work (academe, not art fraud) and no reason why I should have submitted to her blandishments. And yet I did. As my friends were cheerfully making plans to drift off to San Francisco after graduation to "figure things out," I was miserably hammering away at Rhodes, Mellon, Marshall, and grad school applications . . . making arrangements, in other words, not to figure things out but simply to stay in school instead. As evidence of my total unsuitability for academic life, as well as my cheerful obliviousness to what kind of life that kind of life might entail, I offer the following: I applied for a Rhodes Scholarship as an essayist and poet, I stated on all my grad school applications that I was not willing to incur any debt to finance my post-graduate education, and I applied to about eight doctoral programs in English with an essay on Nietzsche.

Worse still, some of these institutions admitted and funded me, mistaking a facility born of indifference for the virtuosity of a true calling. The next thing I knew, as my closest friends cheerfully headed west, I set off on an Amtrak from New York to Boston—my beaming mother waving good-bye from the platform, an overpacked duffel on the seat beside me—feeling as forlorn and as petulant as when my parents first sent me off to camp.

Why? Why, if it felt so much like a defeat, did I go to grad school at all? I was twenty-one, after all; I could make my own decisions; I could fend for myself. And yet, having grown up being told that scholarship was both my destiny and my gift, and having this gibberish confirmed by various grant-making and scholarly institutions, it was impossible to articulate the simple formulation, I really don't want to do this.

Instead, my displeasure expressed itself that first semester in an addiction to over-the-counter antihistamines, an obsessive crush on the Bataille specialist who lived across the street, a weeklong bout of using Jack Daniel's as mouthwash, and a January stint of hypergraphia during which, on a single night, I filled ninety-six journal pages with illegible and self-immolating rantings prompted by my inability to decide which courses to take that spring. Living in the grad dorms (Mom's idea, again), and thus isolated from anyone who shared my temperament or my aversion to obese Sinophiles, orgies in wading pools, international cuisine nights, or the kind of people who live in grad dorms generally, my personality underwent a terrifying regression. I became like the protagonist of William Lindsay Gresham's *Nightmare Alley*, who, appalled by carnival geeks at the start of the novel, winds up geeking himself.

But to judge by external appearances, all was well: I excelled in my courses; I charmed my advisers; I went out for drinks with my "cohort," and I kept everyone entertained with my insouciant running commentary on the perversities of academic life. I claimed, as though I was some kind of Christ Church patrician, that I had no intention of getting an academic job; I just wanted to write the dissertation. And everyone was too polite to ask the obvious question: If you have no plans to become a professor, then what the fuck are you doing here?

I couldn't have answered. My dad had been, according to my mom, a great intellectual who had frittered his talent away before he died when I was eleven. All through my procrastinating, underachieving adolescence, he was the bogeyman she'd use to threaten me: There were tales of walking into his study and finding him reading HiFi magazines instead of working on his doctorate; of her having to type up his field notes because he was too disorganized. Don't end up like your dad, she'd say (unsuccessful, unloved, sentenced, dead), and I, fearing a similar fate, would buckle down and resolve to do better.

His history, as told to me, seems to be patched together from bits of *The Tin Drum*, *Kramer vs. Kramer*, *Legal Eagles*, and *Love Story*. He grew up poor in the

South Bronx. His illiterate, Polish-immigrant parents would lock him in the apartment every morning while they went downstairs to work in their candy shop, leaving poor Morton, who suffered from severe childhood arthritis, candyless, bent, and bawling. Eventually the family migrated to Encino, California. He worked his way through UCLA, became a classical music DJ, got married, got divorced when his wife turned out to be a lesbian, and, at age thirty-four, decided it was time for a change. He would go to grad school. He would become a professor.

So he enrolled in an anthropology program at Harvard. There he met my mom, a Wellesley undergrad studying to become a concert pianist. These were, I'm told, the golden years: full of nimble irony, horsemeat steaks at the Faculty Club, Tom Lehrer recordings, stiff drinks, intellectual symbiosis, and so forth. But really, what eighteen-year-old wouldn't think her thirty-five-year-old fiancé was a genius?

I wouldn't know if he was. I refused to read his dissertation, refused to buy into the idea of the Good Mort, as my mom put it. The one she clearly missed; the one she kinda wanted back. You can't trade punches with a ghost. But neither can you shed their trappings: Here I was at Harvard, in graduate school, where, in my second year, I too rented an apartment in Cambridge and fell in love with an undergrad. Where would this stop? I planned a dissertation on whether characters can ever become real. Unable to leave this oedipal purgatory by conventional means, I got out by being accepted to another grad school—this time in an MFA program. I didn't go—I'd wised up enough by then—but it still did the trick. I handed in my prospectus and got the fuck out of Dodge. Four years later, the department administrator, who had not heard a word from me since I left, called me in New York and asked if I was in or out. "I guess I'm out," I said, and, with no little regret, canceled my university health insurance. I don't miss grad school. But I sure miss that insurance.

So now I'm an artist, and I wound up being made a professor anyhow (of art, not academe. For years, my Berlin institution's website charmingly called me "David Levine, ABD[1]"). My father would be so proud . . . maybe?

---

1 All but dissertation.

My mother is so proud . . . kinda? It's not really the same thing. For one thing, I didn't have to write a dissertation.

My parents' generation saw academe as a safe haven; they placed an enormous amount of faith in the prestige of a PhD and the security of an academic job. To them it was incomprehensible that if offered an opportunity to lock up one's future, one would pass. But in this century, it takes nerves of steel to behold the MLA conference without cringing, or to stare down the barrel of a non-tenure-track job in Wichita. You have to know who you are, and what you're in it for. You have to be clear-eyed about the state of the profession. You have to know the difference between a vocation and an avocation, and you can't be saddled by romantic ideals or family ghosts. You can't, for the most part, be a twenty-one-year-old.

Nancy Bauer

I WAS A HORRIBLE—*HORRIBLE*—UNDERGRADUATE student, the kind of student that, as a professor, I now loathe and shun. It wasn't that I was superdumb or couldn't write my way out of a paper bag or got crappy grades. I was clever, rather than studious or intelligent, and what distinguished my writing from that of my peers, I later learned, was mostly that I had paid attention to groovy Mr. Cole while, in what appeared to be a function of relentless illegal drug use, he spent much of ninth-grade English class dreamily diagramming sentences on the blackboard.

My MO in college was to cut every corner I could. I'd skim about a third of, say, *The Protestant Ethic and the Spirit of Capitalism* and hang back in class until I got a sense, from what the teacher and the other students were saying, of what Weber was probably up to. Then I'd wait for the opportune moment and launch a game-changing conversational zinger. My papers were typed in haste, preceded by neither drafts nor notes, in the newsroom of the *Harvard Crimson* on our beloved thirty-year-old manual typewriters, always in the middle of the night and ordinarily in the company of other frantically typing Crimeds racing to complete their own assignments in the few hours we had for anything other than producing the morning edition. I wrote well—sparingly, inventively, and with sufficiently restrained passion—and over my four years in college was continually stunned to learn that these generic virtues were enough to score me, over and over again, at least an A-minus, regardless of the class or topic or whether I had actually done the reading.

Had there been a contest among my college friends, I would almost certainly have been voted Least Likely to Go to Grad School. And we're talking about a group that by and large went straight into journalism and never left. (Nick Kristof, anyone?) In the summer after my junior year, I had interned at the *Boston Globe*; when I graduated, I was offered a job as the paper's first full-time reporter on Cape Cod. I had a townie boyfriend, a copyboy on the city desk for the paper. On Friday nights, he'd ride down to Hyannis on his motorcycle, swoop me back from the house the *Globe* was renting for me on Bodfish Place up to Boston to see a band at the Inn-Square Men's Bar, and deliver me back to the Cape in time for me to catch a prop plane to the Islands to cover Saturday's story.

In many ways, obviously, this job was too good to be true. But something felt wrong, before and after I moved back to Boston and started working in the newsroom again. In hindsight, I can identify two aspects of my job that rankled. One was the easy-breezy sexism at the *Globe*. Sometimes, when you walked by the interminable iteration of tables that constituted the city desk, you'd be greeted by an all-male group of virtual Olympic judges, holding up handmade score sheets for the body part du jour. This before the term *sexual harassment* had become a category of experience. One simply experienced a haphazard sense of shame, frustration, and confusion.

The other rankling factor is harder for me to identify with any precision. It had to do with all the feature pieces I wrote on kids who had died in various heartbreaking and gruesome ways. There was the young man who had just gotten his pilot's license and decided to surprise his parents by doing loop-de-loops in the air above their house, only to lose control and crash into the backyard. There was the hit-and-run killing of a young kid by a drunk driver the day before the dead boy's family was to head out on a cross-country RV trip funded largely by his penny-by-penny savings over the course of his very short lifetime. And then there was the game stopper.

I sometimes wonder if I would have ended up in grad school had I not been assigned to investigate the death of four-month-old Marie Chu. Marie and her family were recent Burmese immigrants living in a middle-class suburban neighborhood near the Boston line. Her parents, Fred and Siu Chu, worked at high-tech jobs on Route 128, a beltway ten miles from the city, and left Marie and Tom, their two-year-old son, in the care of Siu's mom and dad, Hgo Bee and Chit Khim Ong. One day, while Chit Khim was hanging out at the corner convenience store with friends, Hgo Bee ran upstairs to the bathroom and left a fussy Marie in her baby seat on the kitchen table. Tom, apparently irritated by Marie's crying, took a butcher knife and plunged it into the baby's head. Hgo Bee, who spoke no English, raced downstairs and, catatonic, rocked the baby in her arms until she died. Two days later, I was ordered by my editor to interview the neighbors to figure out whether there was anything suspicious or otherwise interesting about the family.

I drove to the house; I got out of the car; I walked around a little. I couldn't bring myself to ring a doorbell. When I got back to the newsroom, I avoided my editor and started calling child psychologists to ask them what life might end up being like for a two-year-old who had stabbed his baby sister to death. The story made page one, and my editor forgave me for not delivering on his assignment. I went on to other shootings, other fires, other features on congressional representatives and Rubik's Cube and nude beaches.

But I couldn't get poor Tom and his family out of my head. I kept imagining myself in the position of Fred and Siu Chu. Should you just rush Tom into the hands of a psychiatrist, as the experts were urging, to help him cope with a lifetime of confusion and mistimed grief? He was so young; he would forget, wouldn't he? Should you even tell him what he had done? Did it make sense, even, to describe the stabbing as something Tom had done, given that he couldn't possibly have understood the ramifications of his actions—and were they full-fledged actions? I had some sense, I suppose, that the questions that haunted me were broadly philosophical. But what struck me was that I, a complete stranger to the family, had written an article that, though perhaps less painful to the family than a (potentially racist) report of the neighbors' speculation and gossip might have been, still presumed to tell them what to do in their thoroughly tragic circumstances.

The more I thought about this presumptuousness, the more messed-up-in-the-head I got about what it was to be a newspaper reporter at all—that is, to have the authority, day in and day out, to tell other people how things that matter to them are. Many years into grad school, this very question, in its more general inflection, became a central intellectual and existential preoccupation for me. But at the time I thought it was a simple matter of ethics, and my sense that what I was doing was often unethical became a serious drag on my work.

So I abandoned my fairly promising career as a reporter, though I didn't have a clue what other sort of life might end up floating my boat. Financially desperate, I took what I thought would be an unambiguously do-gooder job at Boston Children's Hospital co-writing a guidebook for parents about child health. My beat for the most part was the mental/neurological: from tics and sleep problems to sociopathic behavior and psychosis. So when the topic of the hospital's ethics rounds was whether to prescribe lithium for a preteen, I dropped in. At that time, there had been no trials of this very powerful drug on children. But one of the hospital psychiatrists was desperate to help a patient who, barely twelve years old, had already made three serious attempts to kill himself. To my astonishment, our discussion, though riveting, went nowhere. I couldn't believe it: The doctors didn't know what they were doing.

Over and over again in ethics rounds, I was stunned. A moronic doctor had failed to read a child's chart and had given him a blood transfusion—and left the empty blood bag on the top of a trash can—without noticing that the parents were Jehovah's Witnesses. (This was in the mid-'80s, when you still couldn't be certain that the blood supply was HIV free.) Because insurance practices had recently changed so that doctors couldn't be reimbursed unless they gave a patient a terse diagnostic label, the staff was finding that children with just a vague symptom or two were, upon being told that they had, say, bipolar disorder rather than just some markedly good and bad moods, rising to the occasion and developing full-blown psychiatric syndromes.

I was convinced that all of these dilemmas were flat-out ethical ones, even though the ethics rounds participants were relentlessly stumped and even though I of course understood that the problems were complicated. At the same time, I was colossally bored with *The Child Health Encyclopedia* and its "just the facts, ma'am" ambitions. So I was primed to be interested when the convener of the rounds suggested that I think about applying to a graduate program in medical ethics at Harvard Divinity School, part of whose charge was to train hospital chaplains.

My dad is a Lutheran minister, and though I adore and revere him, I had a horror of following in his footsteps. What made me change my mind is that the master of theological studies program (basically an MA program housed in a divinity school) had very few requirements and allowed you to take courses all over the university for program credit. My little fantasy, which turned out not to be entirely unwarranted, was that on top of studying something I found incredibly interesting, I would have a chance to redeem my sorry undergraduate career. The two years I spent in the MTS program were a blissful luxury, funded by the seventeen dollars per hour—a fortune in those days—I earned from prostituting myself for a test-prep company. I took four semesters of Greek just for the fun of it. With the guidance of a radical feminist theologian, I read Luce Irigaray and Hélène Cixous before they were household names. I took an amazing course on Kant, Coleridge, and Schleiermacher from the brilliant Richard R. Niebuhr, who was the first person to demonstrate to me what I continue to think is, besides flat-out luck, the key to success as an academic: taking your idiosyncratic interests seriously and having the courage to explore them in a public forum.

This lesson was reinforced on a minute-by-minute basis in my philosophy courses with Stanley Cavell, who was wont to mention the likes of Greta Garbo, Wittgenstein, Milton's writings on divorce, and *La Bohème* in the same breath. After a semester of unsatisfying courses in mainstream ethics, I enrolled in Cavell's graduate seminar on film simply because it looked fun. There I learned that what had really been gripping me from my reporter days on was the fatefulness of the categories of our experience, that is, what we call things. Had the notion of sexual harassment, for instance, been a part of my grasp on the world, my real-time experience walking by the city desk "judges" would have been radically different. Was what happened to poor Tom Chu and his poor grandmother best described as a case of negligence? Why do we conform ourselves to our concepts rather than the other way around? These became, and still are, questions I could genuinely call my own.

I have stories about how I wormed my way into the Department of Philosophy and ended up writing a thesis on Simone de Beauvoir, even though no one at Harvard knew a thing about feminism or about Beauvoir and the traditions of thought from which she emerged. I have stories about how I met my first husband, a grad student in English, and got married in the second year of my PhD program, had two kids while dissertating, and was divorced a couple of months before I started a tenure-track job. I have stories about why, though I loathe administration and love writing and teaching, I'm composing this essay bit by bit in my fancy-schmancy office during a couple hours I steal early each morning before I start my long crazy day as dean of academic affairs for arts and sciences at Tufts. But I'll just leave you with the moral of all of these stories, which is that the best reason to go to the kind of grad school that's not going to make you rich is that it has turned out in your case that taking yourself seriously as a human being requires it. And the best reason to stay in academia is that, year after year, you find that what's on your mind inspires your students to care about what's on theirs.

Ben Nugent

WRITING A BOOK CONSISTS largely of avoiding distractions. If you can forget your real circumstances and submerge yourself in your subject for hours every day, characters become more human, sentences become clearer and prettier. But an all-consuming obsession with writing can be just as poisonous as an excess of diversion. In grad school, I tried to make writing my only god, and it sickened my work, for a while. The condition endemic to my generation, attention deficit disorder, gave way to its insidious Victorian foil: monomania.

Monomania is what it sounds like: a pathologically intense focus on one thing. It's the opposite of the problem you have if your gaze is ever flitting from your Tumblr to your spreadsheet to your baby to rush-hour traffic. It's the opposite of the problem you have, in other words, if you are a normal, contemporary, non-agrarian thirtysomething. It was when I left Los Angeles for the primeval hush of the Midwest that I became a monomaniac.

I got into an MFA program in fiction and moved to a college town on the prairie. On my stipend, I was able to live like an unprosperous gentleman-landowner of nineteenth-century Russia. There was nothing to do besides read, write, reflect on God, and drink. These were circumstances favorable to writing fiction. But they were also conducive to depravity, the old Calvinist definition thereof: a warping of the spirit.

I didn't set up an Internet connection. I didn't have a TV or an iPhone. For hundreds of miles in every direction, none of the movie theaters were playing movies I wanted to see. I spent my days scribbling long-hand. During the winters, snow piled against my house and made high branches slap against my windows. I was embowered in the graces of Turgenev's age.

When I socialized, it was often with poets, who confirmed by their very existence that I had landed in a better, vanished time. Even their physical ailments were of the nineteenth century. One day, in the depths of winter, I came upon one of them picking his way across the snow and ice on crutches, pausing to drag on his cigarette.

"What happened to you?" I asked.

"I have gout," he said, his tone hail-fellow-well-met. "It still happens, apparently."

The disaster unfolded slowly. The professors and students were diplomatic, but a pall of boredom fell over the seminar table when my work was under discussion. I could see everyone struggling to care. And then, trying feverishly to write something that would engage people, I got worse. First my writing became overthought, and then it went rank with the odor of desperation. It got to the point that every chapter, short story, every essay was trash.

I could not imagine why; conditions were ideal. It took me a long time to realize that the utter domination of my consciousness by the desire to write well was itself the problem. Monomania, a nineteenth-century malady to which my twenty-first-century immune system had developed no defenses, had crept into my soul, like gout into a poet's foot, and spoiled it by degrees.

When good writing was my only goal, I made the quality of my work the measure of my worth. For this reason, I wasn't able to read my own writing well. I couldn't tell whether something I had just written was good or bad, because I needed it to be good in order to feel sane. I lost the ability to cheerfully interrogate how much I liked what I had written, to see what was actually on the page rather than what I wanted or feared to see.

It's no coincidence, I imagine, that writers of the nineteenth century wrote deathless novels about monomania. When Ahab speaks of the white whale, he shouts "with a terrific, loud, animal sob, like that of a heart-stricken moose." Victor Frankenstein, longing to "penetrate the secrets of nature," and idolizing "men who had penetrated deeper and knew more," grows "pale with study" and "emaciated with confinement."

There is a scene in *War and Peace* in which Napoleon is so focused on reaching Moscow, so busy with his map and field glass, that he barely notices a group of his soldiers, Polish Uhlans, who have tried to impress him by attempting to cross a frigid river. Forty of them drown or freeze to death to show him their valor. "The little man in the gray overcoat," writes Tolstoy, "began pacing up and down the bank . . . occasionally glancing disapprovingly at the drowning Uhlans who distracted his attention." Tolstoy ends the chapter with a Latin aphorism that applies to the soldiers and their leader both: *"Quos vult perdere dementat."* Those whom God wishes to destroy he drives mad.

When Napoleon's army takes Moscow, it loses its discipline, starts looting, and begins to fall apart. When Frankenstein's creature opens its eyes, Frankenstein is repulsed and runs away. Ahab's confrontation with his whale does not restore his self-esteem.

I purged myself of monomania slowly and unwittingly. I fell in love, an overpowering diversion, and began to spend more time at my girlfriend's place, where she had Wi-Fi, a flat-screen TV, and a DVD player. I joined a cover band that held live karaoke parties. One morning, after I diversified my mania, my writing no longer stank of decay.

I've spent the two years since I graduated working as a full-time creative writing professor, and it's easier for me to write well now than it was when I had nothing else to do. I've come to believe that one of the worst mental illnesses a writer can acquire in grad school, up there with alcoholism and morbid competitiveness, is the unwillingness to fail. There is bad work that is lazy, and there is bad work that is written in a state of delusional obsession, and the greater danger for a writer in grad school is the latter. If you use an MFA program as a period of experimentation, in which you're happy to throw out a month's or year's worth of work and start over; if you're content to view it as a time in which you may not write anything that sees the light of day, and it's nothing to kill yourself over because there are other things that make life worth living, you will probably surface as a better writer. Whereas if you write with the notion that this is your moment to write your book and that therefore the book you are working on is all that matters, your manuscript will become too big to fail, that is, too emotionally high stakes for you to accept the possibility of its failure. And as soon as you lose the ability to accept the possibility that something you are writing is irredeemably bad—as soon as you lose the ability to listen to your dread—you are well and truly fucked.

I'm glad I went to nineteenth-century Russia. But I wish I had been more careful, more humble, and kept one foot in modernity.

Nikil Saval

A PHD PROGRAM IN the humanities isn't an education but a finishing school. You emerge from it speaking an entirely different language, with a different tone of voice and maybe even an accent, like Eliza Doolittle post–Henry Higgins. The symptoms are unmistakable. You might begin to pose every declarative statement as if it were a question that you're not actually asking, by ending every sentence with " . . . right?" As in "But Zygmunt Bauman has already problematized the whole notion of 'politics,' right?" You learn that the only sort of behavior appropriate to professional life is cold politesse, so you develop the habit, almost instinctively, of adopting an elaborately formal discourse in e-mails to professors, or colleagues you don't know well; you find yourself often expressing the sentiment that you would be "perfectly delighted to have a coffee sometime"—the kind of phrase you would have once been ashamed to use. You cease to read for enjoyment, except furtively and shamefully. If you get caught carrying a book around that looks off syllabus, some policing colleague will check your papers by asking you, "What are you reading that for?" For which professor, what class, what career reason? The only pleasure you allow yourself to speak openly about, and again only in tones of boisterous embarrassment, is a predilection for bad television. "Ohmygod, I watched eight hours of *Law and Order: SVU* last night!" you splutter. This is how you signal you are an intellectual.

If you come to graduate school after any time spent, say, at an office job, you'll notice the atmosphere in the academy is palpably different. Offices are filled with false cheer and desperate bonhomie, gossip and glad-handing; by contrast, the academy can seem a chilled and airless place. Long ago, the sociologist David Riesman characterized this distinction in work-places as "false personalization" versus "enforced privatization." The former is the pseudo-friendship of the white-collar world that serves to mask real hierarchies; the latter is the friendship-killing frigidity of the academy that exacerbates vast power differentials that don't really exist. No professor, however young, would make the mistake of treating you, a graduate student, as an equal, socially or professionally, even if very little separates you in intel-lectual terms. They spent years having their psyches crushed by their professors, and it seems only fair for them to do the same to you.

Your compensation for all this is that you can go out later with your fellow students, blow your stipend on booze, and talk shit about the profes-sors behind their backs for hours on end. But the next day you return to school, aching and sober, and all the hard words you leveled at the faculty in private suddenly dissipate into meekness before figures of authority. Passivity: graduate school's most lasting and universal gift to its students. Man hands on misery to man.

The most important story to tell about graduate school, one that people can't tell enough, is one about academic labor: underpaid doctoral students with unsupportable teaching loads, the ongoing adjunctification of the professo-riate. Of course, the undergraduates you teach are also working. Politicians often talk a great game about working to pay their way through school (when they didn't, à la Mitt Romney, "borrow money" from their parents), but this is true of most of the undergraduate workforce; a majority work, and one third of American undergraduates clock in thirty-five hours a week or more. If they aren't working to pay for school, and often even if they are, they're going into debt servitude, with loans that they will service their entire lives. (The best explanation I've seen of how all this interconnects is Marc Bousquet's hand grenade of a book How the University Works.)

As far as grad student exploitation goes, I happily escaped it, and there-fore can't speak to it directly. For the past few years, I've been a doctoral student in the English department of a staggeringly rich university in Silicon Valley. You know the place: enormous and sunny, full of red-tiled roofs and sandstone archways like an oversized Taco Bell, with names like Gates and Hewlett and Packard spelled out on the lintels. I went to graduate school because I had been groomed for it as an undergraduate, had had many professors tell me that I should continue my studies. The same professors told me I should take "time off" to work; and so I did, during the day in publishing houses and nights for a fledgling literary magazine. As usual in New York, I found myself attending literary parties, where I talked about the writing I should have been doing instead of attending literary parties. This got old, so I made sure to get into a school far from New York—in the state where I had grown up, as it happened. There, I promised myself, I would make time to edit and write more for my journal.

I have gotten writing done, lots of it. This is because, in material terms, the university has treated me nicely. My fellowship is incredibly high compared with most programs, and I haven't had to teach much at all. Money seems to be spilling out of the seams of the institution. Ask for a certain honorarium to bring a speaker to campus, and the authorities in charge of the cash box will immediately beg you to take more. The library is capacious and well stocked. The undergrads are smart, if uncurious, and generally work hard. This should have been an ideal setup.

And yet graduate school has been a drag. This is because I allowed myself to get caught up in the banalities of professionalization, the most common feature of graduate education in the humanities. From day one, you learn not what and how to read, but rather how to position yourself as a candidate for the dwindling number of humanities jobs. It's assumed from the outset that there's nothing new to discover, only positions to take and status rewards to acquire. (For this reason, humanities students have come to love the lacerating sociology of Pierre Bourdieu, who is always surreptitiously talking about the social life of academia, even when he is ostensibly describing the hard sciences or politics.) Any scenario where you might be educated is quickly transformed into a competition for prestige. Departmental seminars are little more than occasions for students to outcompete each other in conspicuous displays of intellectual plumage and toadying to professors. Conferences, panels, and lectures sometimes result in a good paper or two, but more often they're scenes of ostentatious back patting and ass pinching by the audience, each "question" prefaced by breathy testaments to the brilliance of the work on offer: "I want to thank you for that wonderfully nuanced paper." "What a brave interpretation of *Middlemarch*." "That was a delightful and vital exposition, but forgive me, I have one quibble . . ." (Check out the humanities blog *Arcade* to see how the post-and-comment form of online discussions can reproduce this grotesquerie to a T.) It's no wonder that, in such an environment, the research itself has the tendency to become pinched, narrow, and gutless.

My suspicion is that the academy has become this way in the past forty years—between the generation of baby boomers, for whom the major book was Herbert Marcuse's *One-Dimensional Man*, and the Generation Xers currently taking over the academy, who grew up in the shadow of Tom Peters's *Liberation Management*. In that period, the narcissistic boomers, who had benefited from the last fruits of the postwar growth in universities and the lingering radicalism of their youth, produced some interesting work. But they allowed the academic job situation to go to seed, and left the Xers with a terrible situation. So the Xers conformed, learning to internalize the human resources guru in their head, smoothing all their rough edges, adopting the safe habits that would get them careers in an increasingly dicey environment. The boomers were wild and destructive, but at least they left a strong intellectual legacy. The ensuing generation, however, is a tragically underformed group of middle managers who make the academic atmosphere the chilly place that it is today.

Yet despite the increasing professional tone of the academy, the fundamental problem with the academy is in fact its *incomplete* professionalization, its refusal to understand and submit to bureaucracy. For when graduate students are not being exploited by ruthless university administrators, they are being infantilized by their professors. Freud, rather than Marx, offers the best guide to the psychological minefield of academic life. For unlike the transparent world of bosses and workers, where people are compelled to come face-to-face with their real conditions of life, the academy is obscure and feudal, with graduate students as apprentices seeking entry to a guild. The professors aren't employers but rather masters of a craft; the stability of their position rests on impalpable levels of prestige and claims to knowledge that the guilds have certified. Between the master professor and the apprentice graduate student lies a rich field of psychic hazards whose keywords—*neurosis, paternalism, incest*—are ones that early twentieth-century Vienna would have known well.

The result of this space of total unaccountability is the professor who attempts to psychologically discipline his or her advisee. I've heard professors speak about needing to "break" their graduate students, and I've seen students get—and have myself enjoyed the privilege of getting—broken in by faculty. Usually this means professors attacking their students' work on personality (rather than intellectual) grounds, suggesting that they're mentally unfit for this line of work, or simply by failing them on an exam that they would otherwise have passed. Every graduate student I know has enjoyed one or more such features of the professor-student relationship. Some get over it through bouts of alcoholism, others by increasing their quotient of fawning and self-flagellation, debasing themselves into some version of Edgar from *King Lear*. Still others have found themselves on a psychiatrist's couch, and soon after on heavy medication. The most common response, however, has been a resort to what Peter Sloterdijk has called *cynical reason*—rationalizing the masochistic system as simply the way things have to be, even though one knows better. Except for labor unions, graduate students have few means of expressing solidarity when it comes to the kind of psychological warfare professors conduct against them. The result is a crippling paradox: isolation on the one hand and an increasing dependence on the institution on the other. If you've ever wondered what catastrophe intervenes in the life of the normal and sociable graduate student, lobotomizing her into the arrogant and insecure professor, this graduate school hazing ritual is your answer.

This isn't to say that there isn't any recourse at all; graduate students *can* band together, and the profession *can* be changed. At a certain point in my graduate career, it became evident that my department had decided to initiate a systemwide crackdown on students it no longer had faith in. Several students who were on temporary leave, and who were seeking to return to

the program, were expelled by an authoritarian director of graduate studies. Several others were given disciplinary warnings about their professional
demeanor. And finally, one student, an exceptionally young first-year, was
singled out for being excessively combative in his seminars and put on
academic probation. He was given a set of goals to complete: The administrators asked him to find a set of faculty who would act as his advisers, two
years in advance of everyone else, and he was asked to complete a set of
unfinished papers. He completed these goals handily, but students began to
hear rumors through the faculty gossip mill that the graduate studies
committee planned to expel him anyway. A number of us circulated a petition insisting that the student be kept in the program, which, under steady
and organized pressure, a majority of students signed. (The ones who
didn't often said that they feared to append their names to a document that
might later be used by professors as an informal blacklist.) Observers waiting outside the faculty meeting where this student's fate was being decided
could hear professors screaming at each other through the closed door. In
the end, the student was spared; an official letter cited the petition as a key
document in his salvation.

Though this bit of collective action is a small source of pride to me, it's
also depressing. It reminds me that too little of graduate life is actually spent
reading or thinking; in fact, the years of graduate school are often intellectually vacuous ones. Even when they're not dodging expulsion, graduate
students are forced to spend an inordinate amount of time worrying about
their advisers—Do they like me? Do they think I'm stupid? If I insert the
right keywords in my dissertation, will they like my work?—rather than
working patiently through texts and through conceptual problems. The
consequence is that you develop research—and a corresponding personality—that pleases everyone but is alien to yourself.

No one who goes to graduate school now can be wide-eyed about the
"life of the mind," let alone the possibilities of getting a job. Still, compared
with the working world, graduate school offers tons of unstructured time
and usually a pretty spectacular library in which to spend it. Institutes and
fellowships let you travel frequently and study obscure languages. These
things are the unadulterated goods of graduate school, its purest pleasures.

And you get paid to indulge them. It might still be possible to carve out an independent existence in graduate school, reading widely and well, and, far from the madding crowd of the academy's gatekeepers, to write an enriching and satisfying dissertation. And if you're willing to endure insults and humiliations, the social world of graduate school may offer you a career. This is, however, very unlikely. So, if you must, go to graduate school, but only to read what you want and learn what you want. Avoid every other blandishment, every grooming technique, every bit of professional advice. Get in, take the money, and run.

John Quijada

IN PONDERING THE QUESTION as to whether a newly minted recipient of a bachelor's degree should or should not pursue graduate studies, an image springs to my mind of Ts'ui Pên's "garden of forking paths" from the famous Jorge Luis Borges story of the same name. Taking one path in the garden leads to one reality, while the other leads to a different reality, equally irrevocable.

In my case, the path *not* taken was the route to graduate school. Having developed an interest in language and linguistics as a teenager after discovering the foreign language section of my local public library, I decided to pursue linguistics as a career path in college, the idea being that I would follow it through to a master's and a PhD, leading to a life of wondrous adventure in the wilds of the Amazon headwaters doing linguistic fieldwork on previously undocumented languages and publishing paradigm-shattering articles in linguistics and anthropology journals worldwide. Ultimately, however, following receipt in 1981 of my bachelor's degree, the reality of family circumstances, poverty, and complete ignorance on my part about things such as grants prevented me from attending grad school. Instead, after taking a civil service exam and spending six months as a truck driver while waiting to get to the top of the hiring list, I wound up as an entry-level petty bureaucrat in California state government.

I spent thirty years five months as a civil servant, doing work which kept me employed and which guaranteed a solid middle-class existence of

97

physical comfort, achieved at the mere cost of having to endure forty hours a week of intellectual and spiritual lassitude, and learning firsthand how and why government work achieves its reputation for inefficiency, short-sightedness, and incompetence. At least I was able to take advantage of frequent exams to promote or transfer into different jobs. Indeed, over the course of my thirty-year tenure, I managed to have six different careers: clerk at a public counter, licensing examiner, administrative hearing officer, administrative assistant to a deputy director, trainer, and IT manager. There were even occasional respites from the mental drudgery—the four years I spent during the mid-1990s training administrative-hearing officers were both mentally challenging and spiritually rewarding (which, of course, only served to remind me what a great time I would've been having as a university professor).

Yet, over the course of those thirty years, my view slowly changed. For the first decade or so, I secretly longed to return to grad school and pursue my dream of a life in academia, but my comfortable pseudo-yuppie exist-ence and penchant for expensive European vacations never allowed that dream to make it off the back burner. As the years accrued, I began to view my garden of forking paths through the lens of a pragmatic pro-versus-con analysis, and the results allowed me to eventually rationalize my long-simmering dream right off of the stove. I mean, after all, by the last decade of my civil service career, I was in middle management, comfortably ensconced in a suburban Sacramento house I owned, making probably twice the salary I would've been making brownnosing my way to tenure as an assistant or associate linguistics professor at some snowbound midwest-ern university (and having grown up in L.A. and not having seen real snow until I was seventeen years old, well . . .)

Nevertheless, in July 2010, in a case of real life being stranger than any fiction, I was allowed a brief glimpse of the path not taken. The surreal events that led to that glimpse ultimately stem from my discovery, at age fourteen, of J. R. R. Tolkien's Elvish languages, as well as the music of the French band Magma, whose lyrics are sung in a fictional language called Kobaïan. As a result, I found myself smitten by what Tolkien called the "secret vice," that is, the idea of inventing one's own private language.

While I subsequently created several private-language sketches over the next few years that were little more than re-lexified English (or French or Russian or whatever foreign language I was studying at the time), it was my formal study of linguistics in college that allowed me to take language creation seriously. As I became increasingly familiar with the formal structures of language and the fascinating ways that human languages (especially those outside of the Indo-European family) grammaticize and lexify reality, the idea came to me to work on what in linguistics circles is known as an *a priori philosophical language*—specifically, an experiment to see if it is possible to create a human language that conveys deeper levels of cognition and semantic exactitude than are found in natural languages. I had no idea that this endeavor would end up consuming countless hours of my spare time over the next quarter century.

After graduating from college and realizing I would not be returning to academia anytime soon, I initially put my language project on the shelf. However, within a year or so, I found myself once again opening my private notebooks filled with linguistic arcana. I soon developed a routine that remained constant during the course of my thirty years as a civil servant. I would make quarterly forays to university bookstores (Amazon.com did not yet exist!) for doses of new tomes in linguistics and other academic disciplines, subsequently spending several evenings a week and occasional weekends studying and consuming them, then applying their lessons to my ever-evolving language. While some might see this behavior as utterly geeky and obsessive, to me it was simply a choice as to whether watching sports on TV or shooting pool with the guys at the bar was a worthwhile way to spend my spare time. If my day job had been intellectually fulfilling, I might well have liked nothing better than to spend my off-hours in such pursuits. But such was not the case. So in order to keep my mind alive, I sat at home or in a coffeehouse several hours a week reading up on the latest in cognitive linguistics, semiotics, fuzzy logic, even quantum theory, then returned to the notebooks where my brainchild was slowly and painstakingly taking shape. By 2004, I finally considered my progress sufficient to post the project on the web, thinking that a few linguistics geeks might take a look and comment on it.

The language did indeed achieve a brief fifteen minutes of fame among fellow *conlangers* (i.e., hobbyists who construct their own languages), but, as I expected, my work was largely ignored by academia. However, in early 2010, I received an e-mail from a group of Russian and Ukrainian academics inviting me to attend a conference on "creative technologies" in the Russian Republic of Kalmykia. (No, I'd never heard of it, either.) This group of academics had discovered my work and apparently believed it to represent a major intellectual achievement. Accepting the invitation for the sheer prospect of adventure, I ended up spending an all-expenses-paid week in Russia, courtesy of the Kalmykian government, where I met the aforementioned academics and their students. They treated me as a respected professor and colleague, gathering in the evenings to ask me questions about my work and to hear me expound my views on language, cognitive science, life in America, life in Russia, life itself. After the first of these evenings of cross-cultural academic exchange and intense intellectual conversation, I walked back to my room, took a shower, and burst into tears, imagining the same idyllic evenings being spent in my university office or in my off-campus domicile, surrounded by adoring students and trusted colleagues. The experience was utterly surreal, euphoric, and devastatingly humbling.

Nevertheless, upon returning home, I managed to regain my equilibrium and to recover my comforting rationalizations about my life-as-it-is. I understand how idealized my view of academia really is. Friends and various articles I've read remind me what a cutthroat, political, conniving, backstabbing, and jealousy-ridden reality professorial life at a university can be. I assume the truth lies somewhere in the middle, as usual.

Recently, I caught a few minutes of one of those daytime talk shows, and the ladies were interviewing Rob Lowe, the actor and onetime bad boy, whose morally checkered past has often haunted him. One of the hosts asked him whether he'd live his life differently if he had the chance to do it all over again. I was struck by Lowe's response: He pondered the question for a second or two, then said no, because he realized if he went back and lived his life differently, he'd likely now be in a different place and in different circumstances, and given how content and at peace he is with his life today, he wouldn't want to risk giving that up.

It is the same with me. I have a beautiful wife of fourteen years whom I met through work, two outstanding stepsons and their lovely wives, and four beautiful granddaughters who have become a true source of joy in my life. If I had pursued graduate school, I would have none of those things. Or, more likely, I might have something equivalent—a different wife perhaps, maybe children of my own, a different house in a different part of the country. Yet they would be different from what I have now. It wouldn't be my wife or my granddaughters, and now that I know and love them, I wouldn't want to have lived without them. Not to mention that, for all I know, had I gone to grad school, I might well be dead and buried already from a case of malaria courtesy of the Amazon jungle or an indigenous spear through my chest as the result of my well-intended efforts at first contact.

One should not try to second-guess the past. Nevertheless, I have been privileged to have been allowed to follow both paths in the garden in a manner of speaking, one of them in my public day-to-day life, the other in my private mental life, which for a brief time manifested itself as part of day-to-day reality. It makes me treasure all the more my life as it is.

Erik Lindman

GROWING UP ON THE Upper East Side of Manhattan, I was shuttled to museums, not soccer practice. Art was a fact of daily life. Whether collected out of status anxiety or genuine enthusiasm, art was always around, hanging on the walls of my wealthy friends' apartments. My own family owned art books, but I saw Rothkos in friends' dining rooms. I remember a Picasso sketch hanging in a guest bathroom at one friend's home; at another's, Warhol's Mao loomed without irony above the desk of a Wall Street tycoon. As a teenager, I would sneak off during parties in these apartments to stare at these paintings, my mind racing with admiration and possibility. My family was neither rich nor poor, and I felt that I lacked an identity in this social scene. My ability to talk about art gave me a way to fit in.

One summer, I went along with two of my cooler friends to a precollege art program. Most nights I sat alone in the quad gazing at rising columns of cigarette smoke and rehearsing the chatter of students and faculty. "You have three choices for grad school, but who wants to be in New Haven?" "Chelsea picks the next stars from their open studios." I wanted to be a painter, but art school turned me off: My time on campus felt like a cult initiation into a place where everyone was an individual in exactly the same way.

Despite my reservations, I applied to an art school alongside a few liberal arts colleges. I was accepted at the art school and was set to enroll, but an offhanded comment from my mother changed my plans: "Now I can't brag to my friends that my son goes to [prestigious university]." I ended up going the liberal arts route partly to please my mother and partly out of fear: I knew that at a competitive art school, my unique status would be lost, and I wouldn't be such a big deal.

At college, I received attention from the faculty and started to intern for artists in the city. Working for them, I learned what the life of a profesional artist could be: You begin drinking at noon, go to openings (where the beer is free) at six P.M., and then crash a dinner where you continue to eat and raid the bar on someone else's dime. I loved the scene, and I loved a free meal. By my twentieth birthday, I never thought twice about what I wanted to do with my life.

At school, talking about MFAs with other students occupied more time than actually making art. From both teachers and peers, I learned that attending a selective MFA program is key to a successful art career. Left and right, artists were being poached straight out of MFA programs by blue-chip galleries. I wanted what these programs seemed to offer: money and status.

But although I was living what I thought was the life of an artist, I wasn't doing much else. At one point during my college career, while attending yet another prestigious summer program, I was taken to task by the head of the art department for my perceived squandering of his time and wealth of experience. "I don't know if you are rich," he said, "but when you graduate you're going to have to find work. And if you go out after work, you'll postpone going to the studio. Then the same thing will happen the next day. Soon enough, you won't be making any art."

After graduation, I ended up living out the department head's prediction. I didn't know what to do with myself, and I couldn't get the answers I was looking for from my former teachers or peers. Leaving a structured environment, even one I resented, left me in a state of shock. Over the next few years, I worked various jobs and spent most of my time drunk at bars, imagining a future in which graduate school would solve the basic conflict of everyday life. Instead of reflecting seriously on why I wanted to be an artist, I drank to distract myself from the realization that I had a lot of trouble with day-to-day activities and a paralyzing obsession with the future. I wanted to succeed, and MFA programs were easier to worry about than actual art making.

When I did get it together to apply to one program—a non-degree-granting one—I had serious doubts about whether I would be able to function in an academic environment, or if I could even interact with people while sober. My concerns proved irrelevant: I wasn't accepted. Soon after receiving my rejection notice, everything else started to fall apart: My girlfriend threatened to leave me, I couldn't get properly drunk, my parents divorced, and I realized I didn't really care about what my attitude toward modernism was.

But getting rejected did lead me to sober up. It also prompted me to finish a series of paintings that I had started in a drunken blackout. They were the first pieces that really felt like my own, and the process made me realize that graduate school was not the spiritual solution I had been looking for. After that, things started to change: I took jobs that taught me basic carpentry skills and art techniques. Duccio became more interesting than the dog-eared copy of *Vitamin P* in the studio common area. I cleaned up my studio, which had previously resembled an aluminum can recycling facility, and I learned how to handle unstructured time. Once I started to make art for the right reasons, I started meeting the right kinds of people. While I had been expecting grad school to help me construct a new identity, I realized what I really needed was a break from myself. When I had my second solo show in Europe two years later, I didn't e-mail anyone about it.

Fifteen years later, I can still see that teenager wandering out of the kitchen at his friend's party to discover the de Kooning in the living room. While gazing around the room, he quickly finds his reflection in the view of Central Park in the adjacent black window. There was so much to see, yet he was so easily distracted.

Peter Coviello

ON A LATE-SPRING DAY sometime in the mid-'90s, I found myself sitting
with a friend on a stone bench overlooking a prospect of estimable pastoral
loveliness: green valley and distant hills, cinematic cloudscapes, placid lake,
etc. The friend was then at the collapsing end of a love affair, and because
she was a few years older than I, and much, much smarter, I experienced her
distress with a kind of baffled shock. (She was, alternatingly, angry and sad,
inhabiting each mode with force.) I can remember looking at her and thinking, "If that much articulacy and worldliness and fierce intelligence didn't
insulate you from such vehement heartsickness, then, jesus, what would?"

I was young.

We looked at the scene before us and took in its failure to be restorative
in the ways much of our reading had suggested it ought to be. We talked, I
am sure, about Elvis Costello. And so, unable to countenance this much
sorrow in a person I found so comprehensively winning—keen-witted,
generous, beautiful, so easily possessed of the mysterious knowledge of
how to be brilliant *without being a dick about it*—I tried to say something I
thought both consoling and true, something about sadness and happiness
and the world. "It's hard to get too sad," I said. "Because whatever else
happens, you're never going to run out of books and bands and songs you
love. I mean, nothing can happen to take those things out of the world, you
know? They'll always be right there for you, always."

We'd not been friends for all that long. But she loved me enough, even
then, to let it go.

*

I assume that if you're considering with any real seriousness whether to go into a doctoral program, you don't need to have the litany of reasons, from the Marxist to the karmic, recited to you about why not to do so. If you cannot say those reasons off to yourself like beads of a rosary, then perhaps you have not given the matter enough thought. Jeremiads like those of, say, William Pannapacker in the *Chronicle of Higher Education* and *Salon* are prominent and well circulated enough that they don't need to be rehearsed at length here. (Summary: DO NOT GO.) I have no real wish to dispute these naysayers, nor do I want to argue with their appraisals of the exploitative machinery of institutional higher education, even though I do think that such dire accounts can be a bit monochromatic.[1]

But even though I don't have a dog in this fight (whether or not going to graduate school is good for *you* is likely to depend upon variables too numerous and case specific to generalize about), I'd still like to offer a small testament to at least one of the ways a graduate school education might be of real human use. I'd put it, at its briefest, like this: One day, at some unanticipated juncture on the trajectory of your adult life, something cataclysmically bad is going to happen to you. It will be, in the ordinary way of things, shattering and unendurable. And when this comes to pass, you may be startled to find that you have an extraordinary resource in, of all improbable things, your years of graduate education. In the people you loved there, of course, but also in the ways you learned to think there, and in the worlds that, by loving and thinking and talking and fighting in a common shared space, you learned to make together. That's not everything you might wish for, after many costly and laborious years, I know. But neither is it nothing.

In some ways this has little to do with graduate school. Live a vibrant, vital sort of life and the people to whom you are drawn in your twenties will, it is fair to hope, come forcefully to your aid in moments of need. Maybe this isn't true of law school or business school—which, god, is one sad fucking thought—but I'm ready to believe it is, just as I'm ready to

---

1 No one, I think, has written a more thoughtful, subtle, or moving rebuttal to the Pannapackers of the contemporary scene than Jonathan Senchyne in his exquisite piece "Working Classes."

believe it is true for those who pass their younger years outside the expensive confinements of institutional life. And yet, I do feel inclined to make a case, however partial and biased, for the special sorts of provision made by years of graduate life. Keep my bias in mind, and keep in mind that, in the cautionary words of late-night advertisements, your experience of the product may be different.

Unlike some wiser and more deliberate peers, I did not enter graduate school with much of a career trajectory in mind, or even an especially solid sense of what I wanted to study within my discipline. Modernism? Twentieth-century poetics? Nineteenth-century America? Shelley? They all beguiled. To the degree that something like a rationale could be retrospectively assembled, I'd say I was there chiefly because of an ardor I'd come to feel in the presence of certain kinds of objects, an ardor I could not fully explain to myself, but in which I suspected, with dim wordless intuition, something of a real, lasting kind of value lay concealed. That such an impulse is alarmingly proximate to, say, an undergraduate's simultaneous belief in (a) the generalized coolness of, like, *books* and (b) the preciousness of his own insights, is not lost on me now, and probably was not lost on me then.

But listen: I went to graduate school and several very great things happened, and happened particularly to my object-love. Two of them seem in retrospect to have been the most sustaining, though they are so interwoven it's difficult to think of them in sequence or isolation. For the sake of clarity, we'll put them in order. First, my avidity for certain kinds of objects, for what they did and what they promised and what they complicated, forced me to find *languages*, analytic vocabularies that offered precision and conceptual density in the place of inchoate enthusiasm. Contrary to what I was told, I was struck to find that these difficult conceptual languages did not cancel my delighted captivation by professionalizing it. (I had been assured by more than a few well-meaning professionals that the cumulative effect of graduate school—if not the actual point—was to smother all sparks of untutored enthusiasm you might bring to the scene of your education.) An idiolect, I came to know, is not the opposite of ardor, just as articulacy need not be the graveyard of pleasure. The languages you learn to speak with assurance and agility, and to make more completely your own: These are ardor's vehicle. They can give coherence to the complex delight you feel in relation to certain objects, and above all they give that delight a versatile, usable form by which it can be sustained, elaborated, and enlarged.

That's one way of thinking about what you're doing in graduate school, whatever field you're in: You are being trained to see the world in the grain of a spectacular, inexhaustible complexity. (Be warned: Academic discourse prefers complexity in explanation even when—ethically, politically, affectively—simpler accounts may be more appropriate or effectual.) You are enjoined to develop an analytic vocabulary that equips you, first, to see the world as possessed of a detailed, finely textured intricacy and, second, to describe that intricacy, and why it matters, with clarity and precision and grace. One can see why the acquisition of such languages might be described as an arduous, solitary, joy-dampening sort of work, made even unhappier by the often exploitative conditions that mediate that labor.

All that's true. But it's also true that you are learning to inhabit these languages in concert with others. And this is the second great thing that happened to me in graduate school: I found that one might cherish not only objects—books, passages, arguments, etc.—with a sustained, lifewide devotion, but also the scenes that kindle around them, scenes forged in the heat and friction of contestation and knit together by the languages that we students learn to inhabit. The collaborative quality of graduate life matters greatly—or it did to me—because talking about why you love what you love with other passionately interested parties, or why you find one idea generative and another hackneyed, or why one book's political intervention is clearly superior to another's, does more than just give you improvised training in the use of critical languages. Making a language together is another way of describing what happens when you fall in love: with friends, with lovers, with entire scenes. We all know how this goes: In your besotted ardor, you and those you share it with invent a baroque terminology that carries within it your styles of apprehension, your delights and your disdains, the whole fabric of a scene that you elaborate into a language that is refined and reworked and reanimated over years.

In this way, if you're lucky, the trade language of your discipline can become interfused with the heated, ambulatory, extravagant kinds of talk that sustain the intimate worlds you assemble during these years. These worlds are marked by frustration and fear, without question—it is graduate school—but also by intellectual exhilaration, hilarity, and care. Eventually, of course, time and the various demands of life will have their dispersive effects. But one of the things you're left with in the aftermath of upheaval and displacement—along with a degree of questionable value—is your mixed and variegated language. You may find that continuing to speak it across expanding distances is one of the ways in which the best, most energizing aspects of those worlds can be nurtured and transformed into unforeseen futures.

And then, one day, you will encounter something that is outsized and terrible, something that devours ardor at the root and will not be dislodged by even the most venerated of objects that have for so long nourished you. Language itself, no matter how conceptually rich or steeped in the history of your dearest affections, will seem like the thinnest and most friable of scrims between you and this horror. And I promise you, though you may not recognize it at the time, the voices calling you back to a scene of language making, back to this patient discrimination and the wringing of clarities from messy indistinction—they won't cure you. But they will act as a testament and a reminder. You will need both.

Sara Marcus

I ALWAYS TOLD MYSELF I'd go to grad school when I hit a wall, but I wondered how I'd know when I hit it. Then I was twenty-six and I knew. It wasn't anything too serious—I got word that a promising magazine assignment had fallen through—but suddenly my life plan stopped making sense, and I didn't know how to go forward.

Running out of other ideas might sound like a bad reason to get something as inherently worthless as an MFA in nonfiction writing. But that's only true if a degree is just a degree. If you play it right, grad school can call forth better ideas about how to live your life, rather than just substituting for them. Everybody says an MFA program is merely a tool to help you do what you could, in theory, do on your own, and this is basically true. But there's a reason that the development of tools marked a huge leap forward in human history. They can actually be stupendously useful. Even though I did what everybody says you should *never ever do* (attend an expensive program without being independently wealthy), I've always been happy with my decision.

So, back to my archetypal moment of despair. It was late October. I sat at my kitchen table in Brooklyn, a dull hour near sunset, feeling life to be an endlessly still body of water that went for miles on all sides. The newly lost assignment was only the latest in a string of signs that my beloved plan was in trouble. I had moved to New York two years earlier, intending to work a job for a while, write on the side, build up my contacts, then quit the job and write for magazines full-time. I saw ex-classmates scoring themselves writing careers by way of unpaid internships or grad programs, but I couldn't afford to work anywhere for free, and I wanted to teach myself to write—with the help of editors who were paying me, of course—instead of paying somebody else to teach me. I was proud of the path I'd chosen: eschewing the ritualized shortcuts of privilege, triumphing on elbow grease alone.

This worked for a while, and it might have kept working if I'd been content to take any assignment that came along, or if my interests had been more middle of the road to begin with. But there was a fundamental disconnect between me and the editors who offered real paychecks. "Why is this radical synagogue *cool*?" one editor had asked after I'd sent in a commissioned draft. "Do any famous people pray there?" Now my latest gig, a piece for a teen magazine on a girls' rock 'n' roll summer camp, had died unceremoniously: "We saw photos of the girls, and they're just not pretty."

Hello, wall, I thought, relieved, like somebody whose so-so lover has just done something unforgivable.

Since the only plan I had left was this IF {WALL} THEN {GRAD SCHOOL} operation, I downloaded MFA applications without quite knowing why, other than the fact that I wanted to write and had run out of ways to do it. As I worked on my application essays, the real reason became so clear it was ridiculous I hadn't seen it all along. After years of writing for newspapers and magazines, I was impatient to write something in my own voice on a topic that I had chosen for myself, something long and impossible—to write, in other words, a book. I wanted a book the way other women want a baby: an ugly, growing thing that will obliterate the rest of your life with its unending demands, something that frees you from making any difficult choices once the first, determining choice has been made. My book-baby would anchor me in the world, a reflection of myself, traveling places I never could. Some Palestinians take familiar names based on their children's names—father of Hassan, mother of Ahmed. I wanted that.

For almost a year, I'd been telling people I was thinking of writing a book about Riot Grrrl, a punk feminist movement I'd been part of in the 1990s as a teenager and whose history was getting distorted and forgotten. Before the grad school idea entered the equation, I had thought I might just quit my nonprofit day job and write the book while living on savings, but I had saved up only about six months' worth of living expenses. My real, bedrock problem, then, was a simple one of time and money. I did the math. An MFA would buy me at least two years, plus community, structure, mentorship, connections, and deadlines. The deferred costs would be enormous—there weren't any stipended nonfiction programs in the Northeast—but I needed a few years of dedicated time to get my book under way, and racking up decades of debt for it, seemed like, while certainly not a just or ideal trade-off, a livable one. The debt would be a drag. But not writing my book—never even knowing if I *could* write my book, given enough time and space—would be a much bigger drag.

Lots of people tried to dissuade me. I got the sense, especially from older writers, that an MFA was kind of a shameful thing to get, like scabies, something that the really smart people with real talent managed to avoid. But nobody had a better idea of how I was going to interview a hundred people, get ongoing access to obscure resources and electronic databases, and write a book that I didn't know how to write, before my savings ran out. That's because there was no other way. I thought I heard a Calvinist undertone to people's admonitions: If I had really been chosen by God to write a book, I would have written it by now. But when? At twenty-two and twenty-three, I was still learning how to write, in a very basic way. I look back on the pieces I published right after college and I feel shuddering relief that I didn't try to write a whole book back then. That's one of the great things about writing: People often improve at it as they get older. In my four years of freelancing, I had taught myself a lot, studying literature that I liked and gradually developing a style of my own. After all that, I still wasn't ready to write a book. But I was ready to learn how. And, reader, that's just what happened.

When I started at Columbia, I had a vague plan of attack for the book. I knew how to write magazine articles, so I would just write a dozen or more magazine-article-type things and then I would have a book. Simple, right? Trouble is, while most magazine articles about musicians require only one major interview, a book chapter might require a dozen or more. I quickly realized that in order to submit my twenty or twenty-five pages to workshop a few times a semester, I would need to spend all my spare time and all my school breaks doing research and interviews. I talked to a band's frontwoman in her kitchen in D.C. while I was back there visiting my parents for a weekend. I brought my tape recorder and notebook to a Brooklyn basement where a key zinemaker and organizer, in town for just a few days, was doing her laundry. I drank tiny cups of genmaicha with a reviled and defiant rock critic in a second-story tea salon just off St. Mark's Place.

Even with all this, I ran out of material sometimes, and I envied my class-mates who seemingly could just open another vein every time it was their turn to share work: a college breakup, a trip abroad, a family crisis. I tried my hand at personal essays, and the experience of submitting these pieces to the scrutiny of some of the squarest people I had known since high school instilled in me an anxiety about writing personal essays that contin-ues to this day. But the essays also gave me a place to experiment with form and tone and structure, free from the pressure of conveying facts about other people's lives or the temptation to revert to my utilitarian freelancer habits. I started hanging out with the poetry students. They looked at the essays my workshopmates had squinted at and they said, "Oh, you're writ-ing poetry!" I started writing poetry on purpose. The book-bits I kept grinding out started to breathe a little more.

During my two years of MFA coursework, I generated a book's worth of words. I learned how my writing went over with readers very differ-ent from me (a young man who seemed to have never actually listened to a woman, a genial suburban dad, many kind-hearted young women in sweetheart blouses from Club Monaco), what was unclear to them, what I couldn't count on them to understand unless I committed to the work of getting it across to them. Half the people in my workshops were probably never going to pick up a book about punk rock feminists. But I could endeavor, anyway, to make sure the book would be legible to those who might happen to open it. I probably wouldn't have done that without grad school.

Each time my writing was workshopped, I'd meet with the workshop leader right afterward. Sometimes my classmates' comments had been helpful; sometimes they'd been discouraging or flat-out insane. "Is this working?" I'd ask the professor. "Is this going to be any good?" They told me it was. They told me to keep going. "Don't just say that because I'm paying all this money. Don't just be nice to be nice." They swore they weren't doing that. They told me how to widen my claims, address an audience of more than me and my friends, tweak the pacing, tighten up the paragraphs. They were frequently right. Other teachers had me read Edmund Wilson, Joseph Mitchell, Charlotte Delbo, Lyn Hejinian—writers who burrowed under my skin and into my work.

I finished coursework with a stack of messy drafts, and that's when the real work began. Since Columbia gives MFA students three extra years to finish their theses, I was still technically in school. I kept my health insurance. I took out more loans. I paid off the private loans with public loans so I could consolidate them all at lower interest rates. It was (and remains) a stupefying amount of debt. Many of my classmates immediately took full-time jobs to start paying it off. I became a freelance copy editor and applied to residencies—and, to my extreme relief and amazement, I got into one. In the middle of a winter of record snowfall for New Hampshire, I marooned myself for six weeks inside a studio that I came to think of, affectionately, as my padded cell, listening to the oil heater switch on and off while I paced the perimeter of the room. I used to fall asleep at night with my drafts still spread out on the floor, and when I woke up I'd sit back down in the middle of them. The workshop submissions I'd written detached themselves from the pages and shimmied around and arranged themselves into something that looked more and more like a book: Single-voice sections melded into chorales, isolated incidents clustered into chronologies. And I wrote new sections, jumping off metaphoric docks at metaphoric midnights, experimenting desperately the way I used to do halfway through a hated personal essay that was due the next morning to my workshopmates in double-spaced stapled copies. In spurts and stallouts, in leaps and stumbles, my book was being born.

After I left MacDowell I moved to upstate New York for several months, where my rent was $250 and the phone never rang. I stayed away from the city as much as I could; home was too expensive, and it brought too many distractions. Once, on returning to Brooklyn to work a few jobs, I asked a writer I admired for her secret of getting writing done in the city. "You have to give up on having a social life and get up really early," she said.

"You mean like eight?" I asked innocently.

"I mean like six," she replied. It was excellent advice.

I graduated from Columbia in May 2009, five years after starting course-work. My parents came up from Maryland for commencement, which I thought was very sweet of them considering I didn't quite believe I was getting a real degree. Six months later, I turned in the manuscript to my publisher, got into bed, and slept for twenty hours straight. *Girls to the Front: The True Story of the Riot Grrrl Revolution* was published in September 2010, six years almost to the day after I had begun my MFA with only enough money in the bank to last six months. Yes, it was a very expensive MFA. It was also a Chanukah miracle, an uncanny stretching of a meager resource: I had made six months last for five years. And as they taught me in Hebrew School, you can't have a Chanukah miracle without faith.

What makes me the chirping dissenter from all the MFA cautionary tales? A few things worked in my favor:

1. I had been out of school for five years before starting grad school. I'd worked a bunch of jobs, helped edit a magazine, freelanced all over the place. I knew how to write and I had ideas of things to write about besides my college years.

2. I had a strong sense of what I wanted my work to look like. This allowed me to avoid the commonly cited pitfall of MFA students trying to please all their classmates. Anybody who's trying to please all their classmates in workshop has a backbone deficiency that can't be blamed on grad school. As for me, I learned quickly that one or two people in each workshop would have good comments on my

work all the time, another one or two would come up with a gem every so often, and the rest were just not my audience.

3. My parents were able to chip in on my rent during the two years of coursework. I lived very cheaply, in a short little room in a loft with my roommate rolling around in his desk chair right above my head all the time, and that parental help represents a fraction of the overall cost, but it did help make things feel a bit less drastic at the time. I also received a couple fellowships in my second year. Am I saying that this can't work for you if your family can't contribute financially? Not at all, but I believe in being honest about these things.

4. I had a book idea going in, I was determined to make it work no matter what, and I spent all my free time researching it.

It's that last item that made the biggest difference for me. If you have a project you're sure you want to finish, and if you believe that taking on all that debt is a bargain whose terms—however grotesque, however unjust—you won't regret as long as you get your work done, and if you think grad school will help you get your work done, then go to grad school and get your work done.

Getting an MFA in order to write is like wearing flippers in order to swim. Plenty of people do fine without it, and some people might think it makes you look foolish. But it forces you to put in extra effort, it makes you stronger, and it zooms you through the water with a power you didn't know you had. Before going to grad school, I didn't know any of this for sure. I just knew that I wanted time and room to hear my own voice and to know how far I could go with it. I suspected school could give me those things, and I made it give them to me, and years later I am still pleasantly astonished to see that this, at least, went exactly according to plan.

Ross Perlin

TO MAKE A GAP IN THE GALAXY, AND ADMIT A COMMON FOX WITHOUT
A TAIL, WOULD BE A DEGRADATION IMPOSSIBLE TO BE THOUGHT OF.
—WILLIAM JAMES, "THE PH.D. OCTOPUS"

HAPPY GRADUATE STUDENTS ARE all alike; every unhappy grad student is unhappy in her own way. When I was still a bright-eyed undergrad, I was haunted by the specter of the accidental grad student: wistful and distracted in section, too tipsy at happy hour, quashed by conferences and seminars and brown-bag lunches. They were mostly PhDs—self-pitying, ironical, veritably postintellectual creatures—but the rest of the alphabet soup crowd (MAs, MBAs, JDs, LLMs, and the like) seemed little better off. Some dressed for job interviews before even buying their first textbooks. Others shopped potential classes and mates even more awkwardly and desperately than we did. If the saddest docs and postdocs were the long-suffering stylites of the holy Academy, exposed to the elements on the pillars of their hyperspecialized dissertations, the worst of the master's types were televangelists in the making, nefarious credentialists angling for a quick hit.

In spite of these impressions, I caved. I'm the kind of person who likes to dispatch unpleasant duties straightaway, get the nasty doings done with—in short, I headed straight to grad land. I remembered the words of Mike Davis: "University campuses are often little quasi-socialist paradises around rich public spaces for learning, research, performance, and human reproduction." I consoled myself that I was doing it in the UK, two master's degrees for one year each, and on someone else's dime. The contemplative life! A respectable pretext! Time for all the Great Books! I soaked myself in theories and ales. Friends outside the warm circle of collegiate life begged for my JSTOR access.

Turns out I was prolonging the agony, delaying the inevitable. Procrastination is not only the pervasive condition of campus life, a hallmark of daily experience, but the master idea of higher education, the very substance of what you're doing there. I bathed myself daily in theory and delusion, ignorant of money and power. I uttered the word *prosopography* more often than *career*. It's true, I liked the lingo and I read course catalogs for pleasure on the john, but I found I had little taste for faculty meetings and peer-reviewed perishing. The more my "field" came into view, the greater my discomfort, the more evident the traces of academic groupthink. Moreover, I gradually understood the beast whose belly I had entered, and the price of academic detachment. What passes today for a professoriate is a tiny elite of tweeded Superstars, pressed on all sides by the eager reserve labor army of researchers and pedagogues. And all of them are treated increasingly as a mere ornament of an Educational-Industrial Complex controlled by Boards and Bureaucrats and (Funding) Bodies, concerned with capital flows and petty politics and pecking orders. If you're planning to stick around, study the beast itself: the instrument before your eye, the armchair from which you think you're expounding.

Then, just as I was leaving the Academy for a desultory series of "real-world" posts, my friends were beating down the door to get in. Some had tired of precarious or freelance lives. Others sought a higher pay grade, sojourning in Ann Arbor or Princeton in order to jump the line in New York or D.C. One enthusiast proclaimed it his last chance at a real education: He would read Plato, learn Chinese, understand Darwin and Freud, and grapple with a world too complex to speed-read on weekends and evenings.

What became of me? Exile from the kingdom, or some would say a fate worse than death: I departed the (supposedly) empyreal realms of pure ideation for the (so-called) grubby marketplace of sound bites. I became a quasi academic. An independent researcher. I maintain an affiliation with a university in Europe, where autonomous all-but-dissertation-style field-work is the norm. Nowadays I duck into the occasional symposium, ever so gingerly. I nourish an unresolved tension, entertain an ongoing flirtation: a standoff with the ivory tower, whose libraries, seminars, and vanishing ice cap of tenure I still surreptitiously crave.

Ask yourself: Do you prefer pedaling an abstract or ad-libbing an elevator pitch? Forget the interdisciplinary hooey. Are you ready to pledge your allegiance to one discipline or another? Do you relish Bloomington and Boulder over Brooklyn and Berlin? Are you paying them or are they paying you? How's your *zitsfleysh*? (Yiddish for buttocks; hence, patience). How do you feel about moving somewhere cheap (could be Spokane, could be Bangkok) and awarding yourself with what a friend of mine calls the "poor man's MacArthur": working on a crazy project of your choosing until your money runs out?

You can survive without grad school. Few nonlifers contemplated the grad school grind until the 1960s, when money poured into the Academy and degrees began to multiply like three-letter pests. The multiversities and college towns became bastions and refuges, gilded cages coaxing thinkers from the cities. Can one imagine the landscape of American poetry today without the dubious patronage bestowed by higher education? The world of classical music without the largesse—and the limitations—of the conservatories? Horrible to relate, but people once did business without MBAs, preached without degrees in divinity, made films without MFAs. Are our works any better than those produced by the benighted unfortunates who moved in less-formalized (and usually less-expensive) realms of apprenticeship, tutelage, and life experience, of try and try again?

The truly academickal will out: the ones who lap up the Big Annual Meeting shit shows, the ones who can't tear themselves from the archives, can't get enough of the lab work. For the rest of us, a graduate degree is a fig leaf to cover up nakedness, no more and no less. Better we had never felt the first pangs of shame! A hundred schools of autodidacticism are just starting to flourish—open master's schemes, alternate credentials, dubious silicon universities, intriguing institutes, free schools, lifelong learning schemes, Chautauquas without end. The overcredentialed will be outcredentialed soon enough—new letter combinations, ever pricier, will never be lacking. The overproduction of degrees, the exploitation of grad student labor, these matters will only get worse until someone sticks a spoke in the wheels. The handwriting is on the wall, and you shouldn't have to subject it to a five-year metatextual, model-theoretic, poststructuralist analysis.

Kenneth Goldsmith

WHEN I GOT OUT of undergrad in 1984 with a degree in sculpture from RISD, the only people who went to grad school were those who wanted to teach. And in my mind, if you knew before you got out of school that you wanted to teach, then you had already given up; there was no way you were going to be an artist. Only losers went to grad school. Everyone else went to New York and clawed their way into the art world, which at the time was open to anyone who wanted to be a part of it. There was a very specific way to get studio visits and to get into group shows. In the mid-'80s, the path to being a New York artist was very clear, and an advanced degree was never going to help you with that. In fact, it might even hurt you.

How different things are today, when you need an advanced degree from a good school to even get galleries interested in your work. This is proven each spring when gallerists and collectors descend upon open studios at some of the hotter grad schools to recruit and purchase the freshest accredited talent. Many a painter's studio has been sold to the bare walls by the end of the day, ensuring them a smooth on-ramp into the commercial art world.

For me, the turning point occurred about a decade ago, when a dear friend of mine who had pretty much single-handedly invented the art world as we know it was forced to go back to school to get a PhD in order to get a better job. In the 1980s, he was the director of a high-profile alternative space that acted as a feeder to commercial galleries, much the same as MFA programs do today. During his decade-long tenure, he discovered some of the biggest names in contemporary art. After leaving his New York City job, he became the chief curator at a renowned institution outside the city. And while he flourished there, he began to desire a better position. Upon applying, he found out that he was not eligible because he had only an undergrad degree. Despite the fact that everyone knew who he was and that he had more street cred than anyone could ever want, his lack of a piece of paper prevented him from moving up; call it the parchment ceiling. At forty years old, he enrolled in night classes and over the course of several years finally obtained his PhD. He is now working the job of his dreams.

Similar stories emerge from the literary world. A renowned poet was tired of supporting himself as a limousine driver and wanted to get into academia. He was absolutely erudite, having taught himself scads of philosophy, theory, and poetry out of sheer interest, but no matter: He couldn't get a job. So a highly placed academic friend admitted him into a fast-track PhD program where he did his coursework and completed his comprehensives and was given a degree within two years, instead of the usual seven. Today, he runs a major poetics program. Again, without the piece of paper he'd still be making runs to the airport in his limo.

I ended up in academia by happenstance. My artistic practice was recognized as valuable by the institution where I now work, and I was given a position there with just a BFA. For a poet, this was amazingly useful. Having worked dreary day jobs for decades, I was relieved to be able spend my days in what is, to my mind, unalienated labor. But meritocratic placement today is the exception, not the rule. With academic budgetary concerns and so many properly accredited people desperate for work, honorary positions have more or less fallen by the wayside.

Sadly, I tell my students that an MFA isn't really going to do them any good in the job market; they've got to get a PhD. I can see a time when the current gold standard MFA will be replaced by newly minted PhDs in studio art or poetry. In a time of rampant professionalization and fear underscored by the true lack of a social safety net, the only things our culture seems to be able to recognize are standardized litmus tests. This has resulted in deadly dull and overly cautious artistic practices. It's time to ask: At what price culture?

Alexander Nagel

MY ONLY EXPERIENCE OF depression was during graduate school. I don't mean I was down or drinking too much or getting up late. I mean I was unable to do anything. I would find myself at social events without the capacity to open my mouth. I experienced an entire interview for a post-doctoral fellowship from above: I was looking down on myself saying incoherent things to a jury of world-famous scholars. I cried a lot. It was my last year in graduate school and I knew it. I knew it because I had received a finishing grant, which meant I was to complete my dissertation (about the origin of the easel picture in Renaissance art, at least that was the idea) and leave the program by the end of that academic year. That was twenty years ago, yet I have never in my life felt so old as I did that year.

For five months I sat at my desk, or just lay down, and did not write a word. At some point in December, I approached my adviser to explain that things were not going well, really not going well at all. This was a miserable capitulation, as I had always been pridefully independent, only ever going to him with some good news or focused question or accomplishment in hand. His jaw hardened and he shifted around in his seat. The department has just been allocated these finishing grants from the Mellon Foundation, he said, fixing me with his cold blue eyes; successful performances during this first round will ensure that the department will retain the grant and, thus, will be in a position to offer it to students after me.

I nodded, left his office, and continued not writing, or doing much of anything. By that point it had also become completely clear that there were no prospects for teaching jobs in my field for the coming year—except, that is, for *one* job, in Kansas, and I would rather starve closer to home than move there. So there I was, on a terminal grant, hurtling toward unemployment.[1] Maybe not writing was my lame gesture of resistance in a wind tunnel of futility.

By mid-January, inertia was accompanied by a gentle but constant hyperventilation. Desperate, I remembered a technique my adviser had described in another context: *When your back is up against the wall, write two pages every day, no matter what.* Even if you know they are terrible, write them out. I think that is how he put it: *Write them out.* So I started. I was pretty much writing "la la la," but I did it. And then I did it the next day. And the next. The thing about this technique is that the first two months are an uphill climb; the more you climb the more you tire, and then you realize the hill is also getting steeper. It is fairly easy to write two pages on any given day, but it is hard to do it day after day, harder to get to ten days, and harder than ever to get from ten to fifteen days. For one thing, you run out of things to say; also, you are now putting effort into making various two-page bits link up with one another. At thirty days, you are in the fog of war, exhausted, dirty, wounded, not sure which way is forward. Some days I would writhe all day, come up with nothing, then see that it was eleven P.M. and in a dry-mouthed panic scrabble out the two required pages before midnight. With minor projects like a seminar paper, you are turning a fairly small crank; there are some weeks of chaos and then you see more or less how you are going to write twenty pages, bad or good, on the subject. I had never turned a crank this big before, and most of the time it felt like there was no way to make it move.

After about two months, however, I had more than one hundred pages lying on my desk—a pile of crap, but it was editable crap. It was a *draft*. On a sunny day, one might even call it half a dissertation. Now, on some days,

---

1 Do not listen to those people who say that job prospects for academics in the humanities have been consistently dwindling. They have not. They are certainly better now than when I was in grad school.

the slog to two pages would result miraculously in five. The crank was getting to where it could be pulled back around. It was like work on a puzzle, which speeds up when the missing parts start to look like holes.

"He never had an unpublished thought." I remember hearing this said about a prominent professor whose unstoppable output demanded a decisive response from the graduate student shark pool. To a student about to embark on a teaching career, I will say, somewhat more sympathetically, "There are times when what you say will be exactly coextensive with what you know of the subject." It is also true, sadly but not surprisingly, that such coextensive presentations usually please the audience much more than your disquisitions on a subject you know well.

But the point of being an academic, rather than a journalist, is not to write that way. We get to look into a subject from various angles before writing something about it. We get to hold things in reserve. Only about 10 percent of the reading, archival digging, and note taking I had done in the years of "dissertation research" made it into the dissertation. Which is not to say that it was useless, or not relevant. It was there, the way the paper is there in a drawing. Graduate school is a very good place to build up reserves. You can tell when you're talking to someone who has reserves.

I didn't think too much about going to graduate school. Like many undergraduates doing liberal arts degrees, I was generally artistic and literary, and I had also been politically involved. I had been a history major, mostly because I thought it was a good basis for anything I might do in the future. I had already decided, after some working and wondering, that I was not an artist, and certainly not a writer of the sort who made things up. Beyond that, I wasn't sure what I was. I liked books and art and I felt I wasn't done devoting lots of time to them. You can do that outside of academia, of course, but I did believe that advanced ideas get worked out in structured dialogue.

I had a friend, Josephine, who was a lot like me, inordinately devoted to art even though she didn't make it herself. When I told her I was going to go to grad school to study art history, she responded like someone trying to dissuade a naïve youth from enlisting in the army: "But Alex, you know what they're going to do to you, right?" I knew she meant that they were going to discipline me, make me memorize vast quantities of things, and generally turn my vibrant, dewy, poetic self into a dried-up writer of footnotes.

We didn't stay in touch, but what Josephine said worried me in a lasting way. I went into grad school determined not to dry up. I would engage in bibliomancy, flouting scholarly method. I kept a hand in contemporary art, and I kept reading my French surrealist poets. Whenever I did something poetic and irresponsible, I would think, "In honor of Josephine!" But the fact is, she was right: Graduate school did eventually catch up with me. By the end of the dissertation, I was narrowed, stiffened, older than my years. Luckily, I was able to finish before this condition became irreversible, and I eventually regained some of the springiness of my younger years.[2]

These were real challenges. I certainly wasn't worried about the other kind of concerns, how this was possibly going to help me make a living, or on a more general level, whether it is really worthwhile to devote oneself to thinking if it is not going to have a palpable application in the world. Mind you, my response was never to say, "But there *are* good opportunities in the field!" or "But my ideas *can* change the world!" It was just clear to me that getting a PhD was going to be very interesting and challenging in a real way, and getting a job probably would not be.

Undergraduates are different from grad students primarily because most of them are not there by choice. Undergrads are nervous, increasingly nervous in the era of performance-oriented parenting, but one thing they generally do not worry about is whether they should be in school. Grad students in the humanities, by contrast, get up every day, look in the mirror, and think,

---

2 Very important! If you stay in graduate school too long, it marks you as a person. It is a corridor where you are half living in the present-day world and half in your world of study. That is a wonderful thing, but it should not be allowed to last beyond two years for a master's, seven years for a master's and PhD.

"Why am I here?" "Was this really a good idea?" "I really feel like I'm fall-ing behind my professional friends." "I've been in school since the age of four and I'm fucking sick of it." "Clearly I am not as smart and driven as X; I should just get out now." The exceptions to this rule are the few who know that there is nothing else they would ever want to do and the ones who return to school after some exposure to the depredations of the real world.

Above all, grad students of the past five to ten years seem to want grad school to be professional school, even in the humanities. In art history, most are headed toward museum jobs and various branches of the contem-porary art world and the publications that surround it, i.e., a world of commerce. They are not headed into academia, which is seen as a machine designed to deliver perfectly intelligent people into poverty, depression, and oblivion. Increasingly, I find that students want to be professionals even while they're in school. They want a contractual understanding of what is expected of them. They want to do a good job. They want a tran-script with no strange looking marks on it and a CV with lots of nonacademic professional experience on it. Above all, they want to not be wrong.

Now my students are some of the best there are, so I don't often get bad papers. What I do get, increasingly, are efficient, intelligent, neat papers that have a reasonable point to make, and make it effectively. The reader is taken from point A to point B along a frictionless path. But only rarely do I read a paper and think, "This is a mind that has been on an adventure." Rarely do I feel that the writer has made contact with real complexity, has felt the panic that it induces, has seen that it is beautiful and terrifying and that it cannot possibly be dealt with in twenty pages, or in a few weeks. (Those that do give some sense of having understood the unmanageable complexities of the topic at hand, and then spend twenty pages saying something really smart about it.) It is getting harder and harder to convince students that contending with exceptions, contradictions, and other wrin-kles strengthens rather than weakens an argument. In sum, I am not seeing enough blood on the ground. I believe that the internships students do during their studies—purportedly to enhance their employability after grad school—are deeply affecting the way they undertake their academic work.

*

Gabriel Winant

LET ME INTRODUCE MYSELF in the customary way: I'm a third-year PhD student in history at Yale. I focus on the history of labor in the United States, American capitalism, and the politics of everyday life. Or, to present a more familiar figure: I'm an East Coast left-wing bearded Jewish academic who uses words like *hegemonic* and *subaltern* in regular conversation. I am, I imagine, more or less what Liz Lemon and Jack Donaghy had in mind when graduate students came up on an episode of *30 Rock*:

> DONAGHY: We might not be the best people.
>
> LEMON: But we're not the worst.
>
> TOGETHER: Graduate students are the worst.

The decision to go to graduate school today is not one to be taken lightly. It often entails a decision to inflict significant wounds on oneself—financial, emotional, and otherwise. Yet we've slipped into thinking of this as the norm, the cost of going into academe. It doesn't need to be this way. Our status—the worst—is something that's happened relatively recently. Specifically, it's a product of the gradual depoliticization of academia over the past decade or two, in a context of general economic and institutional disintegration. Academics in general have fallen victim to the same trends paralyzing and disfiguring so much of American society; graduate students, as the most vulnerable subset of academic workers, are particularly vulnerable. So to understand how academia got this way, we need to correct the misconception of the university as a world apart and see it for what it is: a mirror, albeit a distorted one, to the rest of society.

(A word of clarification here: When I talk about graduate school, I mean PhD programs, and when I talk about academia, I mainly mean the humanities and social sciences. I suspect much of what I say may go for the natural sciences as well, but I'm less sure.)

Since World War II, academia—or the part of it I know something about, anyway—has undergone a series of dramatic shifts. The story goes something like this: Prior to the war, universities were the preserve of young rich men. Their faculties were, to draw a caricature, populated by the third sons of industrialists—the eccentric lads who did not inherit the family business or become lawyers, instead developing an interest in ancient Rome or ornithology.

The war and its aftermath ruined this country club vibe. Emerging from the social struggles of the Depression and the mass mobilization of World War II, broad swathes of the American public demanded access to civic institutions from which they had previously been barred. In higher education, the GI Bill sent millions of young men to college whose fathers were farmers and factory hands. The professoriate changed, too, cautiously accepting some scholars of less exalted social extraction, and even the occasional social critic.

But certain aspects of postwar society—endless economic growth, Cold War anxiety—ensured that these new entrants didn't get any ideas. Across disciplines, a certain caste came to power during the postwar decades. Ideologically liberal, universally male and white, and professionally smug, the great scholars of 1945 to 1965 more or less led the professoriate through the doors that had opened in the 1930s and 1940s, securing tenure and influence. Yet, in retrospect it seems that postwar academics won their intellectual freedom by promising not to use it: They committed themselves to defending the American mainstream. Lionel Trilling, Clark Kerr, Paul Samuelson, Talcott Parsons, and Richard Hofstadter come to mind here as pillars of the postwar consensus. Some of these guys were Jews, some had flirted with communism in the 1930s, but by the 1950s, they were mainly wearers of bow ties—overly fond of status and power and dedicated to the institutions and ideas that had allowed them to earn their positions. Their work held in common a belief in the evident superiority of American society and the permanence of the liberal tradition.

In the mid- to late 1960s, the grip of this consensus began to weaken, and over the course of the 1970s, it collapsed entirely. Entire disciplines lurched to the left. Sociologists turned en masse toward neo-Marxism. Literary scholars began to embrace a new historicism—the analysis of culture as the product of the historical forces of its time, rather than the singular creation of the author. African American and women's studies achieved major breakthroughs, opening the academy further to those whose existence and opinions had long been deemed irrelevant at best. In history departments, the first generation of critical scholars, the so-called social historians, emerged out of the New Left and rapidly undid the notion of an all-inclusive liberal tradition. They retold history "from the bottom up," reconstructing how ordinary people in the past preserved the values of their own communities and drew on them to contest the world around them.

Although it was hardly obvious at the time, it now seems clear that the same shock waves undermining the postwar consensus in politics, culture, and economics were also at work within the academy. Slowing economic growth, widening claims for recognition, rights, and citizenship, and increasingly bitter social and political polarization—the hallmarks of the 1960s and '70s—appeared inside academic disciplines as well as in undergraduate quads, workplaces, neighborhoods, and streets. (It's important to mention, however, that at the same time, political science and economics took a sharp right turn. Rational choice theory and its corollary, free market politics, assumed a dominant position among economists, who rapidly subjugated much of political science into their methodological colony.)

It wasn't long, though, before blowback came for these earnestly radical scholars. By the early 1980s, the next generation of scholars began asking how these heroic workers, slaves, women, and immigrants had apparently remained uncontaminated by the broader values of their cultures. Were these people not, like us, stuck in the webs of culture that they themselves wove? Is society, these critics wondered, something that can even exist outside the notions in people's heads and the words they use to articulate them? And if not, what on earth did social historians think they were "reconstructing"? So we arrive from reconstruction to its more famous successor, deconstruction.

This was the form that postmodernism, or more accurately, poststructuralism, took in history departments. (Anthropology, sociology, literature, art history, and the languages all had their own versions of this argument.) It was a critique devastating enough to stop social history in its tracks in the late 1980s. With it came a new generation of so-called cultural historians, who, armed with difficult, largely French theory (Foucault, Derrida, etc.), again rewrote the canon with a radical edge. Their version of history was not an account of persistent repression and heroic resistance, but a kind of war of all against all, in which historical subjects were constantly spinning and struggling to escape from webs of meaning that effected their own domination and that of others. The long arc of history, once seen as bending toward liberation—the main feature of the scholarship of the 1970s—disappeared in this account, and was replaced by a grimmer understanding. Freedom, for these cultural historians, is never really free. The more one runs toward liberation, the farther off it seems to get.

The arrival of poststructuralism rendered previous paradigms in many fields inoperative; its critiques were too powerful to ignore. But it also had little further guidance to offer. In one classic poststructuralist formulation, we do not read the text; the text reads us. Which is to say that there is no "real" object of analysis out there to discover—neither the past, nor the intentions of the author, nor the dynamics of a social system. It is not really possible to ever gain a more fully true understanding in this schema, only to develop a new subjective vantage point for criticism. This grinding pessimism has meant that, after gaining control, this "cultural turn" has spent the last twenty years slowly dying of exhaustion. For if progress is an impossible, even malicious, concept, then why even bother? By denying the possibility of a grand historical advance, poststructuralism killed any seeds of a new paradigm emerging from within it. This situation feels something like how I imagine the Soviet Union did in its final years: The old model has worn itself out, but any change would probably be even worse.

What we are left with today, across the human sciences, then, is a somewhat barren theoretical landscape. After taking a right turn in the seventies, much of political science and economics are increasingly detached from reality, bunkered down in a libertarian ideology that is almost entirely unconvincing to scholars outside these fields and has instead found allies in corporate boardrooms and government agencies. On the other hand, fields that went through the radical convulsions of neo-Marxism and poststructuralism in the 1970s, '80s, and '90s have found themselves not only without political influence but also oddly depoliticized. Although individual members spent decades fighting political battles, as these fields lost their faith in progress and liberation, they also lost their energy and vitality. In history, where Marxist theorists like Antonio Gramsci and Jürgen Habermas were universal touchstones in 1977, and poststructuralists like Michel Foucault and Judith Butler were on every bookshelf in 1993, there is now simply no successor. No common agenda unites the field, politically, theoretically, or methodologically. We may not yet be in free fall, but we are certainly stalled out.

This state of inertia should sound familiar. It's the prevalent political situation across the board in the United States: deepening freeze, with crises going unanswered. It characterizes the economy, too, seemingly in quicksand up to the waist. And it's a decent enough description of the problems that have befallen universities themselves, stuck in an administrative-bureaucratic mire to match the intellectual one. Student debt is piling up, faculty hiring has slowed to the point of standstill, administrative bloat is expanding, online teaching is taking off, and federal funding for research remains stagnant. As things stand, it seems beyond dispute that universities have gotten themselves into an unsustainable pattern with no clear alternative.

Here, then, is the general situation facing today's would-be graduate student. Also clear by now, I suspect, are all the grim personal reasons you shouldn't go to graduate school: You won't get a job, you'll spend at least fifteen years getting treated like shit, and nobody you used to be close to will know or care about what is, increasingly, your only subject of conversation—your work. If you're seriously considering taking the GRE and filling out an application, then you've likely heard all this already. All of these are the ugly faces of a university system that has increasingly revealed itself to be broken beyond easy repair by the same forces that have brought about upward redistribution of wealth, decaying democratic institutions, and a general social and cultural stalemate and drift.

But none of this means that you shouldn't go to graduate school. It just means that if you do go, then you have to go *pissed*. If you come in ready to meekly accept the fate decreed for intellectual life as we know it, you'll resign yourself to the fundamentally conservative slur that academia is slothful and indulgent and is only getting what comes its way. You'll shuffle your way through graduate school with your self-respect—indeed, sense of self—barely intact, only to enter a job market that will heap further indignities on you. By the end, you'll be thirty-five or forty, living in the middle of nowhere, with weird hair, alienated friends, and the income of a high school teacher—without the job security.

Academics consent to the personal rigors of this work because we care enough about the ideas at stake. If this is true for you, by all means, come to graduate school. But you have to come ready to scale a wall. To succeed, you'll have to break the sense of identification you probably have, as a heretofore successful student, with those in charge. Instead, you'll have to develop an awareness of the fact that the people running the show—in your field, in your institution, and in your society—have blown it. If you want to get anywhere, you'll have to be ready to take things back. You'll need to join the graduate student union and get involved. If there isn't one, start one. Find the progressive community, find the labor, racial and social justice, environmental, and feminist groups where you go to school, and throw yourself into them. No matter what you study, *there will be no better way to get a new angle on your subject.* The only way to see things fresh is to do the work required to imagine a different academy. That, in turn, is only possible for those who are willing to imagine a different society. If that seems outlandish, then forget your sterling recommendations, your perfect score on the GRE, your brilliant senior thesis, and go to law school. But if it does seem exciting, then you could do nothing better than to get a PhD and help figure out what the next big thing will look like—because it's about to happen.

Dale Stephens

I DROPPED OUT OF elementary school, so I might have a slightly different perspective than most on the question of education. When I was in fifth grade, I went to my parents (one of whom is a former public school teacher) and told them that I didn't want to go to school anymore. While they were not exactly pleased with me or thrilled with the idea, they said, Hey, it's your life, make your own decisions. If you want to leave school, go ahead. The worst possible thing that could happen is that you could go back. School isn't going anywhere.

And so I did. I left school after that year. I wanted to escape the strictures of the public school system and have the freedom to learn how and when I wanted. My family investigated some private schools with engaging curricula, but the logistics just didn't work out, so we became convinced that homeschooling would be the best option. At the end of the first day of homeschooling, I exclaimed, "Mom, I've learned more today than in all of fifth grade!" and I never looked back. I intended to return for high school, but somehow that never happened. While my peers sat in class copying words verbatim off the blackboard, I found mentors, built businesses, did internships, took college classes, and explored other interests. For example, photography. I love photography. Being out of school gave me the flexibility and resources to pursue it, and I began selling my work at local art fairs. I started a website to promote my work, and I learned entrepreneurial, marketing, and web-managing skills that I still use today.

Despite my six years of happiness outside the classroom, I still decided to go to college, at a liberal arts school in Arkansas. I went because my peers were going, my parents had gone, and that's what I assumed you do if you want to lead a successful life. After all, college-educated people are less likely to be unemployed, right?

While that may be true for now, it's also true that college requires you to spend four years of your life and tens of thousands (sometimes hundreds of thousands) of dollars for what is still ultimately a risky venture.

The people I met at college didn't know what they wanted to do with their lives. And while I knew what I ultimately wanted to do, I didn't know how I should be spending my time in college. My fall semester, I took a required freshman seminar, a Holocaust literature class, a history class, and French. College seemed like a very expensive way to spend time without direction.

Was it worth spending time in school when I could have spent it working on projects in the real world? Did I really want to graduate with tens of thousands of dollars of debt and be forced to take a job to pay it off instead of having the freedom to explore my interests? After six months in school, I still knew that I wanted to move back to San Francisco. I had offers for tech jobs. There was no reason for me to stay in Arkansas.

Around that time, I applied to the Thiel Fellowship program, which offers promising students under the age of twenty financial and professional support to drop out of college and pursue their own projects. I also started writing about my frustrations on my website, UnCollege.org. I was promptly rejected from the Thiel Fellowship. A month later, however, the Thiel Foundation reached out to me and asked me to reenter the final round because they had noticed my work with UnCollege. When I was granted a fellowship, it gave me access to $100,000 and connections to the top entrepreneurs in Silicon Valley. In grad school, students can develop a project and have access to university funding and mentors. I had an accelerated version of this in the real world. It was an amazing gift.

More than a year and a half later, my plan seems to be working out. I run an organization that empowers self-directed learners to take charge of their education. I've written my first book, *Hacking Your Education*. I do some consulting with universities and have given talks around the world about the future of education and how to make universities more geared toward self-directed learners. At twenty, I am financially independent from my parents.

By baseline metrics of success, I'm also doing well. I'm literate. I can balance a checkbook. I'm not smoking pot in my parents' basement. I've learned to communicate clearly. I've learned to engage in public dialogues. I've learned how to manage relationships with people. I've learned to convince people I can do things I have no experience doing. I've learned how to deal with jet lag. I've learned how to negotiate contracts. I've learned how to persuade people. I've learned how to sell.

I wouldn't call myself a patient person. If I'd had more patience, perhaps I would have lasted longer in school. Sometimes people ask me, if you had stayed in college, if you had gone on to grad school, what degree would you have gotten? What grad program might have helped with what you're doing now? I don't think a program exists that covers all the things I've learned in the past year. An MBA, an MFA, a design-thinking program: Any of them might have covered some of it, but I don't think it adds up to the same knowledge and skills. They certainly wouldn't have taught me how to apply my skills in the real world.

So will I ever go back to school? There's always a chance. Maybe in the future I'll want to study neuroscience, and I won't be able to keep cadavers in my garage or afford an MRI scanner. Not everything can be done on your own, but for now, I love my life.

Michelle Orange

MY GRANDFATHER USED TO say, "Whatever decision you make is the right decision." I'm taking my mother's word on that; it's not something he used to say to me. Aphorisms weren't my family's thing, and I suspect the few plausible candidates were ratified by a kind of default. Over the years, I've heard the above one a lot. My otherwise morbidly pragmatic mother offers it—always with the crucial attribution—when circumstance requires a wise and gracious, generation-tested piece of advice. My part of the tradition is to silently curse the sentiment's total uselessness, especially as applied to life's binding dilemmas—to go or stay, to quit or keep on, the blond or the brunet.

My mother's applied serenity did not extend to my decision to attend graduate school, probably because the decision involved very real things like emigration and plundered bank accounts. Now it was I who pointed to that elusive higher plane, promising that the answer lay just beyond it. It was easily the single biggest decision I had ever made, and I didn't have a business case to back it up. Facing down my late twenties, I had a decent public broadcasting job and was writing on the side; it was comfortable and mostly accidental and making me nuts.

You know what it was? It was this one exact day, when a particularly odious managerial type commented in a meeting, in response to I-forget-what, about how my team didn't have to worry about me bailing in the middle of another interminable project because "Michelle's a lifer." In my memory, she delivered that sentence looking me dead in the eye, with a cold, clown-rictus smile. Twenty-six and condemned to life in a make-work office and the self-loathing projections of middle-aged women? Oh, no ma'am.

So that was the main thing: to get out, press the reset button before it was too late. I'm one of those, I'm afraid; there was no real glory in it. I can't claim that I was driven back to campus by a thirst for deeper knowledge or a desire to inhabit a world where *unpack* is what you do to a text and not a suitcase. Instead, when pressed back then, I'd say my plan was to buy myself two years to try to figure things out. What things? Well, I had a BA and knew I enjoyed and excelled in film studies, but I was only serious about academia insofar as it met my need to enjoy and excel at things. No, the education I had in mind is betrayed by the fact that I applied to a single school: New York University.

It was my dream to attend NYU as an undergraduate, but my parents weren't behind it. I couldn't persuade them that the education I sought depended as much on place as curriculum and reputation, certainly not when the financial stakes were so high. The cost of higher education in my native Canada is a fraction of what it is in the United States; the only Canadian students I knew who went south had sports scholarships. The rest of us had to suffer our unsightly pangs of ambition in greedy, ungrateful silence. Because, though I pushed the idea of NYU as the intuitive choice for an arts degree, it was plain to my parents and other interested onlookers that I had actually hinged my future and the person I might be in it on the less wholesome pursuit of a bachelor's of NYC.

Can I try to describe to you, for a moment, just how far away New York City feels to a suburban Ontario kid? Or do you already know precisely, the longing for a person so cool and thrilling and impossible that it becomes a place, and for a place so sublime and exciting and possessed of your unknown fulfillments that she becomes a person. Our separation was painful to me. I felt certain that if I could just get there, we would seduce each other, play out a turbulent romance, die in each other's arms every night.

And in New York, though I enrolled in film school, what I really wanted to study was Americans—perhaps even become one professionally. NYU's

Office for International Students and Scholars seemed to recognize this
ambition: Before the fall session began, we international students attended
several mandatory orientation classes designed to attune us to the culture
and its expectations. Even those of us who had been consuming American
television, music, and processed snacks since birth, possibly conception,
fell on the International Students' Resource Guide passed around on the first
day like it was a field manual to a rare landscape filled with hungry, high-
strung animals.

Below, I have annotated some of the finer points of that instructional
text.

> *Americans tend to distrust people who do not look into their eyes while talking to them. Americans*
> *prefer to avoid arguments and long periods of silence. Americans are literal, demonstrated by such*
> *expressions as "Just say no," "What part of 'no' don't you understand?" and "Say what you mean*
> *and mean what you say."*

I didn't give myself many opportunities to practice my American in my first
months at school. Shy and preoccupied, I no doubt invited the distrust of
my fellow students. Everyone seemed a couple of years younger than me,
and I felt like I had my own thing going on. I really regret this. The open
secret about grad school is that it can be incredibly lonely. No one lives in
dorms; there's little social infrastructure. The cliques that do form can feel
either too big or too small to penetrate. You're adults but not really, you're
working but not really, you're eating and sleeping but not really. It's structure without structure, where the thickness and tensile strength of a single
ID card is all that separates you from the thinking vagrant.

Graduate school programs, especially if they aren't designed to secure a
higher net income, are sometimes called a cop-out, a place to hide. They
can be those things. They can also be the inverse: a place to grow up where
the lack of structure and status force you into closer contact with your
squirmy basic self. Accepting graduate school as more than a pretext for my
move to NYC meant embracing the free fall, reaching out to argue, weath-
ering awkward silence, making eye contact, and ideally realizing some kind
of decorative formation with my fellow skydivers.

> *As you can readily tell from commercials, Americans have been taught that the natural smells of people's bodies and breath are unpleasant. Most Americans bathe or shower daily (or more often if they engage in vigorous exercise), use an underarm deodorant, and brush their teeth at least twice a day. They will not wear the same clothes more than once during a week, often discarding them to be washed after one use.*
>
> *It is common for women to shave their legs and underarms and to use a small quantity of perfume every day; many men use a scented cologne or aftershave lotion to impart what they believe is a pleasant smell. Most Americans will quickly back away from a person who has "body odor" or "bad breath." This backing away may be the only signal that they are "offended" by another person's breath or body odor. The topic of these odors is so sensitive that most Americans will not tell another person that s/he has bad breath or body odor.*

Well, this is just useful information. Are you also getting the feeling that an international student wrote the resource guide for international students?

> *Doing rather than being: Americans consider activity to be a good thing; thus reflected in expressions such as "keeping busy," "getting things done," "keeping on the move." Rather than simply getting together with friends to spend time together, Americans will frequently plan an activity— any activity—and will tend not to get together without some focus to the time spent with friends.*

Graduate school can be lonely, for sure, but it can also help recalibrate your clock and put you in closer touch with how you like to spend your days. I was lucky to get a full-time job before graduating from university (which I did debt free: My University of Toronto tuition cost 10 percent what NYU's would have, and it was paid as a benefit of my father's professorship at another Ontario school; scholarship money covered the rest of the costs), but I accepted the job because *doing* seemed like the obvious choice over *being*, especially if I wanted to move out of my mother's apartment. I thought it would be a year or two, tops, while I got my bearings; four years later, I was still there. From the outside I looked like a stable, responsible adult, keeping busy and getting things done. But inertia often wears a busy face.

My first year in graduate school disoriented me to the point of crisis. I had given up all the security and stability that I'd had, and it showed. I knew I was no lifer, but it took a while to get the hang of just being without worrying about what I was and wasn't doing. I look back on this as a good and very necessary development. In a way, I came to America to be less "American," and to get on with things in earnest. I haven't held an office job since leaving Canada, and graduate school provided the pause I needed to regroup, reconnect with my mind and its rhythms, and gather the courage to set up a life I might want to live.

> Americans usually think of nature as something that can be altered, conquered, and controlled for people's comfort and use and in order to minimize the effects of fierce weather conditions.

This was definitely written by an international student.

> Americans generally believe the ideal person is self-reliant. Most Americans see themselves as separate individuals, not as representatives of a family, community, or other group. They dislike being dependent on other people, or having others depend on them. Also people act competitively, are proud of their accomplishments, and expect others to be proud of their own accomplishments.

This might be the thing I believed most going into NYU and least coming out of it. Although my program had a healthy competitive buzz, the ambivalent truth about my graduate school experience is that it seemed like students paid foremost for the privilege of meeting the right people, and to gain access to spaces where luck and preparation might bonk together.

In terms of disliking being dependent on other people, I was as good as naturalized on arrival in the United States. Despite this, looking back I can trace a very clear line between a single class I took, in my second year, and every paycheck I have received to write about film since. A fellow student in my criticism seminar snagged a job writing about movies soon after graduation. A year later, he recommended me to his editor based on the work I had presented in class. From there, I fielded a quick succession of opportunities, each new one lit, as it were, by the last.

My classmate grew up dreaming of being a film critic, and he enrolled in graduate school with the intention of furthering that dream. He didn't hoard his opportunities, though, and instead extended them to someone

who showed few signs of sharing his ambition. And after a postgradua-
tion year of making copies for twitchy junior VPs at various temp jobs, I
was grateful.

You should probably be prepared to do that, by the way: to throw your
lot in with the fresh, pointy faces of American individualism and wait for
your degree's enigmatic rewards to present themselves. Because, and this is
the most direct recommendation I will make for graduate school: If you can
accept that there's no guarantee *how* it might affect your life, only that at
some point it will—for the bizarre or unexpected or underwhelming,
maybe, but most likely for the better—then you won't be disappointed. See
also: most of the big decisions you'll ever make.

*Americans often think that other countries should use their example and adopt their ways of doing
things.*

So everything I just said only applies if student debt will not clatter behind
you, like a string of platinum-lined soup cans, for the rest of your life. If
there was one facet of American life that sent me into straight culture shock,
it was the cost of what Canadians (and most other developed countries)
consider basic rights: health care, education, a free and equitable fleece
tuque trade.

Had I been able to find a job in the U.S., I would have, but I couldn't.
Especially post-9/11, when immigration was moved under the purview of
America's newly formed, shadowy Department of Homeland Security. At
that point, a student visa felt like the most viable route to legal entry.
Funding for international students is not a priority, so the aid I received
spanned nil to minimal. I emptied my bank account, borrowed from my
retirement savings, took out loans, and received help from my parents. It
took years to pay it down. Honestly, I think the cost of American education
is a disgrace, and, unless you're wedded to a certain school/program, if
you can go somewhere cheaper in another country, do so. I can't stress this
enough: It's not like this everywhere/anywhere else. I never got used to it,
and I will never think it's okay.

Americans are more inclined to make decisions based on the anticipated or desired future, and they tend to view change and material progress as good and desirable.

So should you go to graduate school? It's not a decision you can base on an anticipated or desired future, I don't think, or the hope of material progress. If anything you should be willing to surrender, at least for a while, expectations of anything but progress and change at their least quantifiable. The program I attended was just okay, the cost unjustifiable, and yet by dint of what seems like luck, my schooling eventually paid for itself. But is that the point?

My American education, which is ongoing, has proven, disproved, and reproved each one of the International Students' Resource Guide's teachings. Except for the hygiene stuff, which, as noted above, is pretty solid. If anything, I'd say its greatest lesson has been to never start a sentence with "Americans are . . ." Or, for that matter, "Graduate school is . . ." For the most part, I pass as one of you these days, which suggests success, though I await the arrival of some kind of heavy stock, calligraphied certificate in the mail.

Not knowing you and your particular circumstances, the question I am best equipped to answer is "Should I have gone to graduate school?" Even there I have some trouble. Looking back almost ten years later, I would say yes, certainly. Not because I chose correctly when faced with a *yes or no* problem, but because I know what it took to make that decision, and in the end, *deciding* was the right thing to do. Grandpa, can you hear me?

Terry Castle

THIS INTERVIEW WAS CONDUCTED BY JESSICA LOUDIS.

Could you talk a little about your own educational history and why you decided to go into a PhD program?

I'D SAY, LOOKING BACK, it was hardly a very rational or intellectually considered decision. My childhood and adolescence had been split between Southern California and England, owing to my parents' divorce, and I'd gone, sight unseen, to a small and somewhat obscure college in the Pacific Northwest—mostly to get away from them and ongoing family complications. When it came to choosing where to go, I was pretty ignorant; having gone to a big working-class public high school in San Diego, I didn't know very much at all about colleges or universities. (It would never have occurred to me to apply, say, to an Ivy League institution—I didn't know what or where they were.) Likewise, my parents hadn't gone to college and, being British, knew very little about American higher education. My father wanted me to go to a two-year community college. It was all pretty inchoate. One thing for sure: I wanted to exile myself—geographically at least—as a way of escaping various crises on the home front.

I chose to go to the University of Minnesota for a PhD in a similarly ill-informed way. Again, I was completely unfamiliar with the place I was going to. I had a vague desire, I thought, to go to the Midwest (it being still further from San Diego than Washington State), but when it came to picking an institution, it was all a bit pin the tail on the donkey. More a stab in the dark (to vary the cliché) than a choice. (I recall that the *Mary Tyler Moore Show* and throwing a woolly hat up in the air somehow figured into my thinking.) On the broader matter of graduate school itself, I was only slightly more sentient. Reading had always been an escape hatch and studying literature seemed familiar—something I knew I *could do*. Books were the substitute family.

Nowadays, I sometimes look back on the grad school path I took with a certain ruefulness. Not long ago, I realized that I've been "in school" my whole life, ever since I was four years old. Every fall, every September of my life, it's all started up again! I've never had a year working on the outside or away from the classroom. No civilian life! Obviously, I found something intellectually rewarding and challenging—not to mention oddly soothing—in my subject and all the institutional trappings. (The people in books often had even weirder problems than I did!) But I have to confess, I went on for my PhD for a mishmash of unanalyzed personal and psychological reasons—and out of a vague sense that I wasn't very well suited for anything else. My stepfather at the time had been in the navy for thirty years, and he kept suggesting that I join the navy. ("You'd get commissioned right away!") So that was a possibility. I also thought a fair amount, bizarrely enough, of becoming a policewoman. I think it was the uniforms that appealed. Either that or an interest in fingerprinting.

Did you ever consider alternatives to going back to school?

It was the early 1970s, and that was a very strange transitional time. When I graduated from my Pacific Northwest college, we were all still belated hippies of one kind or another. I'd also announced myself as a radical lesbian feminist—so the lingo went in those days—so the only alternative that came to mind was that of dropping out and working as a gardener on a women's commune or something. Romantic pastoral fantasies involving pruning shears . . . But studying English somehow won out.

I've heard many academics say that they suspected early on that they were ill-suited for anything else—in your case, how did you figure it out?

Frankly, I read all the time. I didn't have much of a social life. I was pretty much a misfit. I didn't yet know myself, and I read in part to figure out who I was. It all became quite obsessional. I remember one summer in college when I read through the complete novels of Iris Murdoch. (She had written twenty-three or twenty-four at that point.) So I'd go on these private mad binges. I was trying to figure out how to be a grown-up, and school seemed the only place where that could happen. To put it bluntly—or abjectly— nothing else really gratified my rapidly exfoliating fantasy life quite as much as the work I did in and out of school.

In addition to your academic writing, you also contribute to literary magazines like the London Review of Books and the New Republic. How did you develop your nonscholarly voice while working as an academic?

It's been a very slow, thirty-year process of self-transformation. It's not that I regret taking the academic path—it was a lifesaver. I've been extremely happy and lucky in my professional circumstances all of my life. I've taught at Stanford University my whole career, and it's been a wonderful place to work and teach. But were I starting over now, I think I would probably try to figure out some way of being a writer that didn't necessarily involve pedagogy or taking a strictly scholarly approach. I've gradually come to feel somewhat bored with prevailing academic styles, indeed with what you might call the *academic personality*—above all, my own version of it!

For better or for worse, too, I've always felt a strong pull toward the autobiographical—toward an almost psychoanalytic exploration of the self. Needless to say, only very recently has this kind of personalized approach become again quasi-respectable in the academic humanities. (Someone like George Saintsbury could still manage it during the first decades of the twentieth century!) So when I began writing for the *London Review of Books* and the *New Republic* and other "out-of-school" places, I felt I'd been given a license to ditch some of the pedantry in favor of something more expressive and honest, and possibly more appealing to a wider audi- ence—especially with regard to my sexual orientation. True, in the early 1980s, when I was a tyro in academics, I was conspicuous even then for cultivating an interest in the history of sexuality. I was able to take advantage of the fact that this once-taboo area of study was just then, in the post-Foucault era, being recognized as a legitimate topic for intellectual inquiry and research. But even as I wrote my academic books and articles, I was conscious of burying some key part of myself in the work—of unfolding, as it were, only a sort of shadow self. The projects were a very displaced way of insinuating a kind of coded, rhetorically awkward, read-between-the-lines autobiography. After a while, it all started to feel unnecessarily coy and self-concealing. I was dying to be irreverent and real and truthful—as much as I thought I could be.

When I began reviewing a series of biographies of women writers (Austen, Woolf, Colette, Cather, et al.) for literary magazines like the *Times Literary Supplement* and the *London Review of Books*, the veil over the intimate life started to fall away. At a certain point, the biographical pursuit seemed to lead organically toward the autobiographical, and that's where I've ended up. It's been cathartic. I have one academic project I need to finish, but after that I'm not sure I'll write another scholarly book—or not one in the conventional sense. (One also gets spoiled by having—in however minuscule a way—a real-world audience!) Overall, finding a less pretentious style—even a weirdly eccentric style—has become more and more attractive to me.

Do you think people working in academia right now have more freedom to experiment with different writing styles?

Perhaps a little more than once was the case, though still, probably, not very often. Especially for jobseekers and the untenured, it remains difficult to cultivate a truly experimental intellectual mode. You have to realize we're coming—still—out of a fairly repressive, deeply conformist period in university literature departments. For roughly the past three decades, Continental theory and poststructuralism and its various offshoots, including the demon-child known as cultural studies (i.e., a sort of half-baked left-wing sociology), have held sway in just about every major literature department in the United States. Given the *Kritik*-dominated times, one was in danger of being seen as bourgeois, naïve, intellectually unsophisticated, and all the rest of it if one took an interest in anything so retrograde as style and aesthetics or an author's personal history or presumed artistic intentions. Humanism was a bad word; notions of the self emptied of any meaning. The idiosyncrasies of the individual voice were held to be of little or no account. Documenting one's own emotional responses to literature would have seemed unthinkable—you risked being seen as impressionistic and self-indulgent. One was expected instead to concentrate, fairly relentlessly, on larger social and cultural discourses—the material context and/or socio-political settings in which cultural artifacts had been produced. The goal was to demystify, Marxist-style, the abstract power relations supposedly underlying every aspect of human expression. A lot of ideological grand-standing went on along the way and was also part of the mode.

And somehow it followed that one was to couch one's critique in the most deadening, technocratic, and pseudoscientific language available. The Author was Dead; long live the text and its oppressive, usually jargon-ridden, discontents. Any kind of remotely biographical criticism was anathematized as old-fashioned and unphilosophical—unabashedly empirical and too real-world oriented to sustain itself in the realm of high theory. The irony in all of this being, of course, that biography was—and remains—one of the few genres of literary inquiry and explication that could actually still support itself in the open publishing marketplace. A good literary biog-raphy—of Austen, James, Proust, Beckett, David Foster Wallace, whomever—still appeals in some degree, even now, to a nonacademic audience: the much-derided "general reader." If you're good and can write a supple and intelligent prose, you can perhaps make a passable living writing biographies. (This is especially true—or at least has been—in the UK.) It would be impossible, however, to make a living out of books of academic theory if only for the simple reason that nobody really wants to read them if not being paid to do so. In academe we are only just now emerging from what I consider a sort of theory-crippled dark age, and a lot of the jargon is still floating around. Graduate students in particular still think you have to sound convoluted and clinical—speak in a kind of buzzword-laden, often incomprehensible code—to be thought smart or intellectually serious.

Writing simply and directly is far harder and more challenging—and viewed by many (the ones who can't do it) with suspicion.

You've been teaching for so long, have there been any major changes in the way you think about it, or in your relationship with your students?

One of the difficulties I face more and more now is knowing what to say to (often) very talented undergraduate English majors who want to go to graduate school. I'm afraid my outlook on the future of the humanities—writ large—is very pessimistic. Decent academic jobs for PhDs in English are becoming so rare that I feel that I have to be up front about the situation, even to the point of discouraging very keen and gifted students. Unless you have a sizable private income or absolutely can't think of doing anything else, I would say it is unwise to go to graduate school in literary studies. I don't feel good conveying this, of course, but the profession, or what remains of it, has fallen on very hard times—both economically and spiritually. I'm not sure we'll ever bounce back to business as usual. I fear we will see the closing down of a lot of traditional graduate programs in American universities and colleges in the next decade or so.

Have you noticed any work or developments that may have once taken place in graduate school happening elsewhere?

Not so much if one is talking specifically about the discipline of literary history. If young people today are interested in writing—fiction, poetry, whatever—they tend to gravitate toward what's known as "creative" writing and/or blogging. But few of the present crop of students seem particularly eager to learn about the genesis or genealogy of literary traditions or indeed engage in old-school literary scholarship. There are too many other things for them to do—too many flashy pinging distractions. We're in the middle, after all, of one of the watershed events in the history of civilization: the digitalization of virtually every aspect of human experience. Reading Spenser's The Faerie Queen just isn't as alluring as it might once have been! (If it ever was.)

In turn, I don't think U.S. undergraduates necessarily come to college or university now having read a great deal in the way of serious or classic literature. They are rarely well prepared to engage with it. (Or certainly not as much as their predecessors would have been thirty or forty years ago.) The culture at large doesn't reinforce addictive, immersive reading—or indeed, really, any thoughtful consumption of culture. Young people are much more captivated by the digital world and absorbed in finding their place in it. Reading the classics in the old-school way—you might call it "slow reading"—just isn't that appealing or obviously useful. But as I say, I'm a pessimist by nature. I still teach eighteenth-century British fiction now and then, but I can also see why it would mean nothing—or very little—to an intelligent and ambitious undergraduate, even at a top-tier place like Stanford. Your question touches on momentous cultural changes and, alas, I don't even know how to frame the issues involved very coherently. From my own moody and partial and yes, old-fashioned, point of view, however, I'm somewhat melancholy.

And how has the general outlook about going into a PhD program changed since you went in the seventies?

Drastically. Even then, it's true, humanities departments sometimes made it their business to warn potential applicants that employment possibilities in the academic world were becoming ever more uncertain. For some reason, though, one also heard a lot of people predicting that the job market would somehow miraculously improve "in the eighties." But it never really did. In fact, it got worse far more quickly than anybody had anticipated. No one expected the bottom to drop out completely in the way that it has. The grim reality of the past decade has been the almost complete evaporation of job prospects for traditionally trained English PhDs. Instead, the focus has shifted (not surprisingly) to so-called digital humanities, social networking, the business of online courses, etc., etc. American higher education is undergoing a convulsion right now. It may be a good one, ultimately, but maybe not for some of the classic humanistic fields. (History, philosophy, religious studies, art history—all these disciplines are likewise hemorrhaging majors.) At the same time—and anyone who writes relatively well is conscious of it—huge changes are likewise taking place in the everyday use of the English language: Witness things like texting and e-mail, and the soon-to-be total eclipse of the printed book. I feel that we, as literature professors, are at the tail end of an intellectual cycle that has lasted for about a century. Studying "great literature" (of whatever kind) appeared at one time to be an eminently defensible and remunerative, if not uplifting, life-pursuit. That's gone now. No one can predict where things are going to go at the moment, but some other kind of human activity and reflection is going to take its place.

Dare one add a final bit of sourness? The process of actually applying to graduate school right now—in English, say—has in my view become a fairly crass sort of business operation, both for the programs involved and the applicants. It's a pretty decadent world. I don't think it has hit a generation of middle-class parents that PhD programs in the humanities are in the very real economic trouble they are. So even as high-flying PhD programs shrink and lose resources, seniors in college are still being encouraged to flit around the country looking at all the different places they might go to for a higher degree, as if there were no risks attached. Out of self-interest—we English professors require TAs and advanced students for our increasingly specialized courses (or think we do)—we do our part to perpetuate the fantasy. After we have admitted students to the PhD program at Stanford, for example, we lay on a lavish recruiting weekend during which we try to persuade these potential admits (who usually have multiple offers at elite places) to choose us over, say, Harvard or Berkeley or Columbia. Our program is very small, but it's also very competitive, so a lot of effort goes into attracting the best students—the very same students who, paradoxically, are ever less likely ultimately to find academic jobs. Some might say it's a bit of a scam.

When I was a student thirty years ago, such bizarre competition between elite institutions—all of the self-promotional gamesmanship—didn't exist. College graduates didn't travel around (or at least nobody I knew did) to look at PhD programs and compare them. I applied to the six or seven places I selected without ever laying eyes on any of them, not even the one

I eventually chose. People drifted into things in a way that seems inconceivable now. True, I went to college and graduate school in the age of Lyndon Johnson's Great Society; I was able to put myself through school using work-study grants and scholarships. Costs weren't anything like what they are today. The financial risks were not so great. Understandably, students and their parents now are hugely invested in finding the best academic situation available to them and don't want to waste large amounts of time and money on an inferior "product." Potential PhD students likewise still want to be in a hip and stimulating place—usually with intellectual or sometimes geographical perquisites. Hence the commodification of everything. The colossal irony is that most of these young men and women who are being wooed so hard to join particular programs are the same young men and women, I'm afraid, who will later find that the credential they have worked so hard to obtain is not, perhaps, as valuable as they might once have imagined. I feel increasingly uncomfortable being part of this (to me) exploitative and contradictory system. I think we're all in the endgame.

Namwali Serpell

Tractatus Doctoro-Philosophicus

THIS ESSAY DEALS WITH the problems of going to graduate school and shows, as I believe, that the method of formulating these problems rests on the misunderstanding of the logic of our language about experience. This essay is not a guide. It could be summed up somewhat as follows: What can be said at all about graduate school can be said only for each individual; and whereof one cannot speak, thereof one must be silent.

1 I went to graduate school and that is the case.
   1.1 My experience there was a compilation of factors, not of facts.
      1.11 My experience was determined by these factors, and by these being *all* the factors, together intersecting.
      1.12 For the combination of factors determined both what happened to me, and also all that did not happen to me.
      1.13 The factors in their intersection as they played out in time were my experience.
   1.2 Any one factor either influenced my experience of graduate school or it did not, in retrospect, and yet its intersection with the other factors remains the case.

2 What was the case, what happened in grad school, was the murky coexistence of factors.

2.1 A thing can seem independent, insofar as it can happen to anyone, but this form of independence is a form of connection with a factor, a dependence.

2.2 For example, I have always been good at math and English.

 2.21 Being good at both means I have always felt torn between them.

 2.22 I went from being a biochemistry major to being an English major in my first year of college.

2.3 Going to graduate school was a way to straddle these ways of thinking instead of choosing between them.

 2.31 Going to graduate school was also a way to consider what it was that subtended them both, e.g., logic, analysis, symmetry, asymmetry, singular exceptions that reconstitute the rule, an equivocal relationship to the past, the beauty of forms.

2.4 We might say that while either of these things—being good at math, being good at English—can be considered independently as factors contributing to my time in graduate school, they are each connected to and dependent upon the combined contingency of being good at both.

2.5 Let us assume the same traits (independence/dependence) for the following things, which constitute—in their murky coexistence—the factors that shaped my graduate school experience.

3 Let us also assume that factors may coexist, and yet remain incommensurable.

 3.1 In *Physics*, Aristotle uses a physical attribute—sharp—as an example of the incommensurable values that can be latent in a single term. He writes, "May we say that things are always commensurable if the same terms are applied to them without equivocation? e.g. a pen, a wine, and the highest note in a scale are not commensurable: we cannot say whether any one of them is sharper than any other."

 3.11 Incommensurability offers the possibility that these values, while they can be compared, cannot be measured against each other, cannot be forced into the same currency of exchange.

3.2 Incommensurability applies to one's twenties and thirties as well.

    3.21 The value of going to graduate school versus the value of not going to graduate school cannot be placed on the same scale, or within the same rubric.

    3.22 For example, honing the sharpness of one's tongue in graduate school cannot be measured against dulling the sharpness of one's clothing.

    3.23 These two versions of "sharpness" fluctuate during graduate school, but to compare them on the same scale would seem silly, like making a logical equation out of a zeugma.

3.3 The following two propositions—I am a writer, I am a Zambian—hold within them incommensurable values when it comes to their bearing on my graduate school experience.

4 I am a writer.

4.001 I know, you're probably one, too.

4.002 [Isn't everyone?]

4.01 When I graduated from college, having taken only two creative writing classes but absolutely certain that I wanted to write fiction, I did not realize you could get a scholarship to attend an MFA program.

4.02 I did, however, know I could get paid to attend graduate school for a PhD.

4.021 This disjunction of information may seem illogical to you.

4.022 But Google was a new thing when I graduated from college, and I never spoke to a counselor and I barely went to office hours.

4.03 It was my sister—a graduate student at the time—who pointed out that getting a PhD would pay better than bartending.

4.031 Plus, I could write whenever I wanted.

4.032 Plus, my poor parents would be relieved to know that their daughter was institutionalized.

4.033 By which I mean, safely ensconced in an institution.

4.034 I hated the jobs I had after graduating from college. I worked in a bookstore that became a toy store and then I helped other people edit science books.

4.035 Get me to an academy! I often said, echoing in my head Hamlet's words to Ophelia.

4.04 So I applied and got in and went to graduate school.

4.05 I did not write whenever I wanted.

  4.1 Turns out, graduate school is for reading.

    4.11 The value of reading all the time is not commensurable with the value of not reading all the time.

      4.111 Reading all the time steeps you in words.

      4.112 Reading all the time teaches you that you are neither exceptional nor alone.

      4.113 Reading all the time introduces you to things you never would have imagined.

      4.114 One day you will think that hitting your head on a bunk bed in Vermont while staying overnight in a friend's cabin is the reason that you can't see the PowerPoint screen in your pedagogy orientation, only to have your doctor inform you a week later that you have in fact read your eyes into ruin.

      4.115 The first weekend of graduate school, you will have to read The Scarlet Letter and Robinson Crusoe and The Autobiography of Benjamin Franklin and a handful of essays.

      4.116 Your head will explode.

      4.117 In ways good and bad and incommensurable.

4.2 The value of reading is incommensurable with the value of writing.

4.21 The value of reading fiction in order to write fiction is incommensurable with the value of reading fiction in order to write about fiction.

    4.211 The value of reading about fiction, e.g., reading criticism, in order to write fiction always seemed fishy to me; it casts over the project of creativity a pall of jargon and technical terms.

    4.212 The value of writing about fiction, e.g., writing criticism, is offset by a similar contagion of high-falutin' words, Latinate prose, and a proclivity not only for "*howevers,*" but also for "*neverthelesses.*"

4.2121 A fiction writer I encountered while I was in graduate school, an idol of mine visiting from England, told me my diction sounded like that of a "London policeman." This apparently was meant as a critique—perhaps specific to England—of the officious working-class person who aspires to sound more educated than he is.

4.2122 The writer probably could have substituted "graduate student."

4.2123 This writer would later introduce me to others as a "brilliant student," a backhanded compliment, I believe, given the frequent distinction this writer makes in essays and interviews between being intelligent or "clever" and being a creative genius.

4.22 But *thinking* about fiction, e.g., literary analysis, *has* helped me as a writer of fiction. Taking apart a clock is obviously helpful if you're trying to make one.

4.221 The value of writing fiction in order to write *about* fiction is less intuitive (making a clock to take one apart?) but just as valuable, I now believe.

4.222 Writers often see things in fiction that critics cannot.

4.223 And vice versa, of course.

4.3 The nice thing about incommensurable values is that their coexistence can be valuable, as a whole.

4.31 So, one need not decide whether to write fiction or to write about it is more valuable in order to understand that doing both can be valuable.

4.32 That is to say, they don't cancel out, they add up.

5 I am a Zambian.

5.01 I know, you're probably not.

5.02 No one I went to college or graduate school with is Zambian.

5.1 I am black.

5.11 I am mixed race.

5.12 I am a woman.

5.13 I am an immigrant.

5.14 These attributes overlap (they are often subsumed under "I am a brown woman") but are not identical. Nor are they easy to reconcile. Their values are incommensurable.

5.2 My experience in graduate school was contingent on the murky coexistence of these three attributes.

5.3 In graduate school, I was often the only _____ person in the room.

5.4 The worst time that happened, I was in a poetry seminar. We were discussing the William Blake poem "The Little Black Boy."

5.41 My best friend at the time, a Korean woman, gripped my hand under the table and gritted her teeth through her forced recitation of the poem. ("With aplomb, please!" the professor had exhorted.)

5.412 At the end of the poem, the little black boy predicts that when he and the little white boy finally reach heaven:

> I'll shade him from the heat till he can bear,
> To lean in joy upon our father's knee.
> And then I'll stand and stroke his silver hair,
> And be like him and he will then love me.

5.413 But it's an antislavery poem, so, you know.

5.414 However well-intentioned Blake may have been, the other students (and I confess, I myself) found the poem condescending, paternalistic, assimilationist, naïve.

5.415 Strange to say, before any of my fellow students would make a comment to that effect, he or she would glance at me—for reassurance? as demonstration?—and then make a parry.

5.416 The professor was rather taken aback.

5.417 I said nothing.

5.42 No other poem in the course was about, much less by, a person of color.

5.43 I insisted on writing my final paper about Paul Laurence Dunbar's "We Wear the Mask," which had not been assigned. It received a B-plus, my only grade below an A in the course.

5.44 When I inquired why I had received an A-minus as my final course grade, the professor looked surprised.

"But you're a B-plus student."

"But . . . you gave all my other assignments As."

Puzzled, shuffling around of papers on desk. Pulling out of gradebook.

"Oh, I . . . Yes, I . . . I suppose that's true. But you don't work on poetry . . . so."

5.45 Is this the only time that I *looked* like a B-plus student, while my work was that of an A student?

  5.451 And just how many times did that work to my advantage rather than the reverse?

5.5 Another professor once told me that my conference presentations would be better received than my writing. No specific reason for this opinion was proffered.

  5.51 This came back to me when I reread this passage from James Weldon Johnson's *The Autobiography of an Ex-Colored Man* about the oratorical performance of his classmate "Shiny" and other "colored speakers who have addressed great white audiences":

I think the explanation . . . lies in what is a basic, though often dormant, principle of the Anglo-Saxon heart, love of fair play. "Shiny," it is true, was what is so common in his race, a natural orator; but I doubt that any white boy of equal talent could have wrought the same effect. The sight of that boy gallantly waging with puny, black arms so unequal a battle touched the deep springs in the hearts of his audience, and they were swept by a wave of sympathy and admiration.

5.6 The same professor asked me once why I would want to go home to Zambia for the summer, as though the very idea were preposterous. "Do they speak English there?"

5.61 And upon my return from that trip home: "How is Africa? Is it still there?"

5.62 Neither of the two skills most pressed upon me in graduate school—understanding things (analysis) and expressing them (writing)—came to my rescue in responding to these two questions.

5.63 That is to say, I gawked. What would giving answer to his assumptions have accomplished?

5.7 Telling my older sister, who went to Howard for grad school, about these incidents later—we were in a car, she eventually pulled over—she was most shocked by the fact that I hadn't told her about them at the time. They weren't terribly painful, or even surprising, to be honest. But they were so clearly alienating. She couldn't believe I had kept them to myself.

5.71 Again, gas fumes floating in through the open passenger window, I gawked. What would telling her have done?

5.8 My last year of graduate school, a group of us were drinking away (and thereby reduplicating) the tremors and woes of the job market when a conversation arose about the relative merit of African literature. Why, a friend of mine—often a devil's advocate, I should say—wondered, are there critics who study a literature that has obviously not been around long enough to warrant genuine attention?

5.81 This time I did not gawk. I don't specifically work on African literature, but by virtue of the two propositions under consideration at the moment—I am a writer, I am a Zambian—I write it. How could my friend possibly believe that it wasn't worthy of study?

5.811 More to the point, how could she possibly believe it was okay to say this to me? To my face?

5.82 On it went, until tears sprung in my eyes and, "Hey," I finally gestured to the other brown face in the room. "Don't you ever feel . . ."

5.83 "No," the reply was so final, almost flabbergasted that I would even think to ask.

5.9 We wear the mask, indeed.

6 And yet.

6.1 The poetry professor with a love of Blake and better eyesight for letters than for colors also had a conversation with me during office hours that changed my conception of myself.

6.11 "Oh you write, do you?"

"I try."

"And do you write poetry or prose?"

"Well, I used to write poetry as a teenager but it wasn't very good, so I have mostly been writing fiction. But people always say I should really write poetry because my language is so . . ."

"Poetic?"

"I guess I use a lot of metaphors and imagery."

"When you create, do you think in words or in images?"

"I haven't thought about it before, but I guess I would say images—I see things and sometimes I mistake things for other things and then I write them down."

"Ah, then you're not a poet."

"Oh, well I didn't think so, but why . . ."

"Poets think in sound, rhythm, words. The images come later."

6.12 This is clearly a highly reductive dichotomy.

[6.121 Poets and fiction writers both are welcome to roll their eyes at this point.]

6.13 But the conversation helped me make sense of something in my own process.

6.14 I never forgot it.

6.15 When I saw the professor at a talk many years later, and shared some good news about my progress as an assistant professor—my first book had been accepted for publication—there was genuine pleasure and warmth in her eyes as she said, "Mazel Tov!"

6.2 As for the other professor with the epistemological doubt as to the existence of an entire continent and its people, well, he has been a wonderful if exacting mentor to me, his teaching the absolute model to which I aspire.

6.3 And my friend with the scorn for African literature recently offered to publish a story of mine. More to the point, she is still my friend, which says a great deal.

> 6.31 Because you will make and lose friends in graduate school, and it will break your heart.

> 6.32 The ones you keep will have been forged in flames unlike any other.

7 Graduate school is a paradox.

> 7.1 Put simply, why are you still in school if you're a graduate?

>> 7.11 Put more complexly, the term *graduate school* stages a transition (the movement from student to professor) as a conflict, the juxtaposition of two words separated by an ambiguous space, without even a hyphen to clarify the relation.

> 7.2 Graduate school enacts paradox by placing incommensurable values next to each other.

>> 7.21 For example, I traveled a lot in graduate school.

>>> 7.212 I traveled for conferences and for love and for the summer.

>>> 7.213 Who knows which of these was the more delightful form of travel?

>> 7.22 For another example, I was broke a lot in graduate school.

>>> 7.221 I always took public transportation.

>>> 7.222 But I ate and drank and traveled very well on my department's dime.

>>> 7.223 Quote MasterCard here.

> 7.3 Graduate school enacts paradox by rendering time rapid and static at once.

>> 7.31 I spent an entire two months writing a dissertation chapter that I canceled, just deleted completely from the document, which was called The Document.doc.

>> 7.32 I spent an entire two months crying over a terrible relationship with a law student.

>> 7.33 Which was the greater waste of time?

7.4 Graduate school enacts paradox by making you incredibly lonely and incredibly social at the same time.

    7.41 I discovered Goya's *Los Caprichos* etchings alone in a museum after a conference in Spain.

    7.42 I skinny-dipped in a river with drunken graduate students I'd never see again after a conference at Dartmouth.

    7.43 Which is better?

7.5 Graduate school enacts paradox by making you learn way too much but never teaching you quite enough.

    7.51 I have never truly understood Ludwig Wittgenstein's *Tractatus Logico-Philosophicus*.

    7.52 But I have always loved its first and last propositions.

7.6 Graduate school enacts paradox by making you love your own failure to understand.

7.7 Whereof one cannot speak, thereof one must be silent.

Lili Holzer-Glier

THE GLOW OF ACHIEVEMENT eluded me on graduation day. I envied the graduates holding bouquets and the parents beaming with pride. Where was my pride? I too had just graduated from the best journalism school in the country, but I was filled with dread.

I had accrued $25,000 of debt in pursuit of my graduate degree—less than many students are saddled with, yes, but daunting nonetheless. And although several potential employers told me I was "wildly talented" and that their publication "needed more people like me," I was still without a full-time job. So I prepared myself for a return to freelancing, an anxiety-ridden lifestyle that I had been hoping a prestigious master's degree would banish forever.

Part of me yearns for a nine-to-five desk job, a salary, and the increasingly rare health insurance package so I can pay back my loans and not be so preoccupied with money all the time. But the other part of me relishes the freedom freelancing affords, and the powerful motivation that can come from the anxiety of always looking for new work.

I started taking pictures seriously when I was fifteen, and I did my undergraduate work at an art school. My photo projects were usually long form, quiet, and personal—a style far more acceptable in the art world than in the world of journalism. But my work was also too documentary for the commercial art world—I was told that it was not reflexive, conceptual, or transformative.

After completing my undergraduate degree, I thought I should give formal art training one more shot, so I attended the Whitney Museum of

American Art's Independent Study Program. The Whitney ISP is a highly selective and low-cost program in New York led by a faculty of art-world and academic luminaries. Aspiring curators, critics, and artists from all over the world enroll in this program to study theory or make art while continuing their own practices. At the ISP, I photographed life behind the scenes at thoroughbred racetracks, capturing a community that is extremely tight-knit but plagued by poverty, poor housing, and addiction. At the same time, I was regularly inundated with righteous Marxist theory at the ISP's biweekly seminars. The dissonance between privileged intellectuals discussing an imagined proletariat and the reality of the racetrack workers I was photographing made my stomach turn. Making and discussing socially conscious art did not feel like enough for me.

So instead, I went into journalism. I am not naïve enough to think that journalism can change the world or that it might even—as many idealistic journalists love to say—"affect positive change." But maybe it could. I knew that it was a more direct way to communicate stories that I thought were important.

Journalism school did make me a better writer. It made me tougher, braver, and it made me impervious to external pressures. I was writing at least two fully reported thousand-word pieces a week; there was just no time to be my bashful self. I learned to be shameless. A year ago, I was far too shy and self-effacing to reach out to editors; now, I write at least five editors a day, introducing myself and sharing my work. As a result of this, my projects are being published and I'm getting assignments.

Since graduation, I've had some success: I've published investigative stories about the lavish spending habits of foreign diplomats in town for the UN General Assembly. My master's thesis ran on PBS's *MetroFocus*, and my work was featured in the *New Yorker*, mostly thanks to the contacts I made at journalism school. This is all wonderful exposure, but there's an important catch: None of it pays well—if at all—and my student debt looms large.

There are a number of stories I am aching to write—one about the life of a backwoods stuntman, another about the effect that the clean-energy movement is having on the perennially troubled coal belt. But these will take months, maybe years to complete and they will require extensive travel. As a freelancer, I have enough spare time to take on these projects but not enough money to fund them. On the other hand, if I had a full-time job, I might not have enough time to do these stories as comprehensively as I would want. So how do I fund the work I care about? Do independent journalists have to be rich? (Perhaps: The number of independently wealthy students at the j-school was a bit surprising.)

The welcome speech on j-school orientation day is traditionally given by a prominent alumnus. The class of 2012 was welcomed by an ESPN anchor who described the experience of visiting a disaster zone as "amazing" and an "incredible high." He concluded by reminding us repeatedly that we were the "elite of the elite at the most elite institution in the world." Moments later, the class fanned around the Journalism Building's statue of Thomas Jefferson, and we were forced to yell, "Pulitzer!" while grinning for our class picture.

I ate lunch alone that first day, as far from campus as possible. I was already wondering whether I should drop out.

Simon Critchley

THIS INTERVIEW WAS CONDUCTED BY JESSICA LOUDIS.

On His Own Education

I WENT TO UNIVERSITY late, when I was twenty-two. Before that, I worked in various factories and as a lifeguard at a swimming pool. I was also a punk, playing in countless useless bands. There was less sex than I would have liked, but lots of drugs and rock 'n' roll. Right before I went back to school, I worked at a swimming pool in a small town in England called Stevenage. It was an awful town, but it had a library. I had always liked to read, but that was where I discovered how much I liked it. So I enrolled in what was called a further education college, which is basically where you go to learn hairdressing or car mechanics or things like that—similar to a community college, I suppose—and I finished some qualifications and somehow got into university two years later. I went to study philosophy at the University of Essex, which had a reputation for being left-wing and which the government had tried to close down in the mid-1970s. I was four years older than I should have been, and had done a lot of stuff that my classmates only dreamed of doing, so I had credibility. That made things easy.

I worked hard and got a good philosophy degree. I graduated in 1985, which in the UK meant the total hegemony of Thatcherism, and the end of the miners' strike, a movement I had been very heavily involved in. What was called the Big Bang was also taking place in the City of London [the English counterpart to Wall Street]. Before that point, the City had been associated with gentlemen in bowler hats who used to work in a very mannered way. After the Big Bang, the City became the way we think of Wall Street now—full of brash, moneymaking vulgarity, with Michael Douglas look-alikes and all the rest. While nobody went into finance before the mid-'80s, by the time I finished school, a lot of people I graduated with were going straight into the City. There were jobs, and the financial sector was sucking people in.

The economic context at the time for universities was gloom and doom. Between 1977 and 1988—an eleven-year period—no academic jobs opened up in the humanities. None. If you look at the demographics of humanities professors at British universities, you find a gap: There aren't many people between my age (fifty-three) and their early sixties. There had been a hiring boom in the '70s, but by the time I got out of school it had been shut down.

My situation was this: On the one hand, because I got a good degree, I had been told by my teachers that I could get money to do a PhD. On the other hand, I knew that I could also get a good job somewhere—even if I didn't know where—and I worried that a graduate education would make me overqualified and less employable outside academia. At least, that's what people told me. I ended up taking money for a PhD fellowship—which wasn't much, but it was three years' worth of government money from the British Academy—and I moved to France with my girlfriend. I signed up to do a master's in philosophy at the University of Nice, but my real intention was to take the money and run; to see how long we could keep doing this before something else worked out. I had no idea what that other thing might be. I wasn't very serious about going to graduate school: There were no jobs, so there was no future. It made things very pure. Even though we thought we were cleverer than the people who had taught us, we still couldn't get jobs. Academia was a closed system.

When I got to France, I learned to use a library for the first time. I spent eight hours a day there, learning how to do research, take notes in longhand, make a bibliography, and how to write at a greater length. All I could think about were the topics that I wanted to write on. I became obsessed. A philosopher named Dominique Janicaud was my mentor, and for reasons still completely unknown to me, he decided to spend time with me and give me a tutorial every two weeks. He made me explain texts to him in French, and we had conversations about them. My French wasn't very good at the beginning, but it got better.

About midway through my funding, as I was writing my master's thesis, my girlfriend and I decided to go back to England. (By that time, I was already thinking about staying on and finishing a PhD.) I was done with my coursework, so I spent the next year and a half in England reading a lot, meeting with my adviser, and working on my thesis about Derrida and Levinas.

As I was getting toward the end of my funding, someone said, "You should give a paper." So I gave one at Cardiff University in Wales, and on the strength of that paper, they offered me a postdoctoral fellowship. But in order to qualify for the fellowship I needed to have finished my doctoral dissertation, so I pretty much wrote my dissertation in four months. Not long after, my PhD supervisor left for a job in the States, and I got his job. At twenty-eight, I became an assistant professor at the university where I'd done my PhD. It's funny, at no point did I have any desire for an academic career, because it seemed like no such thing existed.

On the Differences Between American and English Graduate Systems

In American graduate school you go to work with specific professors. In England, we had teachers who we were on very good terms with, and who we often really liked, but we didn't really take them that seriously. We took ourselves much more seriously. If you talk to an American PhD and ask, "Oh, what did you do?" they'll say, "Oh, I was at Yale with X, and then I went to Harvard and worked with these people." This is completely alien to me. It sounds like they've turned themselves into dogs trained by people to do certain tricks. This just wasn't the way it was in England. Students would work in groups or they'd work alone, and teachers would drift in and out, but there wasn't a hierarchical structure. The American system is much more like the German system than the English system. There are hierarchies of professorships and assistantships in Germany, and in a funky way, the American university apes that, though in the end, it's always about who you studied with. In England, you'll meet some old bore who taught at Oxford, and after a few drinks, he'll tell you that whoever wrote the latest thing everybody is talking about was his student. Those are always the words: "He was my student," whereas in the U.S., the formulation is, "I took classes with X," or, "I studied with so-and-so at Y." I find that hierarchical attitudes are quite ingrained in the States, and in a way, it's much more formal than what I was used to as a student. People are in it for a job.

I should mention that in Britain, the structure of higher education is very different from the U.S. Britain has no private universities: It has a state-run system that expects universities to behave like private corporations. Because they receive block grants from the government, these universities are completely at the whim of government education policies. I was the chair of the philosophy department at Essex for three years before coming to New York to teach at the New School in 2004. During my time at Essex, there would be a new memo from the Department of Education every few weeks, and we'd be forced to reorganize what we were working on. There was a real lack of autonomy. This bureaucratized market model was eventually implemented across all British universities, and now, through the Bologna Process, that model is being implemented throughout the EU. It's a fatal error for European higher education. I teach in the Netherlands as well, and I've watched that country—in best Calvinist fashion—impose more and more ludicrous straitjackets on itself in order to assimilate. The English model, under the belief that it's an American model because it's somehow linked to the market, has become the European model. In reality, the American model is much more complicated. There are private universities, state universities, liberal arts colleges, technical colleges, community colleges, all sorts of stuff. I rather like that.

On Teaching American Grad Students

It's easy. They're very good students, but they're far too deferential, at least to your face. They're usually well-mannered in class. I'm always trying to identify that student who is willing to push back a bit, but I find that most are too dependent on the opinions of their professors. That mystifies me. I don't see why that should be. I wish students would try to do more original work and take more risks earlier on, but they don't because they're worried about their professions and their careers, and it's bullshit.

Graduate school can be limiting, but getting rid of the fear and anxiety that's connected with it is important. Panic about the future shuts people down. This is a terrible thing to say, but I think that a lot of students are stupider five years into a PhD program than they were just after they finished their undergrad degrees because they've been narrowed down so radically. Education should be the opposite of that: It's about opening up vistas. There are many routes to professional success. One is being a mathematics gradu- ate from Harvard who actually understands the algorithms that make the financial system work. Another is being someone who is generally educated, interesting and interested, open and well-read, and prepared to talk to anyone. That's an inevitably employable person. I don't think our graduate programs on the whole are producing those people. Instead, they're producing shadow puppets of professors who are largely unintelligible to anybody other than a handful of initiates.

Another big criticism I have with graduate programs in the U.S. is the lack of originality at the dissertation level. For the first few years of graduate school, students can get through courses the same way they did when they were undergrads—by taking Adderall or whatever, and speed-writing papers. Most don't acquire the skill of doing research. For me and for my graduate cohort, the dissertation was the only thing that mattered. To get a PhD meant writing a dissertation, and therefore you poured yourself into it and tried to make it as interesting and original as possible. The dissertation in the U.S. sometimes tends to be an afterthought.

Finally—and this is important—if you want to write a dissertation that you think is going to be a success or get you a job, you have to be careful not to produce something that will be passé by the time it appears. In many cases, dissertations are at least ten years out of date because students are working on something that their professors are working on, and professors are usually five years out of date at least. There's an awful lot of work like that. Shadow puppetry again. Of course, thinking for yourself and not making compromises based on some fantasy of what's going to get you a job is a very hard thing to do. Many of the New School students I teach want to make themselves into respectable figures who could have come out of an Ivy League school. But why do that? Why not do something different? I encourage students not to be obsessed about their discipline and to think about all the other potential locations for their work. There are all sorts of possibilities out there.

David Auerbach

IT IS ALWAYS DANGEROUS to refuse one's fate. I was supposed to be a software engineer. I did not speak until I was four, but I showed prodigious enthusiasm for mathematics and computers, programming in Logo and BASIC by age eight. My parents introduced me to the requisite reading for math and science types everywhere: Isaac Asimov, Robert Heinlein, and Robert Sheckley.

But it all went wrong in high school, when I stopped reading science fiction and discovered Vonnegut and Camus and Salinger and Woolf and Melville. The summer after eleventh grade, I took a college course on *Ulysses* taught by an especially empathetic professor. I was enraptured. The study of literature appeared to me as destiny and haven.

It did not work out.

I had imagined the university as a sanctuary of intense study and self-questioning, free of popularity contests and ruthless social competition. I was, admittedly, very naïve. My first year at university, I was in a literature seminar taught by a professor who had never read *Paradise Lost* prior to teaching it to us. I wrote a paper that this professor thought too good to have been my own work, so she accused me of plagiarism. No official action was taken, but I was spooked, made flatly aware of my helplessness.

There were other discouraging moments. There was the literature professor who said that originality was overrated in undergraduate work. He passed out, as a yardstick, what he termed the perfect undergraduate paper: It was mostly plot summary. There was the history and politics survey run

175

by a neoconservative, where Edmund Burke was exalted and Marx only represented by "On the Jewish Question." And there was the writing teacher who never read our work, skipped five of the six meetings I scheduled with him, and ridiculed me when I dared complain about it.

Those small incidents at college did not feel small, and if the life of the mind is not to become a joke, they should not feel small. They represented to me the evisceration of the ideal that John Williams described in his great novel *Stoner*: that the university should be "an asylum, a refuge from the world, for the dispossessed, the crippled."

There were a few professors who showed inspirational engagement, humor, and open-mindedness. One of them, the novelist John Crowley, astutely recommended Robert Musil and Robert Burton to me. I fell in love with their disenchanted intellectualism. This passage from Musil's *The Man Without Qualities* haunted me for years to come:

> Few people in mid-life really know how they got to be what they are, how they came by their pastimes, their outlook, their wife, their character, profession, and successes, but they have the feeling that from this point on nothing much can change . . . In their youth, life lay ahead of them like an inexhaustible morning, full of possibilities and emptiness on all sides, but already by noon something is suddenly there that may claim to be their own life yet whose appearing is as surprising, all in all, as if a person had suddenly materialized with whom one had been corresponding for some twenty years without meeting and whom one had imagined quite differently.

In the end, I took a degree in computer science, a small and strong department. It still came to me so much more easily than literature. My thesis involved writing a Java compiler in ML. A life in academia still seemed plausible for a time—a PhD in computer science—but I eventually realized that I was an engineer rather than a theoretician, preferring to build things rather than prove them, so I left the academy for Microsoft.

Since then I have accumulated a host of stories from friends who did go to graduate school in the humanities. Many of them had experiences far worse than anything I suffered: oral examinations turned into brutal interrogations, capricious advisers betraying or abandoning their students and leaving them with nowhere to go, graduate students used as proxies in internecine warfare between professors, absurd factionalism within departments, students backstabbing one another over scraps of academic prestige, and, most ubiquitously, professors sleeping with their students or otherwise emotionally blackmailing them. The stories kept piling up. They still do.

Of course, such things do happen outside of academia. The difference between academia and the corporate world—the difference that scared me, at any rate—is the unchecked power placed in the hands of faculty and administration and the lack of a safety net should things go wrong. Should the adviser-student relationship fail, should you specialize in an unpopular or overpopulated field, should you fail to please a single crucial person, your academic career may well be permanently doomed. There is little recourse left after that save becoming an underpaid and exploited adjunct. When I met with petty politicking in my engineering career, I simply switched jobs, nearly getting sued in the process but ultimately making a successful escape.

For me, computer science became the haven I once saw in academia; indeed, it tolerates misfits and the maladroit far better. I worked at Microsoft, then at Google. The interviewing process was similar at both: In each of five or six interviews, you would be given a small technical problem and asked to code the solution on a whiteboard. The hiring decisions could still be arbitrary and unfair, but technical skill counted for something. The best-dressed, smoothest-talking applicants tended not to be the most skilled coders. Software engineering is often collective work, and though back-stabbing and corruption exist, the nature of the work did lend itself to mutual support and camaraderie.

At both companies, I worked primarily on servers, so much of what I did was opaque to the outside world. I spent a lot of time dealing with mysterious crashes and performance bottlenecks: I breathed race conditions, hashing/fingerprinting, and load balancing. This meant taking a huge and complex problem, breaking it down into small, simple, highly reusable solutions, and linking them together as elegantly as circumstances permitted. As far as user-facing work goes, I can claim credit for being the first person to put graphic emoticons into a chat program (MSN Messenger Service, specifically) that would show up if you typed a text emoticon like :-) or :-P. That feature took a day to implement, but to most of the world it's far more meaningful than the really hard stuff.

The work paid the bills and was immensely satisfying—at least to half of my brain. I did miss literature, and during these years, I read and wrote in place of a social life. In my twenties, I wrote five novels. I read Ray Davis's blog, *Pseudopodium*—then known as the *Hotsy Totsy Club*—the only place on the web I'd found discussion of Robert Musil and Krazy Kat both. Inspired by his example, I started my own blog, *Waggish*, to gather my thoughts about what I was reading—and to reach out to like minds. During a one-month stint between jobs, I tried to blog through all of Proust. I didn't quite make it, but it was one of the most fulfilling reading experiences I'd had since first encountering Musil and Joyce.

After six or seven years as an engineer, I eventually did attend graduate school, of a sort—not enrolled in any program, but taking literature and philosophy classes of my choosing while debating whether or not to matriculate. I studied *Finnegans Wake* with a brilliant, eclectic Joyce scholar who seemed to have read everything and could sing entire Gilbert and Sullivan operas from memory. I studied philosophy of mind with a professor whose enthusiasms ranged from Richard Hughes's mesmeric *A High Wind in Jamaica* to the eleventh-century Talmudic writings of Shmuel HaNagid. Their examples showed me that there was much to be found in the obscure corners of the humanities, but also that pursuing an advanced degree would have required far too many compromises and sacrifices in the hopes of winning the tenure lottery. A successful academic friend advised me that if I had no pressing need to be employed as a professor, my work was better conducted outside of the university. I agreed.

Having decided that independent scholarship offered the greatest freedom, I went into reading and writing full-time. The ways of this world of scholarship are far more mysterious and capricious than those of technology, and I navigate them ineptly, hoping that some intrinsic worth in my writing will show through past my uneasy self-presentation. The sincere, thoughtful e-mails I receive from appreciative readers mean the most to me. I know some will not take my scholarly writing seriously without academic accreditation or affiliation, but many have been welcoming. When I presented a conference paper last year on *Finnegans Wake* at University College Dublin, the professors and students were friendly and encouraging; they engaged with my paper and challenged me on points, but they were also quite considerate in their comments. The conference was clearly a labor of love for the organizers, and I was impressed by how the other students and junior professors had attached themselves to unfashionable subjects out of sheer passion and found a place for themselves, however tenuous.

These days, I write on literature, society, and technology. Many publications prefer I write about the latter, but I've persisted with my eclectic studies. I hold tenaciously to Jacob Burckhardt's maxim that one should "be an amateur at as many points as possible for the increase of knowledge and the enrichment of possible standpoints."

At their rare best, science and the humanities reveal the false assumptions we hold in the hopes of finding truth and improving the world. In the words of philosopher Hans Blumenberg, "Thoughtfulness means: not everything is as self-evident as before." The university should ideally serve as a focal point for these efforts, but today, success in academia depends far more on luck and social capital than it does on strength of thought. If I resisted this realization, it is only because our most beloved dreams stick as stubbornly as barnacles to our souls, so much that they can only be removed once our spirits have been rubbed raw.

Jake Heggie

IT TOOK ME NINETEEN years to complete my master's degree.

I started grad school in piano and composition at UCLA in 1986 with good intentions, and I dropped out two years later with only my thesis project left to write. That never bothered me. In fact, it proved to me that I wasn't cut out for full-time academia. But it did bother one of my former professors, who nudged me year after year to finish the damn thing. So in 2005, after a seventeen-year gap, I finally did.

Though the actual degree hasn't yet served any real function for me, there is no doubt in my mind that a direct line can be traced from my time as a graduate student to the wonderful career I'm privileged to have today. It had nothing to do with obtaining the actual degree and everything to do with the people I met there, where they led me, and the experiences that followed.

I'm an American opera composer whose stage works include *Dead Man Walking*, *Moby-Dick*, *Three Decembers*, *The End of the Affair*, plus about 250 art songs and other compositions. I make my living on commissions for my compositions, as well as from royalties from international productions, from the occasional performance fee as a pianist, and sometimes from being a guest artist or lecturer at festivals, universities, conservatories, or opera companies. It's an unusual job description.

My story really begins toward the end of my senior year of high school. I always knew I'd head off to college. That was never a question for me as it was for my three siblings. Stop going to school? Why would I stop going to school? I loved learning and was eager to get away from home and break the patterns of self-doubt that had plagued me since my father's suicide when I was ten. I wanted to establish a new and true identity, find "my people" out in the exciting world of grown-ups, and accumulate knowledge and experiences. College sounded like a safe and adventurous place to do all that.

It was 1979, and I already knew that my life would be about music. I also knew I was gay, and the idea that anybody else might also know it absolutely terrified me. In the small towns where I attended schools in Ohio and Northern California, being gay didn't really fly. It was ingrained in me that gay people were inherently bad. I didn't want to be a bad person, but I also never felt like I was, so none of it made sense. It took a lot of work to keep my sexuality hidden, but I did, burying myself in piano and composition—realms in which I felt powerful and successful.

My mother entrusted the college application process to me, thinking I'd apply to several worthwhile colleges. I was a very good student, and her hope was that I would attend UC Berkeley, close to home. But when I graduated, I took off for Europe to attend the American University of Paris. It was the only college to which I applied, much to my beloved mother's surprise. I knew it was time for me to get far away from home, and I wanted to go someplace where I was unknown and couldn't come running back if things got tough. I wanted a fresh start. Plus, I had dreamed about going to Europe for ages: the land of Chopin, Liszt, Schumann, Beethoven, Mozart, and all my other heroes.

It was an incredible experience. My shell cracked a little. I met fascinating people from all over the world, became fluent in French, read and wrote a lot, played the piano, composed songs and lyrics, envisioned writing a Broadway show, and was introduced to classical singing. Even so, I remained fundamentally afraid of myself. Most people likely suspected I was gay. A couple of friends actually knew it, which scared me even more. What if they told somebody who mustn't know? I lived in dread and didn't like myself very much.

In 1981, my mom insisted it was time for me to come back to the U.S. So I left Paris and went to UCLA to study with the great pianist Johana

Harris, about whom I'd heard a lot from friends and former teachers. UCLA was gorgeous, the environment welcoming and invigorating. I also found a lot of people like me: classical and musical theater geeks of all ages. All of us were pursuing the elusive goal of a life in music from within the safe haven of a university. I met a few openly gay men, even fell in love with a male classmate, but I still tried to keep my sexuality hidden. I did well in school, but I wound up hating myself even more. There were times I couldn't even look in the mirror.

At UCLA, my life revolved around the music department. Johana turned out to be the most extraordinary artist and teacher I could have imagined. She saw in me depths of creativity and possibility that I had never seen in myself. More than anything, she thoroughly believed in me as an artist and was incredibly nurturing. She also fell in love with me. I was twenty-one, very vulnerable and completely terrified. She was nearly seventy and I guess scared in her own way. So how did we handle this situation? We ignored all the elephants in the room and got married. In my fearful thinking, being married to her would be more acceptable to my family than my being gay. It was 1982. My mother and siblings were surprised and upset at first, but they came around and tried to be supportive, as they always had been.

Johana and I formed a two-piano team and gave a few concerts. While she continued to be my piano teacher, she also became the most important composition teacher I ever had, encouraging me not only to "go for the gut" in my writing, but also to have another look at pieces I adored. The connections between living human beings and what they created on the page became very real all of a sudden. I experienced magical, transformative teaching like I had never had. I got to meet legendary artists who were her friends: Leonard Bernstein, John Browning, Lorin Maazel, William Schuman, and Isaac Stern.

But a year into our marriage, it became impossible for me to pretend anymore. We both had to recognize what was going on. I told her I was gay. She said she understood but did not want to get divorced. So, we remained married. I knew people had been whispering behind my back, but I suddenly felt oddly empowered: I'd had the strength to tell Johana my secret, and she didn't reject me completely; she didn't die, and I didn't die.

I learned to embrace the controversy that surrounded us, but still, we were living a lie. It was exhausting.

Composition became more important in my life as I let go of the dream of being a concert pianist and began to think of myself as a collaborative artist. At UCLA, I started to make friends who saw me for who I really was, knew what was going on, and still stood staunchly by me. We graduated in 1984. Almost immediately, seven of us joined forces and created a composer's group we called the Lo Cal Composers. We pooled resources and put on concerts of our new compositions, which we paid performer friends from college to participate in. Each concert marked new growth and new possibility. It was an exhilarating time.

I didn't really consider graduate school right after college. I was busy teaching private lessons, concertizing with Johana, and composing music. Yet at the same time, I kept hoping a hero would show up and save me from my false personal life. I needed somebody to put an end to the craziness, to sweep me off my feet and carry me away. Even though I was feeling better about myself as a creative artist, as Johana's husband I worried that I would become complacent and end up leading a sheltered, "kept" life. False and kept: what a horrible, shameful way to live. After a year or so of this, I realized that I missed the opportunities a different kind of nurturing environment could offer. I wanted experience, guidance, perspective, engagement, and direction. I needed to be challenged on a deeper plane. I felt isolated and lonely, and I yearned for the society of others on similar creative journeys. These realizations felt like an alarm clock going off. So in 1986, I went back to UCLA for grad school.

During my first quarter of grad school, I realized that the only hero who could save me was myself, and that I was exactly where I needed to be. Not only was the coursework more focused, challenging, and enjoyable, the environment felt significantly different than it had when I was an undergraduate. I was more of an adult, and I wasn't in grad school because I had to be, but because I elected to be. Being there felt empowering, and I loved it.

Opportunities seemed to be around every corner. Through the UCLA Center for the Performing Arts, I became the guy who turned pages for recital pianists at the university's major venue, Royce Hall, and wound up onstage with legendary artists like singers Leontyne Price, Montserrat Caballé, Kiri Te Kanawa, Renata Scotto, violinist Itzhak Perlman, and many others. I became a staff pianist for the choirs on campus. I started performing regularly, and I was given the chance to hear my compositions performed by excellent young artists and faculty.

As I moved on as a student, I was also able to make progress in my personal life. I came out to my family: nobody was rejected, nobody died. My relationship with Johana evolved, and though we remained married, we lived separately for a year or so.

But nothing's ever easy, right?

During my second year of graduate school—and just as I was coming out—Johana experienced an immense family crisis and wanted me nearby. So, we bought a house and started living together again. At the same time, I developed a medical problem known as focal dystonia in my right hand. My fingers would curl up uncontrollably when I played the piano, and it caused me to make mistakes, so I had to quit performing.

I had just begun exploring new territory as a composer, and suddenly it all stopped. I felt like the world I had been moving toward as an independent creative artist was slipping away. To top it off, I wound up choosing the wrong adviser in graduate school. Things had gotten so crazy in my personal life, I requested at one point that he give me an incomplete so I could catch up. He said, "Don't worry about it!" and gave me a dreaded C-minus. In graduate school that is a failing grade. There it was, clear as day: "You're a failure." And I felt like a failure.

I stopped playing the piano and composing and left graduate school. Was I running away again? I don't know. Maybe. But the world had become almost unbearably heavy, and I couldn't stand it anymore. This was an identity crisis I had never imagined possible. Dealing with being gay was one thing. But my primary identity since childhood was as a musician. If I wasn't a musician, what was I?

I suppose it was inevitable. Though I had always tried to be a good person, I had never felt like an authentic person. Nor did I feel like an authentic artist. For most of my life, I had coasted on being the person I thought other people wanted me to be. Now, I had hit a wall. Graduate school trained a magnifying glass on my life and work, and it made me recognize that I needed to be honest with myself and with others. Over the years, I had met fearless, genuine people who were willing to put themselves on the line and take risks: I finally recognized that in order to find happiness and contentment, I needed to become one of them.

Slowly, things began to change. Right before I left UCLA, I was introduced to a guest speaker on campus who had delivered a talk about pianists with focal dystonia. He connected me with a piano teacher who helped me develop a new technique so that I could play again. A friend recommended me for a job running a private concert series in Beverly Hills. When that ended a few years later, she gave me a full-time job as a writer for her company, which opened up new pathways, new connections, new ideas, and new possibilities. I found I could write about music successfully.

Then in 1991, Johana developed cancer. She retired from UCLA in 1993 at age eighty and her children took up her care. She and I talked about the future and agreed it was time for me to move on.

That year, I moved from Los Angeles to San Francisco to start fresh. I knew that the change would allow me to find out if I was meant for a life in music or just one adjacent to it. A UCLA colleague set me up with a job as a writer for UC Berkeley's performing arts series, and within a few months, I was offered a position at the San Francisco Opera as that company's writer. I finally came out of my shell completely. Amazing friends, great artists, and remarkable opportunities came into my life. My piano technique returned and I started to compose prolifically and to concertize with singers. Johana and I stayed in touch until her death in 1995. As she wished, we never divorced.

In 1998, the general director at the San Francisco Opera took a huge, almost unimaginable leap of faith and named me San Francisco Opera's first composer in residence.

The position came with a commission to create my first stage work: an opera based on *Dead Man Walking* with playwright Terrence McNally as my librettist, Joe Mantello as director, Patrick Summers as conductor, and a cast that featured superstar mezzo-sopranos Susan Graham and Frederica von

Stade. The opera received its premiere at San Francisco's War Memorial Opera House in October of 2000 to great acclaim, and it has by now been produced internationally in more than fifty separate productions. Since then, I've created a substantial body of work as a full-time composer in San Francisco. I don't ever want to leave.

A year before the opera premiere, I met my husband, Curt, and we married in 2008. I've been lucky enough to share in raising his son, who is now about to go off to college.

In 2005, one of my former professors at UCLA called me—as he had many times over the years—and urged me to complete my master's degree. He had always believed in me, and he felt strongly about my finishing what I had started. I could use any of my compositions as a thesis project. I chose my song cycle *The Deepest Desire* with words by Sister Helen Prejean. The cycle traces a very personal story of spiritual crisis and awakening to one's call and purpose on the planet. That felt about right.

That May, I went back to campus to be a grad student for one more day, stood in all the appropriate lines, and received my piece of paper. Mission accomplished.

Going to grad school did not get me to where I am today, but there is no question that it helped me to find my way. It was the ultimate looking glass. It gave me time and opportunities to work closely with remarkable, fearless people who forced me to examine myself and ask the biggest question of all—"Why?"

Ron Rosenbaum

APPARENTLY, PEOPLE HAD BEEN talking. When I received an e-mail from an editor of this book asking me to contribute an essay on the subject of grad school, she told me, somewhat mysteriously, slightly ominously: "Several people have mentioned that you have strong feelings on the subject."

In fact I had recently spoken to a grad school class on Shakespeare at NYU (led by my colleague, the gifted poet and memoirist Meghan O'Rourke) about my book *The Shakespeare Wars*. And if all grad school teachers of literature were like her, I would have no problem with the institution.

But I must admit, I expressed some very "strong feelings" in that class. Specifically about the controversy stirred up by some academics who have arrogated to themselves spurious authority to discard parts of *Hamlet*. I had indeed emphatically warned the impressively bright students in the seminar against the kind of grad school–nurtured exegesis of Shakespeare most egregiously represented by James Shapiro in the section of his book *1599*, wherein he purports to read Shakespeare's mind and discover that Shakespeare would have wanted to cut, trash, delete, and disappear Hamlet's final soliloquy; one of the high points of the play and of Shakespeare's entire oeuvre.

It's true that the fourth-act soliloquy ("How all occasions do inform against me / And spur my dull revenge . . ."), which is present in the so-called Good Quarto of *Hamlet*, the one published during Shakespeare's lifetime, was omitted from the posthumously published Folio edition. But there is no evidence that this was *Shakespeare's* preference and not that of, for instance, a theater manager who wanted to speed up the action of one of the Bard's longest plays, which in fact revolves around extended delay.

As I suggest in my book, the mind reading case Shapiro makes for the excision is no small matter. It's emblematic of a whole academic mind-set, of the sort of tin-eared arrogance that would consign to the dustbin on no good authority thirty-five eloquently tormented lines of self-reflection by one of the greatest characters in world literature—a character defined by his penchant for introspection and self-reflection—on the basis of a half-baked theory. In this case, the theory that Shakespeare decided he wanted to revise *Hamlet* to make Hamlet more of an action hero! Like Schwarzenegger in *True Lies*! Or maybe a Bruce Willis vehicle: *Die Hard with a Vengeance: The Elsinore Conundrum*.

In this analysis, Hamlet's last soliloquy slows down the action, makes Hamlet too "dark and existential," as Shapiro disparagingly notes. Wouldn't want that! That Shapiro's theory has been taken seriously by academics and that none have objected to his ludicrous mind reading of Shakespeare's supposed intentions is not merely an intellectual scandal.

It is the perfect exemplar of the way most graduate study of literature in America diminishes it. The way the graduate study of literature has become something to be avoided like the plague.

I've tangled with Shapiro before, and I will never cease condemning his grad school–bred disembowelment of *Hamlet* 'til the day I die and, like Hamlet's father's ghost, pledge to return to haunt those who advance this meretricious attempt to pour poison into the ears of grad students, to deface one of the high points of English literature.

Yes, I guess I do have strong feelings.

But I told the editor that I couldn't speak about graduate school education in general for two reasons. First, it seems intuitively true that for subjects such as history, philosophy, the hard sciences, and even some of the softer ones, it would be hard for me to make a case against graduate study.

But grad school for literature, I can't advocate. I escaped Yale before it became the center of the frenzied fad for French literary theorists, as a result of which students read more about the arcane metaphysics of language, textuality rather than texts, instead of the actual literature itself. But even though many of the most sophisticated contemporary intellectuals who once bought into this sophistry (such as Terry Eagleton) have abandoned it, the tenured relics who imposed this intellectual regime are still there, still espousing their view that literature itself is only to be understood through their diminishing deconstructing lens. I can testify to it, having sat through enough seminars at the Shakespeare Association of America conferences to last a lifetime. Please don't waste your life this way.

The second reason for my reluctance was that the editor told me she was asking two kinds of writers: those who had, and those who had not gone through graduate school. I fell into neither category: I had only spent a year at Yale's graduate school (in English literature), and then fled the institutional comforts it offered for an unknown future.

All the better, she said. I'd looked at life from both sides now.

And so return with me to the moment I made the choice about whether to stay in graduate school; the moment when two roads stretched before me. I don't suggest anyone take the path I did—I don't want to ruin any lives—but maybe it will help some see if it's the road for them.

It was the spring of 1969, around midnight at a lovely house on a comely cove a few miles up the coast from New Haven, a place I shared with a couple of Yale friends. I was sitting at the kitchen table. I had been up late paging anxiously through the classified ads of the *Village Voice* (long before they became a porn emporium), looking for a traveling salesman job, not finding one, and wondering if I should accept what seemed to be my fate and continue on in graduate school.

Traveling salesman job? Yes, I was desperate, looking for anything to get me out of the dusty, drowsy seminar rooms of graduate school and the endless succession of other dusty, drowsy seminar rooms that choosing an academic career portended. Anything to get me on the road, any road. I was in grad school because I loved reading literature, but literature does not, cumulatively, make the case for spending your life in classrooms studying and teaching literature. And abjuring graduate school does not mean you must end your romance with literature—in fact the opposite could be true. There's this thing called "reading," which can be done, according to my understanding, outside dusty seminar rooms.

(In fact, if you're interested in learning as opposed to credentials and career, I would advise, immediately upon leaving college, taking out a subscription to the UK *Times Literary Supplement*, which has been for me a vastly useful way of keeping in touch with the greatest minds and clearest thinkers and writers in academia—and finding copious reading recommendations—which will serve you better than most graduate schools and is far cheaper.)

In any case, those with souls so dead they stay in graduate school literature programs as they are now taught are precisely the ones who shouldn't—but do—end up teaching literature and telling students things like Hamlet's last soliloquy is superfluous. Needless to say there are exceptions. I single out some brilliant Shakespeare scholars such as Ann Thompson and Russ McDonald in my book. But it is a sad fact that it is the people too timid to taste life without the prospect of tenure who stay behind and ruin literature for the students in graduate school who have any life left in them.

And, in fact, as many have noted, the choice to go to graduate school may only offer the illusion of comfort and security—these days it's an arduous path that only rarely leads to tenure; for the unwary it's a wild and expensive gamble with no guarantee of security.

Looking back, I'm still amazed that I'd acted on my impulse to get out of there, because I was not a venturesome soul. Not timid, but no swaggering badass *On the Road* type, either. It is a testament to the degree and the quality of the boredom I felt that I found myself flipping through *Village Voice* classifieds.

Indeed, I'd found myself in fairly cushy circumstances at Yale that argued for staying on. I was there on a Carnegie Teaching Fellowship, which was designed to lure Yale undergraduates into graduate school life by giving them a seductive package of perks, including official appointment to the Yale faculty (as a subassistant junior instructor or something, but still). And I was given junior fellow privileges at my residential college, where one of my fellow fellows was Stephen Greenblatt. (Go ahead and go to graduate school if you think you're as smart as Greenblatt. Even Greenblatt, though, needed to escape the jargon-throttled pages of the journal he founded, *Representations,* before writing his later intelligible works.)

The responsibilities were not especially onerous—teaching just one freshman literature seminar (although I used to get up at four-thirty in the morning to spend hours preparing for each class) and taking one graduate seminar a semester.

That fall, I was pleased that I'd been accepted into a Yeats seminar taught by none other than Richard Ellmann, known as the Yeats scholar of our time, whose biographies of the poet and of James Joyce are still monuments.

What a disappointment! A great writer, but as a teacher Ellmann was sedulously, reductively, droningly biographical in his approach to Yeats. Every luminous poetic line was dragged down to its mundane source in Yeats's life, just the opposite of what Joyce did with his Dublin, which was to raise the mundane to the sublime.

And all around me the graduate students in my seminar silently nodded, not with weariness but with what seemed to be careerist sycophancy. With one exception, a young woman who was, like me, seething with boredom. Her name: Camille Paglia. Need I say more?

The second-semester seminar was somewhat better, a Shakespeare class with Howard Felperin, whose small renown in academic circles came from becoming a hardcore deconstructionist and then, years later, having second thoughts and making a rare escape from the cult. I liked him. I liked Shakespeare, but again the students, the dusty, drowsy seminar rooms . . .

And there were the grad school sherry parties, the faces flushed with alcohol, the musty smell of damp tweed, the jockeying for position around such rising stars of sophistry as Harold Bloom, who many forget invented his own hermetic jargon before donning the mantle of humanist (remember "clinamen" anyone?). And the grad school culture, beery, sneery sessions with fellow students who seemed to evince no love of literature, just a lack of imagination. Was this what I wanted from life?

But I could have stayed; I could have played the grad school game. I had a good life with the prospect, after some thesis labor, of a secure tenured lifetime.

But it was beginning to feel like a life sentence.

Fortunately, I had had two experiences of life beyond grad school before then; one romantic, and one hard-boiled.

The first came the summer before I started grad school, when I had scammed second-class press tickets to the Democratic National Convention from a hometown local daily, the *Suffolk* [Long Island] *Sun*. The *Sun* was a short-lived Cowles Publishing Company venture that nonetheless got the DNC to recognize my press pass. I drove out to Chicago in a beat-up Chevy and found myself in the middle of the wild riotous '68 Democratic convention. Shifting from the posh interiors of the convention hotels to the tear gas and billy clubs in the street, I met a woman and convinced her we should leave the hectic violence and head for the lakeshore where (according to some sketchy info I had) Allen Ginsberg was going to be chanting for peace at sunrise. We never found Allen Ginsberg, but we did find ourselves alone on the beach as the sun rose.

It was an impossibly romantic dream of a first newspaper experience, and you can probably see why it spoiled me for the dusty seminar rooms.

And then in the middle of my graduate school year, something else happened that proved to be even more decisive. I didn't think it would be possible to replicate the romance of Chicago and had kind of given up on the idea of being a writer, when the same Suffolk paper offered to let me work as a daily reporter during winter break, where I was given the job of underassistant police reporter.

This was what I wanted, this was what I found I loved. Hanging out with cops and criminals and reporters. Being up close and personal with crime and punishment, not just writing papers on it.

Maybe my favorite part was getting a front-page byline on a story about a Long Island Rail Road strike. The managing editor, a classically grumpy veteran Irish newshound, taught me the art of "bouncing quotes"—repeating some management-bashing quote from the union leader (Anthony D'Avanzo—I still remember his name) to the management spokesman, then reading his retort back to D'Avanzo, who upped the ante. I stirred up a fight, actually reporting the underreported union point of view. I thought I was part of The Struggle. Almost as important, my father, who commuted to the city on the LIRR for forty years and hated the incompetent line, was proud I was giving them a hard time with my byline.

Still, curiously, that night in the spring, the night I had to decide whether to re-up at Yale or . . . what? I didn't think I could become a writer. It was just blessed luck that when I couldn't find a traveling salesman job, I kept flipping the pages in Help Wanted and my eyes alighted on the tiny type of a small classified ad for a job as assistant editor at a summer weekly called the *Fire Island News*, which was published in Ocean Beach on the barrier island right across from where I'd grown up in Bay Shore. I drove down to the interview in the Chelsea Hotel with a guy named Bill Redding, a novelist who had taken the job as editor, and got the sense that a number of writers took summer gigs with the paper despite the nearly no pay, in return for the room and board (I lived in a room behind Karl the barber's shop) and the sun, surf, and other beach enticements. I signed on. But then Redding had trouble with the publisher and I was suddenly left as editor, having to write practically the entire weekly for the rest of the summer.

Again, I don't necessarily suggest you try this at home; I was very often very lucky to be in the right place at the right time. The founding editor of the *Village Voice*, Dan Wolf, had a summer place in the next town over, and his wife, Rhoda, called his attention to the unconventional copy I was throwing into print, ranging from a very deep exegesis of Bob Dylan's country-pie album *Nashville Skyline* to profiles of the hippie cast of *Hair* visiting the haute gay enclave Fire Island Pines. And I covered a march led by the great Nat Hentoff, the *Voice* writer who also lived on the island and led a protest against discrimination by the wealthy WASP Newport Cottage–style colony called Point O'Woods. Hentoff later suggested I write to Dan Wolf to see if there was a place for me at the *Voice*, which was then still in its golden age.

And as it happened, the *Voice*'s last counterculture reporter, the legendary Don McNeill, had walked into a lake at a commune in Massachusetts allegedly with a headful of acid and died the year before. And so I was thrown into the breach.

It was heavy duty covering the Weather Underground types and the acidheads, but I survived it in part, I think, because of the skepticism and distance I had developed from reading my beloved seventeenth-century metaphysical poets and the crazy quilt of visionary sects who surfaced during Cromwell's Interregnum—the Diggers, the Levellers, the Ranters, and the Family of Love (for more on all of these see the great scholar Christopher Hill's wonderful book *The World Turned Upside Down*)—all of whom anticipated in their dreams and sad fate the '60s and '70s types I was covering and left me less vulnerable to being carried away by their seductions.

I began covering politics, too, and eventually ended up as the *Voice*'s White House correspondent, standing a few yards away from Richard Nixon as he made his weepy farewell speech the day after he resigned, just before he choppered off to exile.

And so began a very fortunate working life, at the *Voice*, *Esquire* (where one of the first stories I wrote was the one on "phone phreaks" that brought Steve Jobs and Steve Wozniak together in what would be the Apple partnership), *Harper's*, the *New York Times* magazine, the *New Yorker*, *Slate*, and other magazines, working for luminaries too numerous to name—to all of whom I owe a great debt for their encouragement and guidance. The point being, again, that without this initial luck I would not have had the fortitude to keep on going and might have ended up going back to grad school or even to law school. Yes, that old quote from E. B. White: "No one should come to New York to live unless he is willing to be lucky."

Seven books and hundreds of periodical pieces later, do I regret that I left graduate school? Do I regret turning the fateful page of the classifieds that night?

What do you think?

In fact, I still recall just one experience that made it all worthwhile, made me realize I'd made the right choice (for me anyway): the chance to see a life-changing Shakespearean production, perhaps the single greatest and most influential in the past century—Peter Brook's staging of *A Midsummer Night's Dream*.

Again it was a matter of luck and being in the right place at the right

time. I'd been following this weird, silly *Medicine Ball Caravan* documentary
that Warner Brothers was filming, about a bus caravan full of San Francisco
hippies that had made its way across America and then accompanied them
over the ocean to the UK for some concerts. (The Faces with Ron Wood at
Canterbury!)

But after all that madness was over I rented a Mini and started driving to
some literary landmarks, such as the place where Keats stood when he
wrote his beautiful ode "To Autumn." And I ended up in Stratford-upon-
Avon, Shakespeare's birthplace, on the very weekend the Royal Shakespeare
Company was opening Peter Brook's *A Midsummer Night's Dream* there. Ask
anyone who's seen it—it was a life-changing experience. I suddenly realized why Shakespeare was Shakespeare in a way I never would have
otherwise (i.e., in graduate school). You can read about it, should you care,
in *The Shakespeare Wars*, a book that was inspired by that experience. Until
then, I'd never understood the power of the spell Shakespeare could cast on
the stage rather than the page—if the players on the stage were under the
direction of a magus like Brook. It was a play about a love potion that was
itself a kind of lifelong love potion. It was an experience that I wouldn't
trade for an entire graduate school education.

Lucy Ives

DEAR WRITERS, THIS IS an essay for you. It may be that I've never *not* written an essay for other writers, but all the same, it feels good to say this up front. This is an essay written specifically and expressly for writers thinking about pursuing a PhD. I am a writer of unprofitable things, and, in addition to an ongoing PhD, I would like to complete shortly, I have an MFA in poetry. This latter degree, along with my BA in English, is worth about as much as the two pieces of faux parchment I keep in the back of my closet; thus the continuing education. Those who are not writers are advised to flip to the next essay—or, nonwriters may also stick around (there is little I can do to prevent them!), but they must bear in mind that this brief essay concerning the perils and promises of grad school is being written for writers and not for them (okay, it may have some general applicability, but I make no promises) because writers, perhaps more than any other kind of person, must think carefully about what they are doing before enrolling in a PhD program.

Point 1: Why is this?

Writers would seem to have all the necessary prerequisites for success in graduate school: They are attentive to detail, driven, quick-witted. In certain ways they closely resemble academics. However, there is a key dispositional and professional difference between the two. It can be hard to spot but has something to do with what or whom one believes writing is for. I think that people usually tell writers to write what they know. I don't know if anyone ever tells them anything like, know your audience. For the purposes of my point here, I will change things up a bit and say, know your audience. Know it deeply, unflinchingly, avidly, and without remorse. You could even sit down one day and create a series of prompts to help you conceptualize the person(s) you might be writing to or for:

1. MY IDEAL READER IS _____.
2. A GENERAL CATEGORY OF READERS INTERESTED IN MY WORK ARE _____.
3. THIS GENERAL CATEGORY OF READERS WOULD READ ME BECAUSE THEY ARE INTERESTED IN/LIKE/WANT TO KNOW ABOUT _____.
4. WHEN SOMEONE READS MY WORK, I WANT THEM TO THINK/ FEEL/KNOW_____.

As a writer, I have rather general answers here: (1) anyone, (2) readers of English, (3) being alive on Earth, (4) something. But on the occasion of this essay, and as I am after all in graduate school, I am going to complete these prompts based on the thoughts and expectations of a successful academic, as I humbly purport to understand them. Let's take a look:

1. MY IDEAL READER IS one of three experts in my field of study.
2. A GENERAL CATEGORY OF READERS INTERESTED IN MY WORK ARE three experts in my field of study and two generalists making use of me in a footnote and three graduate students who will read my work over the course of the next decade.
3. THIS GENERAL CATEGORY OF READERS WOULD READ ME BECAUSE THEY ARE INTERESTED IN/LIKE/WANT TO KNOW ABOUT my research in my field.
4. WHEN SOMEONE READS MY WORK, I WANT THEM TO THINK/ FEEL/KNOW that I am an authority in my field.

Admittedly, it's grim. Admittedly, it's also something of an exaggeration— however, only a slight one! I'd say meditate on this.

Moving on to Point 2, a personal confession:

During my graduate coursework, I became a taker of copious notes. This is not unusual: It's what everyone is doing with his or her pen, tablet, and/ or MacBook around the seminar table. However, my notes were seldom of a very effective variety. Mostly, they took the form of observations concerning what was taking place in the room around me (usually a seminar or colloquium of some kind). For example:

In recitation now. The Phaedrus. White erase boards are very white. Also, I hate the smell of carpeted classrooms, they smell like the inside of pants.

Or: The chairs are real. Plastic leather and some sort of composite, but with "real" metal buttons holding the plastic on. Beige predominates. A poster from the sixties concerning Algeria. Two matching damaged floor lamps. Obviously I spend a good deal of time looking around the room. I am so well trained at this point, however, that I make no effort to record any of my thoughts but rather withstand my boredom by consuming it, avidly even, like a broth.

Or: Before lecture, a student who wants to point out that Roman gods are anthropomorphic.

Or: The rumor is that someone has had/has (do not know what correct tense to use with this procedure would be) Botox. I spend some time admiring her bronzer. She always looks moist, her facial skin that is, without appearing shiny, and I think this must take some effort. Also, her haircut from two weeks ago has at last molted, or settled, etc.

Or: Blinking medievalist hands out copies of footnoted chant he composed—for which other members of the colloquium were apparently on hand and in hoods (?) when he performed in TX.

And so it goes. I've learned in the course of my studies that I'm very interested in other people and, apparently, furniture. I have also discovered that I am less interested in what might be considered the point or purpose of a given conversation or academic course. I'm not really one for argument, though there have been occasions upon which I have pretended to. (Faking an argument is pretty much the same thing as making one.)

What I'm trying to say is that, though I've always been a fairly good and mostly docile student, some demon of creativity would inevitably arrive to torment me the second we sat down to parse Barthes's seminar or Benjamin's epiphanic modernism. I don't know why this happened. I was compelled to write these notes! It's not my fault! However, Writers, let it not be said that I did not warn you.

Lastly, Point 3, most pragmatic of points: Grad school is a job.

One of the odd things about grad school—and this is more true of PhD programs than MA programs—is that it's a job. I say that this is odd because prior to one's entry into a graduate program, it is not likely that one would have experienced school as a job. It's not impossible that middle school or high school or college was a job for some, that these places were unpleasant in some of the same ways that jobs are unpleasant, but graduate school is a job in the nonmetaphorical sense. You are not there to learn, specifically, but rather to enrich the research of professors and generally contribute to the atmosphere of intellectual endeavor. Often, and particularly within the humanities, the job will be performative: one has opinions (one *demonstrates* that one has opinions); one has read (one acts knowledgeable); one attends. There's probably nothing innately distasteful about such performances of academic involvement; however, note that none are optional. Again, let me repeat, graduate school is a job.

If you are anything like me, you may have used books and other textual interfaces in your life as a way of escaping what you privately, in less happy moments, consider the tyranny of other people. You don't wish anyone ill, but the book—the written work—holds a special place in your imagination; it can be a source of relief and/or escape. It's a cliché, of course, but sometimes there's just nothing to replace it. Perhaps I only state the obvious here, but in order to contribute to an academic discussion, you cannot simply read a book and like it. You must instead judiciously apply the book to matters under discussion. It does not matter if matters under discussion are mostly irrelevant to the book itself, or if your relationship to the book happens to be more affective than analytic. Here the book is a tool of under-standing, a piece of evidence; you, as scholar, cause it to give up its secrets.

Anyway, I wouldn't want to warn anyone off of grad school simply because she or he likes literature! That sounds crazy! However, I do want to insist that you not take the realities and pressures of professional writing and reading lightly. Writers, please don't sacrifice what you hold most dear to the exigencies of the academy. Sell out for greater amounts! Or, if you must go through with it, please take copious notes.

Nicola Twilley

THIS INTERVIEW WAS CONDUCTED BY JESSICA LOUDIS.

Could you talk a bit about what you do and how you got into it?

I am a writer and I also run a space called Studio-X NYC for Columbia University's Graduate School of Architecture, Planning and Preservation. I write a blog called *Edible Geography*, which uses food as a lens to explore culture, science, sensory perception, cities, landscapes, history, and speculative futures. I am also working on a book about artificial refrigeration, which came out of writing the blog and also out of an exhibition I curated at the Center for Land Use Interpretation on the geography of the cold-scape—the massive network of artificial refrigeration spaces that store food across North America. A variety of different projects have come out of *Edible Geography*: a journalism career (full-time and freelance at different times); a scratch-n-sniff installation in a Manhattan gallery; an international event series on food and cities called the Foodprint Project; a multidisciplinary independent design studio and exhibition called *Landscapes of Quarantine* at Storefront for Art and Architecture; a pop-up, traveling landscape survey project called Venue; and, most recently, a residency at the largest whole-sale food market in the world, in Mexico City, which led to a publication printed on tortilla paper.

I got into all of this through *Edible Geography*, which I started as a way to make myself think through writing—and as an excuse and a framework to pursue and engage with things I thought were interesting, rather than just consume them.

Did you initially think that you wanted to be a writer, or did you plan on doing something else?

I did always want to be a writer, although nonfiction never occurred to me. (I only read fiction growing up in England, and I am under the un-fact-checked impression that popular nonfiction is still much less popular in the UK than in the U.S.)

However, I didn't have the self-belief/balls/experimental spirit to actually start writing, or even figure out how to begin to do it. I also didn't see journalism as an option because it seemed that you had to get started as a beat reporter, and I was much more shy when I was young and couldn't imagine asking strangers questions all the time. I applied for a job at Penguin in London, thinking that might help, but I didn't get it, so I started down the path of working at museums and nonprofits instead. I didn't get started as a writer until I saw what my husband, Geoff Manaugh, had managed to do with his architecture blog, BLDGBLOG. I wrote a couple of guest posts for him and then we both quit our jobs and spent a summer living on our savings in Rome and Sydney, and that's when I started my blog.

Do you have a background in architecture? How did that become one of your areas of focus?

I got a BA in English literature at the University of Leeds in the UK and then an MA in art history at the University of Chicago. My thesis was on contemporary art and medicine.

I've always been interested in landscape, design, and cities. My two main pastimes as a kid were designing and running room-size Lego cities with my brother and writing, illustrating, and publishing my own newspapers. I was, however, also interested in art and literature, and that's the direction I took with my education. I did this out of a slightly idiotic desire to somehow keep my options as open as possible and to not go down a more vocational path like town planning or architecture or landscape architecture. I always knew I was interested in too many things to commit to a specific discipline.

I applied to graduate school because I had no idea what I wanted to do next, and when I got into Chicago with a scholarship, it seemed like a great way to spend a year abroad and to study something a little different. It was definitely not a decision made with a particular career goal in mind.

So when did things start to click for you in terms of your intellectual and professional interests?

Before I started my blog, I did a lot of other things, some of which were amazing: My favorite was serving as director of public programming for the Benjamin Franklin Tercentenary, where I was in charge of coming up with creative ways to celebrate the three hundredth anniversary of Franklin's birth. I did everything from launching a competition to create a commemorative beer to running a three-hundred-word autobiography project, the thirty best of which were published on Philly bus shelters.

Others were not so amazing. Finally, after a particularly soul-destroying couple of years at a San Francisco–based nonprofit, and, after watching my husband build a writing career on the back of his blog, I decided to take the plunge myself. As a sort of productive constraint, I wanted a beat for my blog, and, after seeing Carolyn Steel (author of Hungry City) speak in London in June 2009, I realized that food would let me write about everything—prisons, fiction, typography, etc.—that I was interested in. I like being forced to use food (in a very loose sense) to get to the things I want to write about.

That constraint has been useful: For example, when I write about something like cow tunnels (lost underground tunnels for bovine transport), I now think about the tunnels in the context of the mechanics of urban food supply, rather than just seeing them as an example of forgotten subterranean infrastructure. The process of writing about something is a way of expanding the ways in which I think about it—I find that describing a thing in a certain way will remind me of something else, and that helps me see the original thing in a different light.

Do you have any advice for aspiring bloggers?

I'd say that a blog can be a platform, a motivation, a training ground, and a great way to introduce yourself to people whose work you admire. I'd advise future bloggers to write about that work in an interesting way and then send to it to the creators, or to interview them—but only if you can be bothered to spend the time to (a) come up with decent questions, and (b) edit the conversation in such a way that both people sound as interesting and articulate as possible.

(I would also suggest using a spell-checker; and try to learn basic grammar. Avoiding obvious mistakes make a big difference in the impression your writing creates. Reading a lot is a prerequisite for writing well, too.)

I personally have been constantly amazed by people's generosity and willingness to offer opportunities, both asked and unasked. I also think that concrete requests are a huge improvement on abstract requests for advice or coffee, which are just laziness disguised as effort.

Finally, if you figure out how to manufacture more hours in the day—or perhaps just how to not overcommit—let me know your secret.

Josh Boldt

I NEVER EXPECTED TO get a degree in English, much less two. When I started my undergraduate studies at the University of Kentucky, I wanted to be a wildlife biologist. I declared my major, and things went well for a while, but by my third semester, I started getting Ds in chemistry. This did not bode well for my future as a scientist. That same semester, I also happened to take an American literature class. I had been an avid reader when I was younger, and reading *As I Lay Dying*, *All the King's Men*, and a Toni Morrison novel—*Jazz*, I think it was—brought me back to literature for the first time in years. I realized I liked reading and writing about ideas, so, encouraged by positive feedback from my professors, I decided to change majors and study English.

When I graduated in 2003 I had no plans. I didn't know what I wanted to do with my life, and I didn't know how to use the skills I had gained in college in a professional capacity. But I also had bills to pay, so I took the first of my many non-degree-related jobs, as a furniture salesman. Over the next two years, I worked all kinds of gigs—from pizza delivery to swinging a sledgehammer on a highway crew. It was pretty much all hard labor. None of the work I was doing required a college degree.

I eventually landed a job at a grocery store thanks to the help of a friend who had gotten me an interview. The place was called Wild Oats, and it was a natural and organic food chain out of Colorado that was later bought by Whole Foods. I was hired on the spot to work on the stock crew, and my first shift started at four A.M. the next day.

From the beginning I worked hard and got in good with the managers. Within months, a position opened up and I was promoted. Then it happened again. Before long, I was running the grocery department, in charge of the crew I had started on a year or so earlier. I was in my midtwenties, finally making decent money, and building a career for myself. It certainly wasn't anything I had expected to happen, but it was working for me. Life was good enough, and I was headed for an upper-level management position.

The problem was I had this feeling that I was not living up to my potential. It wasn't that I didn't like my job; my job was fine. The people were nice and the work was relatively easy. But every morning when my alarm went off at four A.M. and I drove through the quiet darkness to unload a truck full of milk, cheese, and frozen foods, I knew that I wanted more, wanted to use my brain in other ways. I missed the days of discussing literature and spending hours in the library doing research. I thought I'd never miss it, but I did.

Once I made the decision to return to school to get a master's in English, I started researching my options. It had been a long time since I'd been in college, and when I tried to get in touch with former professors for recommendations, I learned that most had moved on or didn't really remember me.

Unable to put together a particularly strong application, I ended up attending a local university that wasn't very selective.

The next fall, I quit my management position at Whole Foods and started work on a master's degree. Leaving the clear upward trajectory of my retail career was a tough decision—one I still occasionally regret.

I thought I had a new career plan when I started school. At the time, I assumed that anyone with a master's degree in English could get a full-time teaching job at a community college, and that's what I intended to do. That strategy seems ridiculous to me now. Why didn't anybody warn me about the academic job market? I might not have listened; I don't know. After all,

I was fresh from the meritocratic world of retail management, where it was possible to climb the ranks simply by working hard. But as I realized too late, it's very different in higher ed.

The reality of the higher education job market started to sink in one semester before graduation. Colleagues who had finished a year before me returned with grim stories about adjuncting. They had tales of missing paychecks, health care debacles, and salaries that were even lower than graduate assistantship pay. Adjuncting sounded bleak, but with no other options, I began applying for jobs.

The position I was expecting never materialized. I soon realized that I was competing against PhDs for teaching jobs in a market already flooded with applicants. I expanded my job search beyond academia, looking broadly at anything in the field of communications, but I still had no luck. I felt stuck with yet another degree that didn't set me up for anything in particular, and once again, I was faced with starting over in a new career. I was in my midthirties and still perusing entry-level positions.

I eventually got a fairly stable adjunct teaching position in the English department at the University of Georgia. It offered health insurance, and though the pay was decent, it was never going to allow me to pay off my student loans. Still, I liked the work and I was good with students. That led me to wonder whether, at the right school, with the right teaching arrangement, I could make a career of academia after all.

I started doing research, but the more I looked around for information about adjuncting, the more I realized how little information was actually available. In fact, I couldn't find anything at all about average adjunct salaries or descriptions of adjunct working conditions at specific schools around the country. All I knew was the pay rates at my former and current schools, the latter of which was *double* the former. If salaries could vary that dramatically at state schools in the South, I figured the same might be true nationally, and that there must be other graduate students and prospective adjuncts out there who also weren't fully informed of their options.

*

The Adjunct Project was my answer to this problem. Now a website hosted by the *Chronicle of Higher Education*, I started the Adjunct Project in February of 2012 as a collaborative Google Document. I created about a dozen categories for adjunct working conditions at different universities—pay per course, health insurance, retirement, union representation, etc. After adding my own information, I began sharing the document with friends through social media. Within a week, over a thousand adjuncts had contributed to the spreadsheet. The Adjunct Project suddenly became the first major source of data about adjunct pay and working conditions at schools across the country, and all the information had been added by the adjuncts themselves.

As I write this two years later, about seven thousand entries have been added to the project, and they have revealed many details about the academic job market that were previously undisclosed. When you look at the numbers, it's clear why universities weren't eager to advertise them. Average pay for adjuncts is about $2,900 per course, meaning someone teaching full-time would earn about $23,000 a year. According to self-reported data, approximately 85 percent of adjuncts do not receive health insurance benefits from their employer. Only about 3 percent of adjuncts reported having a contract that extends beyond one semester. In other words, every four months or so, most teachers are left wondering if they will be rehired.

I strongly recommend that anyone who is considering graduate school with the goal of becoming a professor explore the website at adjunct .chronicle.com. The unfortunate reality of the academic job market is that a slim fraction of grad students will succeed, but the vast majority will not.

For me, learning these facts was enough to dissuade me from continuing on to the PhD I thought I would eventually obtain. I just couldn't risk investing more money and time in a degree that would very likely leave me exactly where I began—only older and broker.

Instead, I've been writing, researching, and doing communications work—i.e., trying to build on what I learned in my master's program without having to invest any more money or sacrifice any more opportunity costs to do so.

*

If you're considering going to graduate school—either because you want to make a go at becoming an academic or because you want to reenter the working world after school in some related field—then start thinking early about how to make best use of this time. Here are a few suggestions, based on my experience.

Make connections with professors. This goes for both graduate students and undergraduates. Professors are the people who can open doors for you in the future. They will write recommendation letters for you and introduce you to the people you need to know. Cultivating these relationships will be hugely important later in life.

Think seriously about job skills. Look, I don't want to sound like I'm advocating for education as a form of job training; obviously, education is much more than that. But I do think that graduate students should be mindful of their goals. If you are heading to grad school with the hope of eventually getting an academic job, then you should be cognizant of the steps you're taking to make that possible.

If you're not aiming for an academic job, think about how you might translate what you're learning into language that the outside world will understand. What does it mean to be a teaching assistant, to spend hours in the library conducting research, to write twenty-page argumentative analyses? What skills are you developing and how might they be useful in another career? If you're smart about it, you can learn to code-switch between academic speak and real-world speak, which will allow you to do what you want and to still sell yourself effectively outside of academia.

Seek out internships and volunteer opportunities. If I were starting over in graduate school right now, I would seek out internships. Even if you have to work for free (and unfortunately, this is often the case), nothing gives you a better shot at getting a job than work experience, and the flexible schedule of a student makes it easier to do this. Also, try to be deliberate about the kind of internship you pursue. If you land an internship at a local newspaper, you will be much more likely to get an editorial position after graduation. If you work as a research intern for a nonprofit, your chances of becoming a researcher or an analyst will dramatically increase.

Once you prove you can do the work, you're much less risky to prospective employers.

My own experience taught me these lessons the hard way. Learn from my mistakes, and be informed about your decisions. The key to getting the most out of grad school is to be intentional. Know why you're going, and have a plan—and maybe a couple contingency plans, too.

Amy Sillman

BETWEEN GETTING MY BFA and going back for my MFA, there was an eleven-year period when I worked in offices doing magazine production. My job was in "paste-up and mechanicals," a now-defunct procedure that prepared printed matter for the printer. The job was custom-made for bohemians: For one week a month, we rolled in at noon and worked all night long. They paid for our dinners, our breakfasts, and our cabs home, and in return we agreeably mocked the hands that fed us, smirking about how ridiculous magazines are; products destined for the recycling bin or the bathroom. Working in an office was genuinely mirthful and comradely, like being on a sitcom, and it's a good thing the job became obsolete, because I had a great time there and otherwise could easily have been lulled perversely into permanent office worker status, in which case I never would have bothered getting an MFA. But in 1990, the good times ended, because paste-ups went digital, and if you didn't want to stare at a screen all day, you had to make a new game plan.

I recall a co-worker at the time who whined at me: Did I think she should spend her last two hundred dollars on a class in computer graphics or just blow it on the rubber dress needed for a job as a dominatrix? Being a prude, I said go for the computers. She got the dress. Seems like it worked out okay for her, since I've seen her books at the art bookstore recently. But I took my two hundred dollars to MFA school, which I now realize is something like getting the rubber dress *and* learning the useful office skills.

I actually didn't get my MFA until after I had a teaching job. Fine art teaching jobs were easier to get back then, and you didn't really need an

MFA to get a position. Through my friend Rochelle Feinstein, I heard that a school needed someone as replacement faculty, and somehow I got the job—not because I was qualified or prepared (I was neither) but because I was friendlier than the other applicants. On the first day, a more experienced teacher rolled her eyes and warned me about the snake pit of intrafaculty politics. I was like, *You've gotta be kidding! I've been a paste-up worker for a decade! This shit is a walk in the park!* Then I tried to muster my authority face while nervous freshmen who had been assigned to work with me lined up for academic advising. What a joke! I didn't have the goods: I lacked the terminal degree myself. I was equally frightened by the other members of the faculty and the stern secretary who ran the office. After a few years of this slightly humiliating charade, I realized that I had to beef up my teaching status from *not one bit qualified* to *remotely prepared.*

So I checked out the programs at Yale and Hunter and Bard. (At the time I don't think Columbia had an MFA program going.) The Yale application asked why I wanted to go to Yale, and I realized that if I were honest, I would have to write that I wanted to go there because it was a famous school. My pride kicked in. What kind of bohemian was I, trying so hard to convince an Ivy League school that I was good enough for them? In a fit of self-pique, I threw the application away. In hindsight, this might have been a mistake, but Yale would have meant moving to New Haven and quitting my teaching job, and I felt like it was a little late for that then. Hunter was of interest, but it took four years if you went part-time, which seemed like an eternity. I considered CalArts out near Los Angeles, but it seemed like only beach-ready blondes belonged in L.A. So Bard College, where a filmmaker friend (Michael Gitlin) was going, seemed like the best choice. Plus, Bard operated only in the summer, so I could keep my teaching job and pay for it with that income. Also, Bard has an amazing interdisciplinary faculty of poets, experimental filmmakers, musicians, and painters, so it seemed like it would be cooler. Bard's MFA is different now from how it was back then—these days it's a highly regarded program with a sophisticated student body, average age about twenty-nine. Back when I went, it was a sleepier, less groovy place where people in their late thirties wearing clogs and braids squeezed MFAs into summer vacations. It was also fairly affordable—I think in the end I got my grandmother to pay for the first year, I paid the second year from my teaching salary, and I got a student loan for the third year.

Bard ended up being the most satisfying educational experience I ever had—though let's not blow things out of proportion, my educational history is checkered at best. In the three years I spent there, I learned how to talk about art convincingly enough, and I met a spectrum of life-affirming people who were more sophisticated than I was, more skeptical, more well-read, more insightful, more sensitive, more skillful, more worldly, and more focused. Among others, I also met many excellent art school types: a tiny woman who painted only eggs, a giant man who lurched into rages and drooled all over his sweater, an urbane kleptomaniac, a Turkish art star, an angry guy who dug a pit in the ground and lived there for a month copying out *Civilization and Its Discontents* with a Bic pen on a roll of toilet paper.

People ask me all the time if I think they should get an MFA nowadays. I guess it's not necessary, but it can make your life way more interesting. I ended up getting a job at Bard, where I still teach, and where probably 85 percent of my social life has originated. I don't think this would have happened unless I had gone there as a student, so it literally shaped my life. I am also drastically underpaid, but that wouldn't be any different if I *hadn't* gone to grad school. To aspiring artists, I would say that grad school is most often not a waste of time or money—even if it might be too expensive— and that you don't *have* to go. But what would be the reasons *not* to go? To save money? Well, for sure: No one should really urge you into tens of thousands of dollars of debt in order to pursue a questionable economic fate. But there are a few good grad schools with fantastic teachers that don't cost all that much. You just need to do your research.

(Caveat: I don't think you should go to *any old* MFA school. You need to find out which schools are good *at the moment*. Schools change, and that will directly impact the experience of attending one. So when you're looking at grad schools, find out if changes are happening in the administration or if there's a new hire going on and wait and see who gets the job before you try to go to that school. Don't read or believe in lists of "top schools."

Nothing is eternal. There are always only about two or three places that are actually worth the time and money. Ask the faculty and recent alumni if they like the school.)

As for the skepticism about MFA programs, it is a paranoid fantasy that all MFA programs are just puppy mills for professionalization. There are plenty of hacks and professionalized creeps who didn't go to grad school. I would honestly say that the two big drawbacks—money and overprofessionalization—do not outweigh the possibility that MFA school will enrich your intellectual life, provide you with the time to think more clearly about your work, and offer the chance to be prompted, challenged, and even productively annoyed by crazy visiting artists and other insightful weirdos who can pitch some great questions and observations at your work.

I really don't think that there are many places in the world that approximate the expansive luxury of art school. Where else will this kind of focused critical attention occur in your life? Are there jobs or communes or reading groups or roommate situations where you are going to be plied with questions, prompted, challenged, given information, annoyed, pestered, informed, needled, called out, or generally provided with concentrated input specifically about your work? If you find such a place, you don't need grad school. But the odds are that you will find a more challenging and more constructive lineup of people and opinions at grad school, and if nothing else, that could be fun. And you will learn about institutions, which will always be helpful for institutional critique.

Rhonda Lieberman

NIETZSCHE SAID THAT SICKNESS is a perspective on health, and vice versa. So what from one point of view is an "education," is from another the depravity of spending the bloom of youth in a PhD program in the humanities while the job market is going into the shitter.

I'm going to a very dangerous place. I may actually have a breakdown. Psychoanalysis says you get cured by remembering. But I was actually cured by forgetting all this . . .

Grad school is one of those awkward stages it's considered unseemly to dwell upon. You just want to get through and forget it—like passing a stone. For those getting a PhD in the humanities, this unspeakable state lasts for an average of seven years (a protracted period of financial infantilization long enough to gestate an elephant; debt accrues, youth curdles, and you eventually learn to hate what you loved) and then, thanks to the corporatized university and the buyer's market for PhDs, it goes on for good!

On jury duty, they ask for your highest degree. I put ABD, which is the truth, but like *Fight Club* nobody knows what that is unless you've been there. It stands for All But Dissertation (some jest: All But Dead), and it means that you've gone through all the discomfort and inconvenience of becoming a doctoral candidate—the course work, the orals, the debt, the indignities, even the dissertation prospectus—but you never wrote the

Horrid Thing. It's like going through the disfigurement and retching of pregnancy, the nausea, the stretch marks—in this case mental—only to start labor and say, "You know what? Never mind."

After years—and years—of therapy, I'm at peace with this.

Yet like a tic, whenever the ABD thing comes up, I feel like the Ancient Mariner, compelled to plague my unwitting trigger with way more than they wanted to hear about the dead albatross that hangs around my neck: my sordid past in academia. In the jury box at the voir dire, I imagine the judge asking, "Ms. Lieberman, what is ABD? . . ."

Inaudible.

Then, "Why didn't you finish your dissertation?"

"Well, Your Honor," I'd regress, babbling something about Derrida, "I must explain myself to the court . . ." The courtroom is filled with good people rolling their eyes at the freak . . .

I was a bookish child. "Stop hiding your face in a book," my mother would scold. "Don't you have any friends?" She was worried I wouldn't meet a husband. I was highly stimulated by the Finkelstein Memorial Library. Something about the aging paper and glue really turned me on. In high school, I fell in with a posse of anxious, overachieving Jews who "wanted to get into a good school." I was in the modern dance club. For our senior recital—"Transitions"—I did an interpretative dance to "Dark Side of the Moon." I couldn't wait to get to the ivory tower, where I would transcend the inherent meaninglessness of my suburban existence: I'd major in Truth and Beauty!

College was an idyll. My professors followed their respective muses and shared their insights with us ephebes. We coveted their lot, which mingled the "life of the mind" with a modicum of security and tweedy dignity. What could go wrong?

I applied to grad school during the heyday of theory: Écriture was an orgy of intertextuality; reading was writing, writing was reading, the world was a text to be de-coded. To read was to bravely insert yourself into cultural contradictions, demystify everything, and speak truth to power! Right on.

But by the time I got there, the party was over: There was a backlash against theory. And worse, the tenure-track jobs that were supposed to open up when the "Baby Boomers retire" didn't. This mythical event, like the coming of the Messiah, would open the heavens and shower the chosen people wandering in the desert with tenure-track jobs. Instead, the decent gigs were replaced by adjuncts: 70 percent of university teaching is now done by adjuncts, contingent labor with no job security or benefits. What was shabby chic in one's twenties was just plain shabby for the foreseeable future.

A few years into grad school at the wedding of a mutual friend, a college pal—a wildly successful interior decorator—was telling his father what a "genius" I was.

The father said, "Seven years for a PhD? If I were your parent I'd kill myself!"

I went to a gynecologist around that time. With his finger on my cervix and unflinching eye contact, he told me he had been a philosophy major at Harvard: "But my grandfather said, 'Whaddaya gonna do, open a philosophy store?'"

Stubbornly devoted to the life of the mind, I was used to dismissing such feedback.

Instead of directing their surplus rage toward the system, academics traditionally aimed at each other. In an old notebook labeled ACADEMIC HORROR SHOW, I found scribbled:

The sick thing about academics is they get put through the ringer during an expensive and protracted apprenticeship, and when they reach their professional "maturity"—which is really a prolonged adolescence since it is so financially infantilizing to be paid the pittance they are paid—the only way left for them to feel their "power" (since they can't hike up the rates for their services)—and thus to feel compensated for their pain—is to shut other people down. Ugh!

Foucault said, "Power is everywhere." And these people had none of it!

Many PhD candidates were ruined for years: Too bewildered and exhausted to leave, they were worked over and deformed by the system, their very identities addled by the reverse coping skills they cultivated in grad school. Like cult members, they saw escape from the Academy as failure.

Among the reverse coping skills required to survive in such a perverse environment is the ability to master the dark art of academic prose. To spend months and years on writing so specialized that only seven gatekeepers could validate it—five of whom would have "doubts" and another who would be "on leave." Rot that would repel any reader with a healthy sensibility was passable fare for the depraved palate of the Cult. To academically kosher a text, one was trained to cultivate the passive voice, offer no point of view, and observe the three golden rules of academic writing: (1) announce what you are going to say before you say it, (2) point out what you're saying while you're saying it, (3) summarize the points you've just said, all the while being careful to throw pseudo-light on nonproblems while projecting an air of being convinced of (their) usefulness and significance, thus lulling the reader into such a state of cognitive dissonance they are too dazed to challenge you.

Another reverse coping skill: disdaining any work outside the Academy as not serious. This creates a big stumbling block for deprogramming.

And the most insidious of all: working for free "because you love it." Giving away your time, energy, and ideas with a misguided sense of altruism and no healthy boundaries to speak of.

All of these reverse coping skills—painfully acquired over years—equip the candidate with the survival chops of a deaf and blind kitten and significantly hobble the process of re-integrating into society.

It was a dark time.

By the mid-'80s it was clear what was coming. We had "blown our youth" being professionalized for a job market in the process of dismantling itself: At the time, they called it the "jobs crisis," and it's still going strong. I was the Norma Rae of Yale. I came to consciousness of my material conditions as academic labor and started the movement to organize the teaching assistants into a union. I rabble-roused—"A specter is haunting Yale! The specter of TA solidarity!'—like Barbra Streisand in *The Way We Were*. I picketed my MA graduation ceremony: "A penny for my thoughts." This was 1985. The Yale TAs are still trying to get recognized as a union.

I was delivered from grad school purgatory when I landed a full-time teaching job with awful pay at the prestigious School of the Art Toilet of Ill-Annoy. I taught courses like Proust and *I Love Lucy*, Trauma and Pleasure, and Paranoid Thought (where one assignment was for everyone to stalk someone else in the class), and I advised grad students for slightly more than I was making as a TA, but I was "doing what I loved."

The dean of the college saw herself as a PC earth mother; she fetishized South Africa and penned a pamphlet about "The Artist's Responsibility to Society" as she nickel-and-dimed faculty. She had an armful of bracelets, a frizzy halo, and the demeanor of a harried Stevie Nicks.

When I first got there, she wanted to bond as two transplanted New York gals. She never picked up the tab at restaurants and she knew I was making next to bubkes. I recall one hideous lunch when she trotted me over to a rich collector's as if presenting a new geisha to *ooh* and *aah* over his stash, which was considerable. He had all the superpricey Germans: a whopping Kiefer series inspired by bombings of World War II, a Gerhard Richter, a wall of August Sander photos decorator-installed on Fortuny paisley silk. He had Jeff Koons's *Michael Jackson and Bubbles*. It went on and on.

(The Moneybags residence was a taupe fortress, all about polished woods and beige and velvety surfaces tastefully enveloping us in the hushed earthiness of wealth. Weird to take all this in with Stevie Nicks.)

As I admired a *Madonna and Child* on his stairwell, the collector quipped, "I'm going medieval. I checked it out with one of my mavens at the U of C . . ."

"Your maven?" I said. "Did you hire him?"

Awkward silence.

He was referring to the chair of the history department. The collector clearly saw scholars as courtiers whose real position was to reflect the greater glory of his hoard.

The corporatized university of the '90s brought the advent of the newly entitled student-consumer. As schools marketed themselves like luxury cruises, administrators emboldened clients to see faculty as part nanny— selflessly servicing the student-consumers like Julie Andrews in *The Sound of Music*—and part happy pedagogical hooker.

One time I took off a week to lecture in L.A. I scheduled makeup classes for all my students. I came back to a mysterious message on my machine from a colleague: "I don't think it was very nice what they left on your door." I was puzzled.

When I arrived at school the next day, there was an installation of xeroxed papers covering the door to my office cubicle from an irate student who had calculated the amount of money I "owed" him, based on the tuition he paid, because of our missed appointment. "I was here prepared to show you work, with my slide projector," it accused, "and you weren't here for the second time. According to my annual tuition of $25,000 (incl. housing) you owe me approx. $741 dollars for 2 meetings, etc." He was docking me! It was a degrading display that my esteemed colleagues walked past every day for a week and no one saw fit to take down. Like an academic version of *The Scarlet Letter*: I was Hester Prynne meets Rodney Dangerfield. For the record, I had nice students, too.

Four years into my ordeal at the Art Toilet I made an appointment with a vice dean to appeal to him for a raise: I was teaching a full load, as they tellingly call it, and I was active in my field—good publicity for the Toilet.

The vice dean smiled at me in a patronizing manner and told me about his wife who "travels to three different schools all over town where she teaches part-time" and made even less than I did. I took this remark for what it clearly was: evidence that his wife was a complete idiot. "Sometimes you have to make sacrifices to work in the arts," he shamelessly added. "Sometimes you have to eat Spam," he actually said to my face.

The last straw came after I moved back to New York for a visiting appointment: My departmental mailbox was too high for me to reach, so to get my mail, I had to jump and grab—like a chimp—while looking furtively over my shoulder to see if the occasional student or colleague caught a glimpse of me in this undignified act.

When it comes to education, one would rather savor the sausage and not think too much about the factory. After years—and years—of therapy, one can take the high road (like I'm doing right now!). But I still ask you: Who will write the academic *Grapes of Wrath*?

Of course, middle-class jobs are collapsing all around us. Job security and benefits have gone the way of Joan Rivers's original face. But only in academia do people undergo this insanely protracted apprenticeship—pissing away their youth, going into debt, cultivating specialized skills and values that hobble their viability outside the Cult (as they provide the cheap teaching labor that props up the system!)—all to prepare for a profession that has hollowed itself out into a factory farm for mental burger flippers. And the system continues to exploit, extracting maximum value from the oversupply of Cult members who still cling to their Ideals and continue to give their best under terrible conditions. Just remember this: Academia eats its young!

David Velasco

"So last year, we all signed a card for Derrida, which was sort of just a gesture of how much we appreciated having him here and his teaching. So this year we have a card again, and there are some instructions." The girl holds up a piece of paper. "We only want to write inside these beige parts. They feel a little . . . The texture's like linen—and I have an ink pen that you should use to sign it with. Just whatever you'd want to write. So I'm going to leave this over by the windowsill with the pen, and whoever wants to write on it . . . You can see sort of anywhere on the beige part takes the ink."

"Thank you," Avital says from the lectern. "That's very thoughtful." We're in a large, third-floor classroom off University Place. Windows overlook the Deutsches Haus. If you crane your neck, there's Washington Square Park. "We are dealing with postcards and letters. From the father, we're reading today. Thank you for your interventions, which I'm still considering and looking at. And the current you had in talking last week." It rains outside.

"So here's a citation from Kathy Acker," Avital continues. "*Great Expectations.* 'I have no idea how to begin to forgive someone, much less my mother.' So we'll keep that in mind. I want to report that one of my scholarly instincts was confirmed today, because I was stuck on the very first word—it is the very first word—of the *Letter to His Father.* What would that first word be? What is the first word?"

"*Liebste*," a girl whispers next to me.

"Liebste," Avital says. "*Dearest*. And I thought, well how many weeks did it take him to decide on that? And why that? And by the way, it was exactly today, 1919, that Kafka sat down to begin the *Letter to His Father*. November tenth to thirteenth. *Liebste Vater*. Dearest father. I thought, what a strange decision. What a necessary—what a jokey decision. What a grammatically already betraying decision, to the extent that strictly speaking—I believe, I don't know if you'll agree with me"—who wouldn't?—"that this already indicates that there is a split. If you are the *dearest*, then there are others . . . perhaps. It's not even comparative. There's dear father. Dearer father. And dearest father, of three possible fathers, or two other possible fathers. So *dearest* father. Don't forget that he's going to indicate that there are three worlds. That there is perhaps already in this *liebste*, dearest, already a split and an intervention into the unicity that patriarchy—the great ür, the original father—might be able to secure for himself. Let's just bear that in mind. This is already a perverse reading. If you have any questions, raise those things . . . hands, or antennae, or whatever you'd like to raise. You will do so."

Gentle laughter.

"So at the moment of the greatest salutation, of the most loving embrace, there's already the possibility there are, grammatically, that there's, um, let's say, a destruction of the singularity of the addressee. Possibly, possibly. *Dearest* father. So the one that I'm addressing now is the dearest of the fathers. So is it already not *the* father? Or is it already the father who is not the guilty father? And it begins as a kind of response, right? 'Du hast mich letzthin einmal gefragt . . .' so 'You asked me, recently . . . you asked me, recently, why I maintain that I'm afraid of you.'"

Our books out, we are practically glowing with earnest intent.

"So this is an answer," she continues. "One that responds to a prior inquiry. Maybe another letter. 'And . . . I wasn't able to answer you in speech, because you freak me out. I stutter. I can't speak when I'm with you. I'm trembling. I have no hold on language. Your hold on me is so powerful that I can't utter a word. So I'm going to try to answer you in writing. Dir schriftlich . . .' I'm going to try to respond to you in writing, but I'm also terrorized in writing, and the greatness—the *Größe*—the greatness—now don't forget that he's going to say time and time again that the father is the measure of all things. The magnitude of the subject goes far beyond the scope of my memory or power of reasoning. So writing is not on the side of memory, reasoning, power. These are kind of little cat scrawls, scratches—stuttering *écriture*. I say *cat* because he's going to say he's more of a Löwy than a Kafka. He's more of his mother's lioness side, but a little baby cat writer. He's not *even* a Kafka. And everything will have to do with the name Kafka, and the scandal that he brings to this name: Kafka."

AR owns the room.

"The pivot will be in terms of—if we could reduce something to it— marriage. 'So I'm you're freaky queer little son, I can't get married, I want to get married, you won't let me get married, you're making me get married. I can't do it, I must do it.' In this sense, the marriage contract that he tries to pass with the father and through the father becomes the crucial . . . *differend*, let's say."

She's got great style. The Lyotard—we're all grateful for that one.

"The marriage is forbidden by the father in the name of the father, in the father's name. Little Franz came up with this last marriage idea. But the father said, 'Are you kidding? You're going to marry this, more or less janitor's wife? I don't think so. That'll stain my name. That'll bring dishonor to my name.' Which remains his name. So Kafka can't even fit in the name of the father. He can't even inhabit this name, Kafka. This would be something to consider in our ongoing reflections because he's, in a sense, on one level—there are many things we're going to ask. What is he asking for forgiveness for? Or who's asking? What kind of text is this? All things we're going to have to raise here."

Coughing. Ernest coughing.

ERNEST: Can we—

AR: Yes. Could you hold on to that intervention for a little while longer? We're going to have more time for that later.

ERNEST: WELL, it's already been a while. Can we talk?

AR: [pause] No. I don't know if that's possible. Not really.

ERNEST: Okay, you're right. I mean, insofar as we're never really occupying the same time as the other, not really. [*cough:* Levinas] But anyway, I'm from the future, just dropping by.

AR: I wish I could say I was expecting you, but I wasn't. I guess this gives you the advantage, except that I imagine that the atmosphere is a bit thin up there. The consequence of our continual hollowing out of futurity.

ERNEST: Yeah, the air sucks. And language has really meandered off the path of grace even since I was in this class. I don't think we had iPhones or Twitter or Facebook or Instagram or any of the other *techne* both attenuating and multiplying discourse. I recorded all these lectures on a Sony MiniDisc player. You can't even recuperate that into nostalgia cool, the shit's so forgotten. I was pretty sure I wouldn't be able to access those old discs, the batteries for the player were literally rotting in the case. But I guess Sony makes things to last. #throwbackthursday. Wait, have you heard of hashtags?

AR: Kid, you know that language has been disembodying itself since long before cybertext and electronic *écriture*. I've tapped the hashtag. It's right next to the zero on a touchtone. But I gather it's now the stock culprit for indexing "experience," for skidding meaning into the long spreadsheet of "social media."

ERNEST: Yeah, I guess you would have anticipated that.

AR: I wrote the book on switchboard transference and umbilical logics.

ERNEST: Yeah, yeah. Okay.

AR: And virtual reality. Don't even get me started on virtual reality.

ERNEST: I won't! No really, I came back to give you an update, and also to warn you.

AR: This should be interesting.

ERNEST: It's not really. Warnings always come too late. Or when you hear them "in time," fate shows up to kick your ass anyway. I learned that from the Greeks, and *Final Destination*. All Cassandras are really narcissists. But I thought you should know that that the art world will eventually swallow not just the underground but academia and probably everything else besides.

AR: Well la-di-da.

ERNEST: You don't sound excited.

AR: You're here to fill *me* in on the obsolescence of the academy?

ERNEST: Well no, it's not so much about obsolescence. I'm talking about an opportunity.

AR: So you're trying to sell me something. Because . . .

ERNEST: Avon calling! But seriously. This classroom we're in right now? It's the temple of doom. Sentimental reflexivities, a nostalgic shoring up of the canon in the name of its destabilization, the rise of the adjunct professor class, the collapse of tenure. The economy's wretched. I mean the readings are great, my mind's blown, but hello! Have you seen your students' loans?

AR: You're preaching to the preacher.

ERNEST: I always thought I was the choir. But I'm here to say that most of your real disciples these days are off frolicking and stirring up trouble in the damnable provinces of the art world, either trying to prompt stutterings in the system or enrolling in media training and learning to regurgitate theory as PR. Now *that's* capitalist alchemy. Art capitalizes on deflated "thinking" qua epic misreadings of still fashionable Frenchies like Deleuze, Derrida,

Rancière. Or maybe they're the best readings because they're the most exploitative, the most bang for the buck.

AR: You sound like an ad man for e-flux.

ERNEST: *Liebste*, if I were that enterprising, I'd have paid off my loans by now. But I think Obama is the only person who's actually made good on his, and he was practically president by the time he did. I heard a rumor that Sallie Mae and her sister Fannie had some wild, molly-fueled ménage-à-trois with him one night in the early 2000s, and that ever since they've been cutting one another slack. Who says politics is bankrupt?

AR: Who's Obama? And you're saying I should leave the academy . . .

ERNEST: And become a curator! Or do Buchloh one better and become an art dealer. Monetize your lucubrations, make a deal with *Denken*. Game the system. Plug "undecidability" into the algorithm for derivatives. Let's really hedge the hedge fund. Forget the European Graduate School and install an Annabelle Selldorf–designed pop-up on West Twenty-Fourth Street. After, you could direct Documenta, top the *Art Shillers* Power 100 list.

AR: Look kid, you may think you're clever coming in here and interrupting my class to blow off some steam about grad school wretchedness, but you can't be serious about the art world. Great waterfront real estate, some good design, even some occasionally complicated itineraries of thinking. But do you really think that it's where you can secure a sheltering space of unconditional hospitality for dissidence and insurrection? Can you still rattle the structure of the art world? Or are you simply shaking it for spare change? You've got another thing coming.

ERNEST: Have it your way. I really just wanted to pop in to say thanks. No really, for everything. I wouldn't be where I am today if it weren't for you. [AR rolls her eyes.] You made my thinking fly. I don't regret a penny of it. But I've gotta run. The art world institutes multiple registers of being, and

I'm on my way to a twenty-four-hour marathon party for "Faena Miami Beach: A Cultural Renaissance," hosted by Baz Luhrmann and Catherine David with a Q&A after by Hans-Ulrich Obrist. Billy Farrell and Patrick McMullan have agreed to set aside their differences for this singular occasion and co-photograph the event. It'll be one seamless documentation, all in 3-D. Awesome.

AR: Sayonara, babe. Don't do anything I wouldn't do.

James Franco

GRADUATE SCHOOLS. I'VE BEEN to a few. They're funny. Each one is different, obviously. Most of the programs I went to were MFAs. I went for fiction—twice—I went for film, I went for poetry, and I went for art. I went because I had spent years as a professional actor and as a mature student of everything else; I wanted to treat my other interests with as much seriousness as I did my acting. Since at one point I had been a mature actor who worked hard and became a professional, I thought I could do the same thing with other fields. Here are a few observations I've made over the course of six years of grad school at six different programs.

With regard to fiction programs, the first thing to consider is that most of the students (if not on scholarship) are paying anywhere from $20,000 to $40,000 a year to learn a profession that isn't going to pay off soon, even if they do get a book deal right after school. The second thing to consider is that writing is a solitary activity, so you shouldn't expect much collaboration with your peers. After classes, students go home and write stories so they can bring them to class to be workshopped. While workshops get criticized a lot, they do allow one's writing to be read critically and talked about. Even if the feedback is worthless, a writer's work changes if the writer knows that it is going to be read.

Film programs, on the other hand, are collaborative: All students work on each other's films. Everyone rotates roles: In one production you're the director, in another you're the cinematographer, in another you're the boom operator. This makes each person invested in his or her classmates' work, unlike in writing programs, where the writer stands alone. In those programs, classmates give each other what is ostensibly constructive criticism, but the situation is still basically one against all.

I'm not saying that writing students are weird, but maybe I am.

Art school is different. It's more like film school. There is more collaboration in art school than in writing programs, though the projects are less structured. It's harder for people to criticize each other along conventional lines because the art world has shattered into so many different kinds of practices. Because writing and narrative film programs usually teach traditional approaches, those programs have firmer criteria for what is "working" and what isn't.

All my teachers have been great. In every program, but especially in the writing programs. There were a few crazy teachers, but they weren't so bad, either.

The great thing about going to a writing program is that most writers teach to supplement their income. So the best authors are usually also teachers. And having Gary Shteyngart or Ben Marcus or Michael Cunningham or Tony Hoagland or Robert Boswell or Amy Hempel or David Shields or James Wood or Jonathan Lethem as a teacher is like acting in a film directed by Gus Van Sant or Danny Boyle or Sam Raimi or Harmony Korine.

In general, if you are in a program that is funded, like a PhD program, everyone is more pleasant. Students don't worry about money in the same way that MA students do, and they know that they're superstars in their subject because they have been chosen over many others and are being supported by the school.

If anything, the best thing about graduate school is that it's a place where the things you consider sacred are also considered sacred by the people around you. There is a lot of love and hate in graduate programs, but at least I've gotten to be with people who speak my language.

Sheila Heti

THIS INTERVIEW WAS CONDUCTED BY JESSICA LOUDIS.

SHEILA HETI: Why are you so interested in MFAs and whether they're a good idea or not?

JESSICA LOUDIS: Well, it's not that I'm interested in MFAs so much as I'm interested in grad school in general, and what it can mean to people who don't know instinctively that they want to be an academic or teach. After getting out of college, I assumed that I would eventually go into a PhD program, but thought that I needed to spend at least a year doing something else first before applying. (This despite the fact that I had no idea what kind of program I wanted to apply to at the time). When that never happened, I started to think about how people regard doctoral programs as a kind of insurance policy; a way of guaranteeing that they will be able to read and think about the things they care about, at least for a few years. Of course, getting a PhD is often very restricting in a practical sense—few job opportunities, committing yourself to a lifelong form of hyperspecialized job training—but it's still a hard set of notions to shake. When I first started thinking about this, and about other kinds of programs, I realized that a lot of people project these sorts of fantasies onto grad school and think of it as a way of trying to reconcile the person they are with the person they might want to be. So to answer your question, I'm interested in how asking people about their relationship to grad school is a way of asking them about their expectations for themselves at a certain point in their lives. It's one of those questions that people tend to react very strongly to.

What about you? What's your educational background, and did you ever think about going to grad school?

SH: I never thought about it. It's really strange for me to read this. It's like you're talking about a handsome, magnetic person who I don't find handsome or magnetic at all. Grad school has no allure for me, never has. I waited a while before going to university—I didn't go till I was twenty-one, and I wasn't even sure I would go—but it was a fantastic experience. I studied art history and philosophy and took economics and political science classes. I just took whatever I wanted and I didn't worry about grades and I read and learned a lot, and I didn't have much of a social life, so it was deeply absorbing. But I feel like one can have all of that as a writer; you're writing, you're reading, you're talking to interesting and intelligent people. Your life is structured around whatever book you're writing, and so is your reading and so are many of your conversations. So for me, grad school has never had much meaning or allure. As well, I have known a lot of people in grad school and no one seems very happy about it.

JL: So in lieu of school, how do you organize your life around writing a book?

SH: Well, if you're working on a book, the book poses a bunch of questions. Maybe it's (in the case of my second book, Ticknor) "What were the early birth control pioneers like?" or "What was Florence Nightingale all about?" Most of your curiosities don't even make it into the book, but you think they will. Moments come where you have to find out about something or you can't go on. So you start reading in that area (Havelock Ellis, Marie Stopes) and you take in the stuff at a really deep level because your need to know it is at once mysterious (why is Marie Stopes so important to you right now?) and really practical (it might help you finish a scene). I guess the main difference is that you are led down reading paths as you go, rather than coming up with a reading list at the start. And it's always changing. Then, in terms of how your life is organized around a book, it's a question of what kind of person you have to be in order to write that book. Do you need to be married, single, traveling, asking questions of other people, alone in your room? What kind of person does the book demand it be written by? You have to become that person.

What else do think you could get out of school that you can't get out of your life now? When we last spoke, you mentioned friendships and mentoring. I like what Eileen Myles said about mentoring—that she prefers "parallel" to "hierarchical" mentoring; that is, learning from one's friends and peers, rather than from more successful, established people. I agree.

JL: A big thing is built-in structure. The idea of parallel mentoring is appealing—though I'm not sure it's an either/or situation—but the reality is, it takes a while to find your peers, and school can be a way of expediting that process. One point that several of our contributors have made is that going into a PhD or MFA program is valuable for the socialization process—either because you find the people who speak your language or because you react strongly to the weirdos you're working with. You seem to have known from early on that you wanted to be a writer, but how did you find the people you wanted to learn from when you were starting out?

SH: I didn't find the people I wanted to learn from until my midtwenties. Before that, I was pretty much alone. I didn't make friends as an undergrad. And though I attended theater school for playwriting before university (after taking a break after high school), even though my program was small (only three other people), I didn't have that collaborative or learning feeling with any of them. (Wait—I'm just now remembering; my boyfriend at the time was in the directing program, and we learned a lot from each other, smoking pot and living together and talking about art and working on an adaptation of Faust.) But when it began to happen on a broader, community level—it was a pretty deliberate choice. I wasn't searching for parallel mentorship, but I was definitely searching for people I could talk to in certain ways and be with in ways that had more to do with art than, I don't know, gossip. Even though gossip is a big part of art! My then-boyfriend (later husband, later ex-husband) Carl Wilson and I began having parties every two weeks. And I started Trampoline Hall (a monthly barroom lecture series), and he had a music show called Tin Tin Tin, and for a few years we were just building this world of people around us. Anytime I met anyone I liked, I would invite them to our parties or to lecture at Trampoline Hall.

We did it because we were bored. We didn't know what to do with ourselves. I remember telling my grandmother about our isolation, and she said, "Have regular parties at your house." I think that's how she and her mostly Jewish, communist, artist friends socialized back in Budapest. She told me what to do, and we did it, and she was right. God, I owe a lot to my grandmother.

It was the regularity of contact that was important—she was right. We threw four events a month, not to mention the times we'd see people at other events. So after a few years, we had gathered a pretty solid group of friends. It took a lot of time, and you often ended up socializing when you don't want to. But it taught me how to have conversations, how to find people, how to work with people who are your friends, and how to turn friendships into working things. I'm just realizing for the first time what an education it was. I think making friends you can work with is a skill like any other; developing those particular kinds of intimacies. They're intimacies like any other, but they grow in a definite direction, not just willy-nilly, like normal friendships. I can't imagine school as having been a satisfying substitute for me. You'd only meet people in your program, and the nice thing about our world was that everyone was doing different things.

How did you go about finding your people?

JL: I guess just by going to talks, to panels, to parties, and by trying to pay attention to the people I met who I wanted to keep around. Your idea of working friendships sounds a little like a version of networking (a truly noxious term) but fundamentally different—more about figuring out yourself in the context of others and learning to identify certain qualities that matter to you. Could you talk a little more about what you mean by it, and how it's happened for you?

SH: Oh god, not networking. I mean something closer to love. Like, who are the people who I art-love? That means admire and want to share my brain with and make part of my brain. It's not like there are a thousand people I can have this ongoing sort of relationship with, as with networking. There are a dozen? Maybe dozens? It's like having boyfriends, except instead of things lasting six months or a year and then you break up, it lasts indefinitely and it's not exclusive and it's less concentrated. I'm in a monogamous relationship, so I can't keep having boyfriends, and I have this instead—with men *and* women. It's better. Instead of having sex, we have art.

JL: It seems like your writerly and intellectual patterns are deeply bound up with friendships, yet you say that you were somewhat reclusive until your midtwenties. What changed at that point?

SH: I suppose I fell in love with Carl. I remember thinking around that time, "Well, now I'm ruined. Now I'll never be able to be alone again." I saw what was wonderful about human companionship. Before that, I was quite content to be alone, to be a solitary wandering person, and I thought I always would be. Love changed that. I mean, I still have my solitary wanderings, but there's that additional dimension to my life, which is love of other people and collaboration and togetherness. It seems crazy to think there was a before and after with something so basic, but, what can I say, there was.

Acknowledgments

PUTTING TOGETHER AN ANTHOLOGY—PARTICULARLY one with this many writers—is a collaborative effort in many ways, and there are a number of people who deserve recognition and praise. First and foremost, we'd like to thank our wonderful contributors, many of whom agreed to write when the book was still in the very early stages, and all of whom have been incredibly supportive and generous throughout the process. For their help shepherding the book from these early stages to publication—and for their wonderful comments—we thank Pete Beatty and Rachel Mannheimer, and our incomparable agent, Mel Flashman, whose insight, patience, and excellent feedback made everything possible. For recommending a number of the contributors in this book, our thanks go out to Jeremy Faust, Claire Lehmann, Kelly Burdick, Emily Greenhouse, and in particular, Mark Greif and Dushko Petrovich. For their excellent and incisive editorial feedback, we are indebted to Benjamin Hart, Maggie Doherty, David Golding, Abigail Deutsch, and Rachel Nolan. And finally, endless thanks to our families and teachers.

About the Contributors

David Auerbach is a writer and software engineer living in New York. He has written for the *Times Literary Supplement*, n+1, *Bookforum*, *Triple Canopy*, and elsewhere. He has coded for Google and Microsoft. He writes at waggish.org.

Nancy Bauer is a professor of philosophy and dean of academic affairs for arts and sciences at Tufts University. She writes about the social value of professional philosophy and is the author, most recently, of *How to Do Things with Pornography*.

Josh Boldt is a writer and editor in Athens, Georgia. He teaches at the University of Georgia and is the founder of the Adjunct Project.

Stephen Burt is a professor of English at Harvard and the author of several books of literary criticism and poetry, among them *Belmont*, *Close Calls with Nonsense*, and *The Forms of Youth: 20th Century Poetry and Adolescence*.

Terry Castle, a writer and literary critic, has taught at Stanford University since 1983. She has published eight books, including *Masquerade and Civilization*, *The Apparitional Lesbian*, and the prizewinning collection *The Literature of Lesbianism: A Historical Anthology from Ariosto to Stonewall*. She is also a well-known essayist and has written frequently for the *London Review of Books*, the *Atlantic*, *Slate*, the *New Republic*, the *Times Literary Supplement*, and the *New York Review of*

Books. Her most recent book, *The Professor and Other Writings*, was a finalist for the National Book Critics Circle Award.

Peter Coviello is a professor of English at Bowdoin College. He is the editor of Walt Whitman's *Memoranda During the War* and the author of *Intimacy in America: Dreams of Affiliation in Antebellum Literature* and *Tomorrow's Parties: Sex and the Untimely in Nineteenth-Century America*. His work has appeared in *PMLA*, *American Literature*, *ELH*, *GLQ*, and *Raritan* as well as in magazines like *Frieze* and the *Believer*.

Meehan Crist is writer in residence in biological sciences at Columbia University. Previously, she was reviews editor at the *Believer*. Her work has appeared in publications such as the *New York Times*, the *Los Angeles Times*, the *New Republic*, *Scientific American*, and *Science*. She is a founding member of NeuWrite, a collaborative working group for scientists and writers, and she is currently working on a nonfiction book about traumatic brain injury.

Simon Critchley is Hans Jonas Professor of Philosophy at the New School for Social Research. He also teaches at the European Graduate School. His many books include *Very Little . . . Almost Nothing*, *Infinitely Demanding*, and, with Tom McCarthy, *The Mattering of Matter: Documents from the Archive of the International Necronautical Society*. A new work on *Hamlet* titled *Stay, Illusion!* coauthored with Jamieson Webster, was published in 2013. He is series moderator of "The Stone," a philosophy column in the *New York Times*, to which he is also a frequent contributor.

James Franco began his acting career in 1999 with the NBC series *Freaks and Geeks*, and he is best known for his roles in *Spider-Man*, *127 Hours*, and *Oz the Great and Powerful*. He has directed, written, and produced films for more than a decade including *Sal*, a feature film about actor Sal Mineo, and literary adaptations of William Faulkner's *As I Lay Dying* and Cormac McCarthy's *Child of God*. Aside from his film career, Franco has attended UCLA, NYU, Columbia University, RISD, Warren Wilson College, and Yale, and he currently teaches graduate film and writing courses at

UCLA, USC, and CalArts. His first novel, *Actors Anonymous*, was published in 2013, and he made his Broadway debut in a rendition of *Of Mice and Men* in 2014.

Andrea Fraser is an artist whose work has been identified with performance and institutional critique. The Museum Ludwig in Cologne, Germany, presented a retrospective of her work in 2013, in conjunction with her receipt of the Wolfgang Hahn Prize. She is a professor of new genres in the Department of Art at UCLA.

Kenneth Goldsmith is a poet living in New York City and the founder of the online avant-garde archive *UbuWeb*. He teaches poetics and poetic practice at the University of Pennsylvania.

Jake Heggie is the composer of the acclaimed operas *Moby-Dick*, *Dead Man Walking*, and *Three Decembers* as well as more than 250 art songs, chamber, choral, and orchestral works. As a pianist, he can sometimes be heard in recital with singers Frederica von Stade, Joyce DiDonato, Susan Graham, and others. Heggie also coaches young singers, composers, and pianists internationally. He makes his home in San Francisco.

Sheila Heti is the author of five books, most recently the novel *How Should a Person Be?* Her work has been published in the *London Review of Books*, *n+1*, *Harper's*, the *New York Times*, and the *Believer*. She lives in Toronto.

Lili Holzer-Glier is a photographer and journalist based in New York City. She received her BFA in photography and imaging from NYU's Tisch School of the Arts and her MS in digital media from the Columbia University Graduate School of Journalism. Her work has appeared in *Newsday*, the *New York Times*, *Quartz*, the *New Yorker*, *Thirteen*, and the *Huffington Post*.

Lucy Ives is the author of two books of poetry, *Orange Roses* and *Anamnesis*, and a brief novel, *Nineties*. A deputy editor at *Triple Canopy*, she lives in New York, where she is completing a PhD in comparative literature at NYU.

Eben Klemm is a founder and partner of the food and beverage consultancy Cane & Maple. He has invented cocktails and written wine lists for Ace Hotel, the Starr Restaurant Organization, and the Marcus Samuelsson Group, and his creations have been published in the *New York Times*, *Food & Wine*, and other dining publications. A resident of Fort Greene, Brooklyn, his book *The Cocktail Primer* was published in 2009.

David Levine is an artist living in New York and Berlin. He dropped out of a PhD program in English literature. He is the director of the studio program at Bard College, Berlin, where he is (cough) a professor.

Rhonda Lieberman is a contributing editor at *Artforum*. She has written for *Bookforum*, the *Baffler*, the *Paris Review Daily*, the *New York Times'* T *Magazine*, the *Village Voice*, and *Spin*. She has taught at the Yale School of Art, the School of the Art Institute of Chicago, Mason Gross School of the Arts at Rutgers University, and Umeå University (Sweden). Her art has appeared in *Too Jewish?* and *Entertaining America* (Jewish Museum of New York), *The Fake Chanel Show* (Stux Gallery), and, most recently, in *The Cat Show* (White Columns), which she also curated, featuring the "Cats-in-Residence Program," which traveled to the Walker Art Center in Minneapolis.

Erik Lindman was born in New York City, where he continues to live and work. Lindman received his BA in visual art and art history from Columbia University in 2007. Lindman's first solo exhibition was in 2009 at V&A Gallery in New York City. Recent exhibitions include the solo show *Human Personality* at Almine Rech Gallery in Paris, and the group exhibition *Pour une grammaire du hazard*. He is represented by Almine Rech Gallery, Paris/Brussels and ribordy contemporary, Geneva.

Sara Marcus is the author of *Girls to the Front: The True Story of the Riot Grrrl Revolution*. Her essays and criticism have appeared in print and online publications including *Bookforum*, *Artforum*, the *Los Angeles Review of Books*, the *Nation*, *Rolling Stone*, and *n+1*. She is currently a doctoral student in English at Princeton, where she is working on a book about twentieth-century American literature and politics.

Alexander Nagel took six and a half years to complete his MA and PhD in the history of art at Harvard University. Life got better after that. He is currently a professor at the Institute of Fine Arts at New York University.

Maggie Nelson is the author of four books of nonfiction, The Art of Cruelty, Bluets, Women, the New York School, and Other True Abstractions, and The Red Parts, as well as four books of poetry. Her next book is a work of autobiography and theory. She currently teaches in the School of Critical Studies at CalArts in Valencia, California, and lives in Los Angeles.

Ben Nugent's fiction has appeared in the Paris Review and Tin House, and his first novel, Good Kids, was published in 2013. His nonfiction has appeared in Time and the New York Times Magazine as well as on the New York Times Op/Ed page. He holds an MFA in fiction from the Iowa Writers' Workshop, where he was an Iowa Arts fellow. He's a creative writing professor at Southern New Hampshire University.

Amy O'Leary is a reporter for the New York Times. Her life almost ran off the rails during the years she coauthored the programming book, WAP Development with WML and WMLScript. She is originally from Renton, Washington.

Michelle Orange is the author of This Is Running for Your Life: Essays. Her writing has appeared in Harper's, the Nation, the New York Times, Virginia Quarterly Review, Bookforum, McSweeney's, and other publications. She lives in New York City.

David Orr is the poetry columnist for the New York Times Book Review and the author of Beautiful and Pointless: A Guide to Modern Poetry. He is the winner of the Nona Balakian Citation for Excellence in Reviewing from the National Book Critics Circle and the Editor's Prize for Book Reviewing from Poetry magazine. Orr's writing has appeared in Poetry, Slate, the Believer, and Pleiades. He holds a BA from Princeton and a JD from Yale Law School.

Ross Perlin is the author of Intern Nation: How to Earn Nothing and Learn Little in the Brave New Economy. He also researches endangered languages and writes on labor, linguistics, and China. He's sometimes found on university campuses but mostly in Brooklyn.

John Quijada is a retired government worker who has been featured in the *New Yorker* as the creator of Ithkuil, a philosophical language. He has a degree in linguistics, speaks five languages, and coauthored the novel *Beyond Antimony*, which explores the philosophical implications of quantum physics. His many hobbies and interests including travel, eclectic literature, music and art appreciation, science fiction, cinema, music composition, astronomy, and protozoology. He lives in Northern California with his wife and two cats.

Ron Rosenbaum's books include *Explaining Hitler*, *The Shakespeare Wars*, *How the End Begins*, and four collections of nonfiction. His writing has also appeared in the *New York Times Magazine*, the *New Yorker*, *Harper's*, *Slate*, *Smithsonian*, and *Punk*, among many other publications. He has taught writing seminars at Columbia, NYU, and the University of Chicago. He lives in Manhattan.

Nikil Saval is an editor of n+1. He is the author of *Cubed: A Secret History of the Workplace*.

Elizabeth Schambelan is senior editor at *Artforum*.

Namwali Serpell lives in San Francisco and works as an assistant professor in the English Department at the University of California, Berkeley. Her critical work has been published in *Critique*, *Narrative*, the *Comparatist*, and was featured in *On The Turn: The Ethics of Fiction in Contemporary Narrative in English*. Her creative work has appeared in *Callaloo*, *Tin House*, the *Believer*, *Bidoun*, *The Best American Short Stories 2009*, and *The Caine Prize for African Writing 2011* anthology. She was selected to be one of six recipients of the 2011 Rona Jaffe Foundation Writers' Award for women writers on the basis of a novel in progress entitled *Furrow*.

Amy Sillman is an artist based in Brooklyn, New York. She began teaching at Bard College's MFA program in 1988 and was co-chair of the painting department for twelve years. In 2015 she will begin a stint at the Staedelschule in Frankfurt. A midcareer survey of her work, *one lump or two*, originated at the Institute of Contemporary Art in Boston in 2013 and traveled to the Aspen Art Museum in Colorado and the Hessel Museum at Bard College.

Stephen Squibb is a student and a writer. He affiliates with Woodshed Collective, n+1, e-flux, and Harvard University and has recently spent time in or near the Martin E. Segal Theatre Center, McCarren Park Pool, the Museum of Modern Art, the SS *Lilac*, West Park Presbyterian Church, Loeb Mainstage, Dewey Square, North Brooklyn, Vassar College, Wayland, Massachusetts, and Camden, Maine. He was formerly the wine critic for *Time Out: Istanbul*.

Dale Stephens is the founder of UnCollege.org, a member of the first class of the Thiel Fellowship program, author of *Hacking Your Education*, and a sixth-grade dropout.

Astra Taylor is a documentary filmmaker, writer, and political organizer. She is the director of two films about philosophy, *Žižek!* and *Examined Life*, and the editor of the companion book *Examined Life: Excursions with Contemporary Thinkers*. She is the co-editor of *Occupy!: Scenes from Occupied America*. She has written about alternative education in the essay "Unschooling," which was published by n+1 and is available as a Kindle Single. Her most recent book is *The People's Platform: Taking Back Power and Culture in the Digital Age*.

Nicola Twilley is the author of the blog *Edible Geography*, cofounder of the Foodprint Project, and director of Studio-X NYC, part of the Columbia University Graduate School of Architecture, Planning and Preservation's global network of advanced research laboratories for exploring the future of cities. With the Center for Land Use Interpretation, she recently curated an exhibition exploring North America's spaces of artificial refrigeration and is currently writing a book on the same topic.

David Velasco is the editor of Artforum.com.

Duncan Watts is a principal researcher at Microsoft Research New York City. His foundational research on network science and computational social science has appeared in numerous articles and books, including, most recently, *Everything Is Obvious (Once You Know the Answer): How Common Sense Fails Us*, and has been recognized by the 2009 German Physical Society Young Scientist Award for Socio- and Econophysics and the 2013 Lagrange CRT Foundation Prize for complex systems research. A former professor of sociology at Columbia University, Watts is also an A. D. White Professor at Large at Cornell University and a visiting fellow at Nuffield College, Oxford.

Gabriel Winant is a PhD candidate in history at Yale University. He is also an organizer with the Graduate Employees and Students Organization, UNITE HERE.

Samuel Zipp teaches American studies and urban studies at Brown University. He is the author of *Manhattan Projects: The Rise and Fall of Urban Renewal in Cold War New York* and is at work on a book about Wendell Willkie and popular internationalism during World War II. He has written reviews and essays for the *New York Times*, the *Washington Post*, the *Nation*, the *Baffler*, *Cabinet*, *Metropolis*, and other magazines and journals.

About the Editors

Jessica Loudis is a writer and editor living in Brooklyn. She has worked at *Bookforum*, *Slate*, the Brennan Center for Justice, and the Center for Contemporary Culture in Barcelona. Her writing has appeared in *Bookforum*, the *New Republic*, the *New York Times Book Review*, the *Believer*, and other fine literary outlets. Before moving to New York, she received a degree in literature from Bard College. Prior to that, she lived in Mozambique, Honduras, Jamaica, and Washington, D.C., among other places. So far, she has not gone to grad school.

Boško Blagojević is a software engineer. In 2008, he cofounded Platform for Pedagogy—a New York–based events listing for serious cultural and academic programming. He also regularly publishes art criticism. He studied at Fordham University, Stevens Institute of Technology, and the Whitney Museum of American Art's Independent Study Program.

John Arthur Peetz is a writer and editor living in Brooklyn. He is currently the studio manager for the artist Martha Rosler and was previously an editor at Artforum.com. His writing has appeared in *Riot of Perfume*, *PIN-UP*, and on Artforum.com. He received a degree in religious studies from Reed College, where he conducted an ethnography of contemporary American evangelicals. As of the publication of this book, he has not attended graduate school.

Allison Rodman is the director of communications for the Armory Show and lives in New York's Chinatown. She is currently a master's candidate in philosophy at the CUNY Graduate Center and received a degree in fine arts from Bard College. She rather likes graduate school.